EDGES
OF THE
EARTH

EDGES OF THE EARTH

A MAN, A WOMAN, A CHILD IN THE ALASKAN WILDERNESS

RICHARD LEO

HENRY HOLT
AND COMPANY
NEW YORK

*Certain names, descriptions, and
circumstances in this book have
been altered to protect the privacy
of those concerned.*

Copyright © 1991 by Richard Leo
All rights reserved, including the right to reproduce this book or
portions thereof in any form. Published by Henry Holt and
Company, Inc., 115 West 18th Street, New York, New York
10011. Published in Canada by Fitzhenry & Whiteside Limited,
195 Allstate Parkway, Markham, Ontario L3R 4T8.

Library of Congress Cataloging-in-Publication Data
Leo, Richard.
    Edges of the earth : a man, a woman, a child in the
Alaskan wilderness / by Richard Leo.
    —1st ed.
        p. cm.
    1. Alaska—Social life and customs. 2. Leo,
Richard. 3. Alaska—Biography. I. Title.
F910.5.L46   1991
979.8'05'092—dc20
[B]   91-589
                                                                CIP
ISBN 0-8050-1575-2

Henry Holt books are available at special discounts for bulk
purchases for sales promotions, premiums, fund-raising, or educational use. Special editions or book excerpts can also be created
to specification.
For details contact: Special Sales Director, Henry Holt and Company, Inc., 115 West 18th Street, New York, New York 10011

First Edition—1991

Book design by Claire Naylon Vaccaro

Printed in the United States of America
Recognizing the importance of preserving the written word,
Henry Holt and Company, Inc., by policy, prints all of its first
editions on acid-free paper. ∞
10 9 8 7 6 5 4 3 2 1

*Grateful acknowledgment is made to Ice Nine Publishing Company, Inc.,
for permission to reprint lyrics from "Cumberland Blues" and "Uncle
John's Band." Each is copyright © 1970 by Ice Nine Publishing Company, Inc.*

FOR
MY DAD

Thanks to White Arrow, Catching Spear,
Crossbow, and Heals With Her Touch,
without whom little would much matter.
Love to you, too, Dancing Cheetah.

EDGES
OF THE
EARTH

1.

HERE

Such great mountains! So vast a forest!
Can they be described?
They must! Here: There!
—HO-SAN

In the morning, when I step out into the forest and look up at the snow mountains, I sometimes try to describe, for myself, what I see.

Even after ten years on a homestead near Denali (Mount McKinley), where, if I skew the grid to one side, there are no people or roads of any kind for a hundred square miles, I find myself needing words to make sense of what otherwise can be, in fact, stupefyingly vast. I wasn't born to this life. It's occasionally overwhelming, still.

"Blue ice in the glaciers," I'll note aloud, stopping to stare. "Cloudberries turning red."

I'm aware that it's eccentric to stand in the front yard talking to myself. But I had to consider suggestions of outright lunacy when I moved from New York City to this land uncultivated and uninhabited by human beings, which is the definition of *wilderness* in my Webster's.

I note, by season, iridescent beetles crawling among the six-foot-tall grasses in summer's constant sunlight or fresh marten tracks in the snowscape at twenty below zero Fahrenheit, trumpeter swans winging low above the trees to or from their proximate breeding grounds, green auroral displays in the star fields before December dawns or copper-coned spruce tops in radiant spring mornings.

A few days ago, as happens often, a Big Animal—probably moose, maybe bear—ambled below the ridge along the creek. The ten sled dogs chained to surrounding trees leaped up to bark furiously.

Their speech was, to me, articulate. "Something's close! It's *edible*. It's right down *there*, see?"

My young son raced down from our sleeping loft in his bare feet, burst out the front door, and jumped into my arms to shout, "What is it? Where is it?"

I saw only what doesn't vary: great mountains and vast forest and the subarctic sky. I pointed to the high horizons. The boy, intent upon the interstices, wanted to see what was immediate, and quick.

He knows the mountains and river canyons. He's seen the trackless landscape around our home. To him it's familiar, neither overwhelming nor stupefying.

He wanted to see something *new*, something unexpected and compelling, the way I used to turn to television when I was growing up to watch Sky King soar into the blue or Lloyd Bridges dive to the bottom of the sea or Marlin Perkins, introducing *Wild Kingdom*, intone, "Here is the elephant."

"The clouds have lifted from Denali," I offered. "There's new snow on the South Buttress. Isn't it *bright*?"

"Yeah, yeah," said my son, glancing up cursorily and then returning to study the direction the dogs were pointing.

I was content to stand on the porch. Right outside the door is what I came north to find, every morning, just here.

The boy, somewhat annoyed at my complacency, said, "Let's *go*! I think it's a bear!"

I was unwilling to pursue what was by now, with all the racket, long gone. "We'll follow the tracks after breakfast," I said.

We went back into the house to light a fire in the cookstove and boil our rice cream. We warmed our feet and our bellies.

But then what? Without the compulsion to meet a job schedule or social obligations, what is it that fills our days in the boreal forest so completely that we don't need to hurry anywhere? How did we even get here?

Let me describe.

2.

GOATS AND CHICKENS
IN THE ATTIC

My lips neared the neck of a young ballerina. Her hair was raised high in a bun. I smelled white flowers and musk.

"Sixty-sixth Street, Lincoln Center," droned the conductor. "Fifty-ninth Street next, change for the B, the C, the D, and the A express. Step lively and watch the closing doors."

The subway lurched to a stop. I staggered a half step back from my dancer. A Rasta man who had Walkman headphones braided through his dreadlocks pushed between us. A businessman who was dressed, like me, in a three-piece suit jostled my *Daily News* out of the crook of my arm as he left the car following the swan-naped girl. A couple of other riders stepped on the paper.

I didn't mind. Since my apartment was only a block from the subway entrance, I had awakened, as was usual, just a few minutes before I stumbled out my door, down the street, and through the turnstile. I was still dreamy and only partly conscious, a lovely way to enter the morning rush hour, the *only* way to enter rush hour.

The price of going slow in the city was getting shoved. The price of going fast was missing the chance to savor, dreamily, a perfumed neck. After three years in New York, I admitted that I was a half step out of sync with those who could step lively in pace with their desires.

I assumed that anything that was meant to be would happen on its own, inevitably, the reward of Right Living. For instance, I held out hope that one morning on the subway a young ballerina would turn her head, gaze fondly at my nose, and whisper, "Your breath is so warm." And we'd live happily ever after.

This is, of course, the absolutely wrong way to live in the city. Scheme and be aggressive! Jostle for position to grab that brass ring before it passes! There are *millions* of people all competing for the same rewards!

I, too, desired the loveliest lover, the penthouse apartment, the means to take a private car to work instead of the IRT Broadway local. But each time that I had to admit my only occasional competence, I wondered what else there might be that would let me, like Faust, cry out in affirmation for nothing more, for just what I had, enough, complete, fulfilled.

That particular morning I was still waiting for something more. But I had been considering lately that the best place to wait wasn't on the subway to work.

I bent down for my paper. "If you watch the closin' doors, you got no problems," said a guy whose knees I brushed.

I looked up from the white candy kiss of pigeon dung on one of his laceless sneakers to his unshaven face. One eye was swollen shut. Between his legs he cradled an open quart of Schlitz.

"If you watch the closin' doors," he repeated, "you got no problems." He grinned. His one good eye sparkled. He'd figured it out.

"Fifty-ninth Street," said the conductor. "Change for the IND trains. Step lively and watch the closing doors."

The bum beamed and nodded like a holy man on Valium.

"This is a sign," I thought. "This is a clear message. The world is filled with signs and here's one staring beatifically right at me. But *what the hell does it mean?*"

. . .

On the thirty-third floor, as the clock reached nine, my staff of four eighteen-year-old girls greeted me in chorus. "Good morning, Mr. Leo," they sang.

I was only three years out of college, trying to work a "real" job after a couple of years in Manhattan working odd graveyard shifts while writing, by day, earnestly puerile stories ("What can you do when you've done it all? Emile sat in his window above 181st Street, startled . . .") and exploring the streets. But my staff was just out of high school in Brooklyn and Queens, glad to have any employment. They earned a few cents above minimum wage, gazing, for the greatest part of their waking hours, at an irradiated console.

The National Industrial Directories Corporation, of which I was, grandly, Editor, relied on them. They entered data, gleaned from direct-mail responses, into their computers, typing in "Company Product" and "Number of Employees" and "Gross Income." My job was, like a galley master, to ensure that they kept up with their strokes. Though I did everything I could to make their salaried lives happier and more fulfilling, they were terrified of me.

Nine months before, when I was hired by the vice-president— an aging divorcée who lived on Librium, black coffee, whole-wheat toast, and vanilla ice cream ("So I see you're single," she'd said, glancing up from my résumé and smiling)—I had ushered "my girls" into the conference room to introduce myself. "I think it's a travesty that you're paid so little," I had said. "So to compensate I encourage you to read good books, use the telephones, take two-hour lunches, and have a good time at work just as long as you finish the week's inputting by Friday. But stay off the roof. I go up to the roof on my lunch hour."

They stared at me expressionless.

"Work should be fun," I added. "These are the most exciting years of your lives."

They thought I was crazy. They worked like slaves.

. . .

On my lunch hour I went up to the roof. I had to disconnect an alarm wire in order to open the stairwell door. Sixty-some stories above Midtown there were grasses that grew in the concrete cornice blocks. I loved that. Their roots were forcing the peaks of skyscrapers apart.

As wind swells carried up the sound of the street in rising and falling waves, I looked out across the towers of Manhattan. I saw Atlantis all around me. I saw a small sea island containing the greatest of the civilization's art and technology and commerce. There were dancers and writers and musicians and actors and artists and poets and the most creative of businessmen, who could think in terms of billions, *everywhere*.

Yet I had visited, before settling in Manhattan, the Pyramids and Angkor Wat and the jungle-encircled stupas of lost Dravidic cultures. And they were ruins.

But here in New York in the last half of the twentieth century was the culmination of all civilization from the time our ancestors first decorated the caves they wrested from bears. From my parapet I could see countless glass-and-steel caves with central heating and electric lighting. Would bears opt for this?

I had a partiality to bears. Bears are everything men would like to be but aren't. Bears are utterly independent and confident; men herd into cities and still worry. Bears sleep alone deep in glacial mountains; we sleep with electric blankets or lug enough plastic into the mountains to insulate ourselves against the dawn. Bears ignore us completely, except when they swat at us as if we were mosquitoes, which is humiliating. Are we not free and uniquely individual?

Certainly I wasn't. I needed to pay my rent.

For the rest of the afternoon I sat at my desk and brooded. Four months earlier I'd taken my summer vacation on the West Coast. On a whim, I'd made a cardboard sign that read FAIRBANKS and had hitched to Alaska. I'd never been to Alaska before.

For a week of thumbing the three—the only three—highways of the state, I'd been impressed by two things: how many huge mountains I could see, and how much nothing there was between the mountains.

There were forests to the horizon, tundra meadows and glacial rivers. Plainly, there was an entire world out there off the two-lane blacktopped highway where few people, if any, traveled.

I had returned to my job not relaxed by an offbeat vacation but curious about the mysteries of wilderness. What *was* out there? What would happen by *living* there instead of just passing through? I had hiked a hundred yards off the road when rides were scarce and had been amazed—and frightened—by how far I was (a hundred yards) from anything familiar. And I could see that if I had kept on hiking away I wouldn't find another road or another person until I was either proficient at keeping myself alive in wilderness or dead. When I admitted that even by dying I wouldn't necessarily be found, I hustled back to the highway.

Above my desk I'd thumbtacked a five-by-seven filing card on which I'd typed a lyric: "Gotta get down to the company mine / That's where I mainly spend my time / Make good money, five dollars a day / Made any more I might move away."

I started singing the song. My staff glanced up at me and then bent back furiously to their work.

The day before, the president of my company had taken me to lunch at the New York Athletic Club. He was a beefy man who wore an American flag pin in his suit lapel. He had a big home on Long Island and carried the *Wall Street Journal* into work every day, and every day he left it still creased on his desk when he went home at three. He let the vice-president run the company.

"I hear you're keeping the ship running at full steam," he had said after we ordered Bloody Marys. "You keep the throttle wide open and one day you could be captain."

It was very depressing. I imagined standing on the prow of my own big home on Long Island with an unread *Wall Street Journal* under one arm and a Bloody Mary in my hand, crying over the manicured lawn, "Full speed ahead! Damn the economy!"

As I sat at my desk brooding, I thought, "Why *not* try to live in the mysteries way out at the edges instead of just traveling through? Maybe there's something essential out there that we can't possibly see from here."

I was, and am, a small-town midwesterner who went from a conventional upbringing to college to a good job, wondering along the way, "Is this all there is?" After my freshman year in college, I'd manipulated the scholarship program to let me spend a year traveling around the world, funded by the anthropology department. It was my accredited *Wanderjahr* in prelude to buckling down to a responsible life. But that experience had made it tough to accept that a promising career complete with a table at the New York Athletic Club was enough.

I'd seen, during that year, that there were unimaginable worlds just beyond the known horizon, but they seemed too exotic to be sustaining. Tourists always go home.

But now, like the presence of pain through an opiate, it occurred to me that what I had been working for in the city (a big apartment, a private car) might not be particularly sustaining either. I didn't *want* to commute from Long Island. But I wasn't sure what it was that I *did* want.

"Have you ever thought of living somewhere remote in Alaska?" I asked the girl nearest my desk.

"No, I haven't, Mr. Leo," she said without looking up.

"Do you know that I really have *no idea* what's out there?" I asked.

"Certainly I don't," she said.

"No real idea at all," I repeated. "But I'd love to know."

After work I went to visit Alexander. I met Alexander when we were freshmen at Harvard. Before starting school I had petitioned the college for a single room without realizing that the only four private rooms for freshmen were reserved for those with the greatest psychological need for privacy.

What I got was *two* roommates, but in the same dorm wing as the only four singles. In a tier, in the corner of my wing, was Bob Markoff, on the fourth floor, a rock musician from L.A. who routinely picked up minor girls from Harvard Square; Horace Matsumoto, on the third floor, a Ninja born in Harlem who collected samurai swords and once tried to ram one through the ceiling to spear Markoff in his bed; Donald Dingle, on the second floor, a Phillips Exeter preppy who introduced himself to me in his room by wiping a Stridex pad across his acned face and slapping it to stick on the wall, giggling, "That's *one*"; and, on the bottom floor across the hall from me, Alexander.

No one ever saw Alexander.

One day I found my way onto the dorm roof, as was my wont even then. Alexander was sitting in a full lotus, staring toward the setting sun.

For a few minutes I stood awkwardly off to the side. Then he sighed, stretched his legs, and said pleasantly, "Hello."

I felt compelled to explain my intrusion. "I like to get up for a perspective," I said, stupidly.

He nodded. His smile was so kindly that I felt even more ill at ease.

"Why do you keep putting bricks in the urinal?" I blurted. No one else on our floor had admitted to doing it. We figured the culprit was the Mystery Man.

"It saves water," he said. "We waste so much in this culture."

He was clean-shaven and conventionally dressed in khaki chinos, a button-down shirt, and deck-soled moccasins, which he slipped on as he stood up. He was male-model handsome: a green-eyed Marlboro Man without the weather-creased face.

We talked about how hard a time we had sitting through classes, what a bunch of ambitious overachievers our classmates were, and other such topics as befitted two loners on a dorm roof at sunset. When our small talk ran out he said, plainly having made a decision to confide, "I'll show you a secret if you promise not to tell anyone."

I promised.

He led me down a dark stairwell through a fire escape door directly into his room. "I cut the alarm wires," he said.

We became friends.

Alexander now lived in a spacious loft near the South Street

Seaport. He had bought and renovated it with money borrowed from his father, the CEO of a large American corporation. The loft was decorated with Tibetan art that he had brought back from India, where he had lived for two years in an expatriate Nying-ma-pa Buddhist monastery. As an acolyte monk, he had done 111,111 prostrations in a meditation cell in the foothills of the Himalayas, seeking absolution from futile desires. He had come back furious with himself for still having desires and had moved to Manhattan to explore every last one of them.

Alexander, when he wasn't investigating the high life to which his birthright and beauty entitled him, built kaleidoscopes in his loft. His kaleidoscopes were so exquisitely crafted that the people who bought them were eager to pay large sums, knowing that such art only appreciates in value. The images through the brass-and-crystal eyepieces were of mandalas.

He maintained a full social calendar and an insistence upon not being disturbed except when he wanted. I thought he lived the ultimate urban life. He thought he should be someplace else. We shared a disappointment with the achievements of our adulthood.

I rang his buzzer and dodged away from the building's surveillance camera.

"I know it's you, asshole," said Alexander over the intercom.

I waved my hand into the camera's field. "Help, Mr. Spock!" I said. "Alien life forms are attacking. Beam me up!" I fluttered my hand at the camera and then dropped it from his sight.

The door lock clicked open. I went up the stairs.

On the final landing before his top-floor loft I stopped to catch my breath and to consider, one last time, my reason for coming. "I'm moving to Alaska," I called.

He leaned against the jamb of his unbolted entryway. "What's wrong with Washington Heights?" he asked.

I climbed the last flight and announced, "I'm going to find some land beneath snow peaks and build a home."

He gripped me by the shoulders and sighed, "Sergeant Preston will track you down. You won't escape. Let me get you a good lawyer now."

I went on inside. "I'm *serious*," I said. "I think. I want a home where there's beauty and wonder, of course, but also the sense that it'll *last*. Do you know what I was thinking about at work today on the roof?"

"The idiocy of giving up a rent-controlled apartment?"

"My unborn children. I don't want them to know this random world as their basic reality. Do you know what's left when the gilding has been worn from men's monuments to themselves? Hulking mausoleums, that's what."

"And simpleminded midwestern romanticism."

"I knew you'd understand."

" 'R*oof*,' " he said, correcting my provincial pronunciation. "The same phonetics as '*fool*.' "

" 'Roof' rhymes with 'woof,' " I said.

Alexander went to the refrigerator and returned with two beers. "I'm going to Studio tonight with some friends. Want to come for a final fling before you get eaten by wolves?"

"Listen," I said. "It's as uncharted out there as the Sea of Tranquillity, and the mountains are as deep as the Himalayas. I'm excited to think that there's even someplace *left* like that on earth."

I accepted a beer. "Anyway, I can't go dancing. I have to tell Melissa what we're doing."

He raised his eyebrows. "She doesn't know?"

"Well. Not yet."

"Then you have to come. You'll need to be a little hung over when you tell her, to mute your intensity."

"I think she'll like the idea," I said.

He choked on his beer and took a while to recover. "Ha!" he said.

At Studio 54 we didn't have to wait in line outside. Alexander's friends nodded discreetly to the doorkeeper and the velvet retaining cord was lifted for us. At first I was held back, but when it became clear that I was, in fact, with the party, I was let pass.

The dance floor was full. A grinning paper moon hung above the stage. It was the size of the Metropolitan Opera House. Or so I thought. It was hard to have perspective. We immediately went up to the balcony to do some drugs.

"Have you ever been here straight?" yelled one of Alexander's friends above the music. "Oh, God. *So* boring."

Down below, a woman wearing red stiletto heels, a red chiffon cape, and nothing else except a red glitter arrow on her abdomen with the tip pointing down pirouetted and shouted.

"He's moving to the Alaskan wilderness in the morning," said Alexander, pointing to me. "To build a log cabin and hunt his food."

His friends looked at the plaid wool shirt and hiking boots that Alexander had dressed me in from his closet, then looked to Alexander, grasped at once that what he had said was at least somewhat serious, and looked back to me.

"Very bizarre," said one.

Before the night was through I was slick with sweat. The paper moon had given way to a galaxy of stars projected on the ceiling and shot through with bright satellite tracks from a mirrored disco ball. I felt odd knowing that there were more constellations visible on the ceiling than were visible from the street outside.

Alexander came up beside me. "I just want you to know that I *do* understand," he said matter-of-factly.

"Understand what?" I asked.

"Why we end up standing to one side looking *up* instead of doing the hustle."

I stared at him. His eyes were clear. I admired him enormously because he had won to America's highest rewards—wealth, style, popularity—and still valued my eccentric dreams.

"Why I want to live twenty latitude degrees closer to the sky?"

He nodded. "There's enough of us here," he said, gesturing with a flick of a hand around the dance floor. "I'm glad there'll be some part of me wandering around out there."

"Which part?" I asked.

He grinned and pointed to my chest. Did he mean the essential heart that sought serenity? Did he mean the sustaining breath of life?

I could see that he was aware of my expansive considerations. As was usual, he deftly sidestepped them.

"My Pendleton shirt, dildo," he explained.

I glanced down at it and laughed. "Thanks," I said. "For that, too."

"We're going to Alaska!" I announced.

Melissa clapped her hands in delight. She had never been north of New York City or west of Hazleton, Pennsylvania, where she was born and raised until moving to Manhattan at seventeen to find her fortune. Now, at twenty-two, she'd become the head chef at one of Columbus Avenue's most fashionable restaurants.

She was vivacious and, by her own wide-eyed admission, vulnerable. "I'm in a vulnerable place now," she had said when I first met her at a party a year before. Her toenails had been painted an alluring red but her great brown eyes were aggrieved. I had never seen such a nakedly honest combination. She explained that, since her estranged father had gambled away the house and her alcoholic mother had died of cancer, she was resolved to make it on her own in New York because she was, in fact, on her own in New York. She made it plain that, though it *wasn't easy* to be so independent, she was handling her life well and had no time for phonies.

Because I was unable to reply, "So, like, you into Donna Summer?" I listened without interruption. She interpreted my attention as caring. I *did* care, but mostly it was to get her phone number. I was smitten by her strong spirit and slender ankles.

She had started me considering honestly what it really was that *I* wanted from the city. Though it took me a year to come to a conclusion, I knew for starters that I wanted *her.*

Now, in her apartment on West Seventy-fifth, with her expressive face lit with excited anticipation, I added, "I thought we'd go to Alaska to *live.*"

She looked, suddenly, confused. "What do you mean 'to live'?" She made it sound like "to disappear down a sinkhole."

"You know," I said. "To . . . uh . . . live."

"Like in 'icicles and polar bears'?"

"Well . . . we might start off in a city like Fairbanks, but then we'll push out into the forest to find our own place—to *build* our own place. Free! Together!"

She nodded. She folded her hands in her lap. "Surely," she said, "you jest."

That night, while I went for a long walk through Riverside Park along the shore of the Hudson (moon in the water! wind from the north!), she planned for Alaska with her roommate, Lamonda. Lamonda, who worked as a Playboy bunny, came from the South Bronx and had wealthy boyfriends who were either a little weird or very weird. Lamonda, therefore, knew more about Life than Melissa did, and mothered her.

"You need some security there," Lamonda said to me when I returned.

"The sky's clear," I said. "The moon is huge."

"You need food if your supplies run out. My grandfather in San Juan keeps goats and chickens. But you can't let them freeze."

"If we build a two-story house we can keep the goats and chickens in the attic," said Melissa.

"Full moon," I said. "It's a sign."

"That way they'll stay warm," said Lamonda.

"We thought about cows but of course they're too big," said Melissa.

"I can't believe I'm leaving New York," said Melissa. "Now I won't be able to open my own restaurant."

We were loading the trunk of our drive-away car, a white Lincoln Continental, delivery address: San Francisco. It was a convenient way to travel cross-country. We planned to take an Interstate 80 tour of the rolling fields of the republic, stopping in Chicago to visit my parents, and then, while Melissa stayed with my sister in Oakland, I'd go north to investigate the possibilities.

"Why would you want to open your own restaurant?" I asked.

"Because then it would be my *own* restaurant," she replied at once.

We were both feeling a little nervous about our journey. Now that we had quit our jobs, the initial adventurous enthusiasm had given way to sobering second thoughts.

"I thought you were fulfilled running the kitchen at Ruelle's," I said.

She snorted. "Working for someone else? I didn't come to New York to work for someone else. I came here to accomplish my *own* goals. Me."

"But for months you've been telling me that work was driving you crazy. You kept saying that you *needed* to get away from everything."

"Work *was* driving me crazy. Nobody knew what they were doing there except me. I had to yell and scream all night to get things served right. I was too exhausted to fall asleep at night. It was horrible."

"I know," I said.

"But Mimi Sheraton gave me two stars. I was meeting people. I was getting to know the business. It was exciting."

I lifted a box from the curb. It clanked. "What's *this*?"

"My pasta maker."

"We're bringing a pasta maker to Alaska?"

"Listen! I'm leaving half my kitchen! Give me a break!"

I looked at the stuff I was bringing. Crammed next to my new felt-lined cold-weather Canadian pack boots ("You sure these'll keep me warm?" I'd asked the salesman at Abercrombie & Fitch. "Hey, whadda I know about Alaska?" he'd replied. "These are the best we got") was my 1948 Royal portable. I also had a box of my favorite books and a framed photo from Alexander of the white Himalayas.

"Sorry," I said.

When we'd finished packing we cruised slowly onto the West Side Highway, windows rolled down, headed north. I felt as if all the epidemic bacteria mutated by penicillin into dormancy, and all other urban pollutants and compulsions, had been exorcised from me and I was clean, clear, *alive*, as alive as I'd been since I was two, before I knew Wonder bread and conformity, when the world seemed so magical that I had to be duped into sleep at night. I was breathing the Manhattan air through filters of such intoxication that I smelled only the trees in Riverside Park and the ocean salt, a very unlikely accomplishment.

We'd started on our pilgrimage, and as with any pilgrimage, God only knew what we'd find when we arrived.

I glanced over at Melissa. She sat bravely erect. Then she turned to me and grinned. "This is just nuts," she said, reaching for my hand.

My father took off his glasses and rested them in his lap. He leaned to the coffee table beside his chair, lifted his glass of sherry, and held it up in a toast. "Here's to you," he said.

My father was the kindest and most gentle man I had ever known. When he wanted to get down to business with his children he started with love.

"Now," he said as he set his glass back down. "How do you plan to make a living up there?"

I wanted to tell him that I had a job all lined up. I wanted to put him at ease. "Well . . . ," I said. "Don't forget that Alaska, with all its oil revenue, is per capita the richest state in one of the richest countries in the world."

He nodded. He understood that I was saying, "I haven't the faintest idea."

"But you do have enough saved to get you started, don't you?" he asked.

"Oh, sure," I lied. But it wasn't a *total* lie. We had left New York. That was a start. I was hoping that the nine hundred dollars I had in my pocket would last until I got the security deposit back from my apartment. Faith has bankrolled the pursuit of more dreams than gold ever did.

He sighed. "I admire your gumption," he said. "But sometimes I worry that you've read too many books."

I laughed. "What does *that* mean?"

He gestured with one hand. "Oh, you're such a romantic. All your quixotic ideas. I wish you could be more *practical*."

"Dad," I said. "You came from Calabria when you were eleven. You spoke no English. Now you're a sportswriter for the *Tribune*. That leap was a lot more extreme than moving from one state to another. Besides, *you're* the one who taught me about books."

I went over to his library and grabbed *Jurgen*, his favorite book by his favorite author, James Branch Cabell. Cabell wrote romantic fantasies during the first two decades of this century, when the rest of America was consumed with material accumulation and sensory gratification. I slapped the cover of the book with an open palm to knock the dust from the binding—one of his familiar mannerisms.

" 'Why, but I yawned and fretted in preparation for some great and beautiful adventure which was to befall me by and by,' " I read, " 'and dazedly I toiled forward. Whereas behind me all the time was the garden between dawn and sunrise. . . . Now assuredly the life of every man is a quaintly builded tale, in which the right and proper ending comes first. Thereafter time runs forward, not as schoolmen fable in a straight line, but in a vast closed curve, returning to the place of its starting. And it is by a dim foreknowledge of this, by some faint prescience of justice and reparation being given them by and by, that men have heart to live. What else was living good for unless it brought me back to love?' " I closed the book.

"Remember how I used to go exploring all the time when I was growing up, past Allanson's farm and all the way down Butterfield Road? Or up the Crick to where they've built that new subdivision now? Remember the time I rode my bike almost to the Wisconsin border and then called you and Mom on a pay phone, collect, to ask you where I was because it was getting dark, and you had to drive for an *hour* to get me? I *loved* that stuff. I was *happy* being out on my own in the fields and the woods. I used to imagine that the summer cumuli were mountains."

My father shook his head. "You know I think Freud was one of our culture's biggest fakirs. I think you're just tired of your job."

I thumbed through his book for a minute. I couldn't find what I wanted, so I pretended to read, and paraphrased, "I can't deny that what you say makes sense. But my explanation is the lovelier."

"And stop quoting my own books to me. I'm sorry you can't be content with normal things like everyone else."

I was surprised. "Really?" I asked.

He sighed again. He took another sip of sherry. "No," he said.

"Dinner's ready!" called Melissa. "Come help us set the table!"

3.

TOURISTS

For three days on the Alaska ferry, steaming up past the coast of British Columbia from Seattle, I stood near the bow watching the sun angle lower with the increasing latitude until it was visible, on the third day, only between gaps in the low mountains that lined both sides of our passage—the Canadian Rockies to the east, Alaskan islands to the west. Spruce forests like carpets of sod covered hillsides down to the water. Dolphins leaped in our wake. I slept alone on the back deck in my down bag.

Most other passengers kept to the lounge, which opened early and closed late. There weren't many of us. Alaska wasn't a popular destination in the dead of winter.

I started a journal. The first line of the first entry was, "Jan. 26, 1981. I'm a little chilled and a little disoriented by the shortness of daylight but yes and yes and *look*!"

The ship docked at dusk at Haines, an isolated community with a road link across a mountain pass to the only highway connecting

Alaska with the rest of the continent. I bummed a ride with a guy I met on the ferry who was headed to Fairbanks, six hundred miles away. He was a retired North Dakota railroad man, bringing a car up to his daughter.

For all those miles, with the temperature thirty below, with the night continuous, I stared out the frosted windows at ghostly land-scapes. My benefactor spoke little. I was grateful.

When I saw a curtain of the aurora turn the sky green I asked him to stop. We were in the middle of nowhere. It was the first time in my life I had seen the aurora. Even at thirty below, with the piercing wind carrying away the sound of the idling car, with swirls of light like luminous sea swells overhead, I ran up and down the desolate road and postured and laughed and knew that nothing in the world could be so exciting because this was merely the *first glimpse*.

At that point we switched seats and, while he slept, I drove the rest of the way to Fairbanks, wide awake.

I got out of the car for good at dawn in downtown Fairbanks.

A bank clock across the street alternately flashed the time and the temperature: 10:52, −36°.

I stood still for three minutes by the bank clock and about an hour on my internal gauges, trying to figure out what was going on. Dawn was, in fact, just breaking. Near midday? But even weirder was the air. It was acrid and so murky I could feel it against my face like spray from an ocean of ashes. Strangest of all, though, was the sound of the city. There was no discernible hum and throb, no urban vibration from the motors of buses and buildings. Things *squeaked*. Tires squeaked, footfalls squeaked, car doors and stray voices. Nothing resonated.

It was like being in some gray sulfurous hell created not by Dante, but by surreal mice.

What few vehicles there were moved ponderously, as if underwa-ter. The occasional pedestrian who passed me walked as if struggling against sheets of dirty laundry that hung from invisible wires above the street.

Then my feet went numb. I started stomping them. The snow beneath them squeaked.

I bent down to lift my pack and realized that I was stiff. After three minutes outside! I felt, suddenly, very tired and very lonely.

I went into a hotel on the corner, flanked by bars. As soon as I stepped through the door, a thick heat made me so exhausted it was hard to move. So I didn't. I leaned against the wall. I wanted to click my heels three times and be back where the aurora lapped against the tops of mountains.

But I needed to find a job. I needed to earn some money first. Why did I believe that I needed money to move out of the city? Because I'd never known otherwise.

The hotel was above one of the bars. From the entranceway I climbed a flight of stairs to the lobby. It looked like a flophouse: battleship gray plaster peeling from a ceiling lit by a bare bulb.

I didn't ask how much a room cost. I just signed the register, gave the clerk a fifty, and got back, to my horror, seven dollars.

He saw my reaction. He had the waxy complexion and pale eyes of a mass murderer, but he had compassion. "Honest," he said, "that's about as good a price as you'll find in town."

I nodded. "But why is the sky so . . . so eerie outside?" I asked.

"Ice fog," he said, as if talking to a dolt.

I didn't have the energy to ask what that was.

"Only happens in town when it's about this cold," he added. "Frozen smog. It'll go away when things warm up."

I was encouraged. "Is it easy to find a job around here?"

He grinned. "Fat chance," he said. "Everyone who worked on the pipeline went home a couple of years ago. Those of us left over take what we can."

I went down the hall to my room. While I fumbled with the key, a drunken cowboy clomped past trailing a short-fingered woman wearing a beehive hairdo. "Ya-hoo," he said, for no identifiable reason, as he bumped into me.

I fell asleep in my clothes.

An hour later I awoke sweating. I changed undershirts and went out to find, before a job, a map. I wanted to see the lay of the land, from within ice fog.

In the Federal Building library I found maps so detailed I ran my fingers over them like a blind man reading Braille. They were bound in large leather volumes called *Regional Profiles of Alaska*. They revealed everything: topography and vegetation, habitation and geology, and hundreds of thousands of square miles of uninterrupted wilderness.

My favorite map, after I'd searched them all, was one that had everything I could want. Beneath the blue-limned glaciers of the Alaska Range was an open circle designating a community called Petersville, which had appended, in parentheses under the name, "Ghost town." It was near the boundary of Denali National Park. On either side of the town were two dark ovals, like panda eyes. "Known grizzly denning area," was the legend. A dotted line ("Unimproved dirt") defined a road—Petersville Road—that extended east from the ghost town under the mountains to the bank of the mile-wide Susitna River. Directly across the river from the Petersville Road was the town of Talkeetna ("Pop. 200"). Talkeetna was on the Alaska Railroad.

"Vegetation: mixed spruce and birch forest intermingled with extensive tundra. Geology: known deposits of gold veined through Cambrian granite. Habitation: widely scattered."

That evening, from the hotel, I telephoned restaurants that had advertised in the *Fairbanks Daily News–Miner* for "wait persons." The first two restaurants refused even to grant me a personal interview. The third said, "Look. We're holding out for a chick with legs. Call back in a week."

In the morning, I walked to the railroad terminal and bought a ticket to Talkeetna. Talkeetna was one of the few inhabited communities between Fairbanks and Anchorage, railheads for the limited Alaska Railroad. I wasn't aware that the train ran, in winter, only once a week. I arrived, by chance, a half hour before departure.

I boarded in stinking darkness. There were three cars: engine, coach, and baggage car. I took my seat in the coach. It was cold. I was alone.

When the conductor came for my ticket he confided, "It's warmer back there," indicating the baggage car.

I followed him to where the other five or six passengers stood around a potbellied wood stove in the center of the otherwise empty car. It was warm.

For an hour we all stood facing the stove. An older man with white hair and red suspenders told stories of Alaska as he remembered it twenty-five years earlier, when the entire Territory had a population about the same as the office building where I'd worked in New York. He'd trapped and had mined gold in the hills outside Fairbanks. He'd run a six-dog team to town when he needed supplies. He said, "Only difference now is that there's more people in the cities. Lots came up for the oil boom and some stayed. But they stayed where it was easy. You can still go out there"—he waved a hand toward the windows—"and not meet nothin' but land for most of the rest of your life, if you want."

We looked where he'd gestured. Daylight was growing. We all turned our backs to the stove to stare out the window.

"Look!" he suddenly said. "Quick! A moose!"

Against a postcard vista of spruce trees and snow, the animal stood watching us pass. I had the immediate sense that it was virtually impossible to travel the rail line in winter and *not* see a moose, one of the most abundant of wildlife in the north. And still the old-timer was excited. That made me feel good.

I said that I'd never seen a moose before except in a zoo, and so the attention turned to me. Where was I from? Where was I going? The basic questions asked of travelers in foreign lands.

I told them that I had tried to find a job in Fairbanks but had gotten so depressed that I was now going to Talkeetna because it looked, on a map, close to where I really wanted to be.

Another man, with a huge fur-ruffed parka, who said he lived in Fairbanks, chided me for not giving the "Interior" a chance. "Sure it's cold," he said. "And ice fog sucks. But as soon as we cross the Range we're going to be fifty degrees warmer and up to our necks in wet snow." He explained that Mount McKinley—which he called by its Athabascan Indian name, Denali—and its flanking massif block the Pacific weather of the Southcentral region from reaching any further north into the rest of Alaska, the "Interior."

I didn't mind the idea of being close to the mountains and their winter snow. I did mind the idea of walking from a plywood-and-plasterboard Fairbanks apartment to a café where I'd serve hung-over cowboys steak and eggs. Besides, the paltry winter wear I'd gotten in New York ("Now, in addition to being down-filled this parka is cut close to make a casual statement . . .") would cost a *lot* to replace with Fairbanks gear.

I said I thought I'd explore around Talkeetna for a few days.

A third man said that he had always admired a handful of cabins up on a ridge about seven rail miles north of Talkeetna. He said that there were probably a number of unoccupied cabins scattered back through the woods surrounding Talkeetna because the town had been established in the twenties, when the railroad was built—long enough ago for settlers to have come and gone.

I don't remember what he looked like or what he wore. I don't remember asking him anything except whether he thought it would be worthwhile to get off the train near that ridge to look around.

"Sure," he said.

He was, as I now know, an angel. He might still be taking the train between Fairbanks and Anchorage to sell ski bindings or to visit the son of his first wife or whatever the hell he was actually doing. But he only does that kind of stuff, I'm sure, part-time, as a cover.

The conductor stopped the train to let me off on the side of the tracks at Alaska Railroad Milepost 233.5, where a foot trail led up that ridge. The baggage man dumped my pack in the snow and the train was gone.

It was balmy and snowing. The snow fell straight down from a windless sky blued by the approaching twilight. The flakes were each the size of a dandelion flower balled into white seed.

Where the trail topped the ridge I could see a cabin. It was surrounded by tall spruce and birch with two-foot-thick trunks. The branches bent heavily over the roof, laden with snow. Behind me, on the other side of the tracks, through a cottonwood grove, was a huge frozen river. Beyond that was a silhouette of forest blurring into the mist of the falling snow.

I felt as though I'd stepped into a fairy tale. I stood for a while trying to fantasize what it'd be like to live in that cabin, but I realized that I really had no idea even how to fell a tree to get wood for the stove.

I started up the trail. The snow berms on either side of it came up to my waist.

The trail forked at the crest of the ridge. The part that went up to the cabin door was covered with new snow. Plainly no one was home, but the cabin wasn't abandoned, either. I went left along the ridge. I was aware that there was not much daylight left, and I still needed to hike the tracks into town for a place to sleep.

A quarter mile later I saw another cabin in a clearing through the trees. It was small and simple and very beautiful. I went closer.

Suddenly a half-dozen dogs exploded from beneath the of trees lining the side of the clearing where I stood. They barked a furiously clear message: Kill. There was a dog on either side of the trail, on either side of *me*, and more surrounding.

I was petrified.

When the adrenaline cleared from my sight I saw that the dogs were chained to their trees. None could reach into the trail.

But then I didn't know whether to go on to the cabin or retreat. I assumed, naturally, that anyone who lived out here didn't want tourists knocking on his door and saying, "Hi!" But I was embarrassed to withdraw and leave him wondering who might have slunk away into the woods.

After a minute, dogs still barking, I walked hesitantly to the cabin. "Hello!" I called. "I'm sorry!" No one came out. I knocked on the door.

A voice yelled, "Come *on!*"

I stuck my head inside. A man with long hair and a steady gaze sat in an easy chair in front of a wood stove. He hoisted a beer. "I'm Marvin," he said.

He didn't bark and he didn't bite. I went in.

"I'm sorry," I repeated. "I was on the train and I got off to look around and I didn't know anybody was home and my name is Rick."

Marvin nodded. "This is Anna," he said. Anna stood at a counter slicing vegetables. She was young and pretty. She smiled.

I didn't know what to do.

"Want a beer?" asked Marvin.

"Thanks," I said. "Sure. Thanks a lot." I shrugged out of my pack.

The cabin was lit by kerosene lanterns that burnished the log walls with gold light.

I accepted the beer Marvin handed me from a six-pack beside his chair. "I hope you don't mind my intruding like this," I said, still standing. "I just came up on the ferry a few days ago and I've been moving pretty quickly since then so I feel kind of jet lag disoriented except it's more like reality lag."

Marvin took a sip. "You want to relax?" he said.

I relaxed in a rush. I dropped on a couch beside a pile of dog harnesses. Next to the couch was a hand-hewn table across from which was a white porcelain-trimmed cookstove. Above us was a sleeping loft with a log ladder leading up to it, and above that a low ceiling of closely spaced poles that seemed to glow.

"This is all very lovely," I said.

"Are you hungry?" Anna asked.

They became my first neighbors. If they'd marched me back down the trail at gunpoint I might now be pouring coffee in a Fairbanks greasy spoon.

Marvin worked for the railroad in summer and hung out during winter. For eight years, after Marvin's air force tour at the big Anchorage base, they'd made their home in this cabin. They seemed as calm and contented as I'd imagined for Alaskan log cabin life.

When I got around to explaining what I was doing in Alaska, Marvin said, "Stanley hasn't lived in his place for years. He's left the country. His cabin's just down the ridge."

After dinner I went just down the ridge. I had to push through deep snow. It didn't squeak. Snow continued to fall, and in the stillness of night I could hear it land on me.

Another quarter mile from Marvin and Anna's I found a tall cabin with a chalet roof. One wall was bowed out. The windows were boarded up.

But the door was unbarred. I looked inside by flashlight.

The cabin was a museum piece: wood cookstove, grain grinder

on a log table, snowshoes hanging from one wall, old books on a shelf.

For a long time I stood in the middle of the cabin's only room with the flashlight off. I was sure that I had never before in my life been aware of such a silence. It wasn't just the absence of sound. It was also the thick silence of isolation, the serene and airy silence when the constant chatter of thought fades, a silence fostered by humility and stunned gratitude.

This was where we'd live while I explored for our own land. I knew it. I started laughing. The sound of my voice was familiar, and anything familiar in such an extraordinary world was droll.

The next morning, after waking at Marvin and Anna's, I hiked the two hours down the tracks to Talkeetna and called the local tax office. "Peter Stanley lists his current address in Virginia," I was told.

I called Virginia directory assistance, then Stanley. "Well, I guess you can live there if you fix the place up," he said. "We haven't lived there in six years and I'm sure it needs some maintenance."

I hiked back up the tracks and unboarded the windows. I made lists of supplies. I took the snowshoes from the wall and made a fresh trail around the house. I swept the floor. Out the front window was the river plain contained by forests that rolled up into the clouds. Marvin said that when the clouds blew off, the mountains were clear.

Then I hitched into Anchorage to buy supplies and a plane ticket for Melissa. I studied the Yellow Pages in a phone booth, made notes, and began running. From a health food store I bought fifty-pound bags of brown rice, wheat flour, dried milk, and red beans, twenty-five pounds each of lentils and honey, and five gallons of tamari. From an army-navy store I bought surplus wool pants and gloves and long underwear and serious Alaskan boots for both Melissa and me, plus down pants. I hit a hardware store and a supermarket. I took it all by cab to the downtown Hilton, where I gave a porter ten bucks to stash it in storage. Then I went to the YMCA.

The next day Melissa flew into Anchorage. I met her at the airport and we went to the Hilton, where I'd booked a sixteenth-floor suite. We watched the winter sun set through low stratus clouds and then ordered king crab from room service.

At eight in the morning we lugged our stuff a couple of blocks to the train station, saving cab fare and getting in shape to be self-reliant. By nine we were riding north. When dawn arrived, the sky was clear.

Three hours later the baggage attendant nudged me. "Comin' up," he said.

The train came out of the woods to run along the bank of the Susitna River. The roar of the train, which had been echoed and amplified by the wall of trees, suddenly fell away across the wide river plain. Beyond the plain, across an expanse of forest, a horizon of snow mountains rose abruptly, like sea cliffs. The peaks were brilliantly white, creased with veins of blue ice. They seemed so close I involuntarily took a step back from the window. To see the summit of the tallest mountain I had to lift not just my eyes, but my whole head.

When the train stopped, Melissa and I jumped to the ground. The attendant began handing us our boxes. Once we'd piled all our stuff on the side of the tracks, he waved as the train pulled away.

I busied myself dragging boxes closer to a little footpath that I'd broken through the snow to reach the cabin. It was a while before I realized Melissa wasn't working beside me. Standing in the center of the tracks, she was watching the distance where the train had disappeared.

I went to put my arms around her from behind. We were surrounded by spruce and overhung, it seemed, by glaciers.

After a minute or two, Melissa turned around to look at me. Her eyes were filled with tears.

I saw joy in her gaze, and also confusion and simple shock, but joy first and last.

"My God," she whispered. "Where *are* we?"

4.

THE LAY OF THE LAND
TALKEETNA, 1981

We woke the next morning with our arms wrapped around each other. Through a strand of Melissa's hair, I studied the log beams above us. They were blue in the early light. The air around us seemed blue. The snowscape that extended up to the windowsills reflected the subarctic sky into our cabin. I felt as though we were a part of the world outside. I also felt cold. My dreamy peacefulness was similar, I thought, to that of the woolly mammoths found frozen intact, embedded in ice.

"I can see my breath," whispered Melissa when she poked her head from beneath the covers.

"Should I start a fire?" I asked. I didn't expect her to say, "No, let me," but I hoped she had an alternative to my getting out of bed.

"You should start a fire," she said.

I groped for my new Duo-Fold thermal long johns. I couldn't find them. The tip of my nose tingled in the cold.

With an effort that reminded me, horribly, of diving into my high school swim-class pool, I jerked out of bed. I tossed clothes around in the dim light until I found my long johns. "I once read that hypothermia is treated by bare-body contact," I said as I hopped around trying to get dressed.

"A warm house works, too," said Melissa.

I climbed down from the sleeping loft, shivering. I had left paper and split dried wood beside the stove. When I crammed it all into the firebox and lit it, smoke poured from the top of the stove like stage fog.

I opened the firebox door, took a deep breath to blow the wood into flame, and gagged. When I'd coughed myself hoarse, I heard the crackle and roar of ignited fire. "It's all right," I rasped. "We'll learn."

That became my private maxim, like "God is love" or "What, me worry?"

It's all right. We'll learn.

An hour later, melted snow water was boiling for tea in a pan atop the stove. The smoke had cleared from inside the cabin. Melissa sat in a rocking chair beside the stove. I mashed eggs that had frozen during the night. We were warm.

Steam rising. Heat radiating. Food cooking. It was Neanderthal nirvana.

"The first thing we'll need is more wood," I said as we ate breakfast. "The pile that was left here will be gone in a day or two."

"I've never chopped down a tree before," said Melissa.

"We'll need an axe," I said. I was aware that I sounded like a fool: "We'll need an axe." What else would we use? Our teeth? But I had brought us here, so I acted as if I knew what to do.

I had found a sharp double-bitted axe in the cabin when I'd first straightened up. The only tool I had purchased in town while awaiting Melissa's arrival was a large-toothed handsaw. I wasn't sure whether axe or saw would be more effective in felling a tree, but I liked the idea of swinging boldly at the trunk, wood chips flying, instead of kneeling in the snow sawing.

We went outside so that I could strap the snowshoes on Melissa. But immediately I was distracted.

The mountains were, as Dōgen wrote in thirteenth-century Japan, right *there*. Or *here*. Translations vary. The mountains didn't. But then they did, even as I stared. The bright wall that lifted the horizon up acquired dimension: The jagged horizontal bands like strata lines along a cliff face became a succession of sharp ridges, each one rising higher beyond the one before. I noticed that the lighter colorations descending wide and unshadowed from near the top of the peaks were glaciers. Then I said, "Oh, *look!*"

We both looked. The light was so intense we had to squint.

"That mountain," I said, without having to point to Denali towering above the rest like the Paramount Pictures logo, "is the tallest mountain on earth measured from its base to its summit. Everest *starts* from a plateau thirteen thousand feet high. Denali lifts from the tundra at seven hundred feet above sea level, which you can see from here."

I had spent a lot of time with the maps in Fairbanks. I felt the need to make my amazement explicable to Melissa. It was as lame as Moses standing before the parted waters of the Red Sea saying, "What you see here is a natural phenomenon unique in the world. . . ."

Melissa touched my shoulder. She didn't say anything. I loved her very much for that.

Then, like theatergoers compelled to leave the show before the final act, I secured her snowshoes and we headed away from the mountains into the forest.

I pushed through the snow ahead of her. I was looking for a tree far enough away from the cabin so that its removal wouldn't alter the landscape we saw from the back window.

Wild lands are often treated with reverence by two very distinct groups: those who live in cities and value the idea of virgin land, and those who have lived intimately for generations beside it. As we marched steadily deeper into the boreal forest, I felt the sanctity of the world we'd entered.

Eventually we found a birch with its entire top hanging broken beneath a snow load. A tree that was dying I would take.

Melissa stood clear. I swung the axe. It stuck in the trunk. I yanked. It didn't budge. I yanked again, grunting. It stayed. I shoved against the handle and the axe broke free. I stumbled up to my elbows in snow.

Melissa didn't laugh.

Three hours later the tree was dead. I had dismembered it after returning for the saw, and we had hauled part of its torso back to cremate after cutting it into small pieces.

My back hurt. My arms hurt.

I wondered how our forebears had kept their caves warm without metal axes and saws, when firewood was not out back from the cabin but miles down the tundra to the trees.

Afterward, while Melissa cooked, I went down the ridge to find the spring that Marvin had said was just below us.

Eventually, by following the bottom of the ridge, I saw the pool. It was two feet wide. Even in the cold it was free of ice.

The powerful Susitna River was frozen. The landscape was deep in snow. I couldn't explain why the small spring pool was liquid. It was magic. It was *alive*.

I went back up to the house to get a five-gallon plastic jerry can. I filled it at the spring by dipping with a cup. As I scooped the final cup, shreds of leaves and ferns on the bottom of the pool curled toward the surface like silt from the ocean floor. Then I spent the last of my energy lugging the can up the ridge.

The next day we did it all again.

"We're not out here to rough it," wrote Nessmunk, a nineteenth-century mountain man. "We're out here to smooth it."

"We'll learn," I kept reminding myself. I hoped I wouldn't contract terminal cramps first. My muscles seemed to be one large knot. I couldn't banish from thought a college science lecture. The professor had described a rare affliction in which all the musculature in the back suddenly constricts so powerfully that the spine is torn apart.

At night, before falling heavily to sleep, Melissa and I talked about New York the way grade-school classmates at an adult reunion talk about their childhood.

On the third day we were going to rest but we decided instead to go into town.

We were curious.

I had whizzed through Talkeetna too quickly to have any sense of who the people were who lived out here. Melissa had only seen the town as a blur from the train window.

After stoking the stove, we went down to the tracks and began walking.

Within ten minutes, just at the moment when we could see up to Marvin and Anna's place ("What are they like?" asked Melissa. "How do *they* survive?"), a snowmachine came up behind us.

The driver stopped. He was so fully wrapped in clothes that I couldn't see his face beneath his goggles and the scarf he wore pulled up over his nose.

"Want a ride?" he said, indicating the sled he pulled behind the machine.

"Sure," I said. Then stuck out my hand. "I'm Rick Leo," I said.

"I know," he replied.

That was our introduction to the network of human society in bush Alaska. Within a matter of days, word had spread that newcomers had moved into the country.

He shook my hand. He didn't offer his name. He waited, machine idling, until we had climbed behind him. Twenty very speedy and very cold minutes later, he stopped at the tiny shack of the railway depot.

When we got off, he waved, revved the engine, and turned the machine down into the small railside parking lot and then on up a snowbound street.

"These people seem very independent," said Melissa.

We walked through the parking area. There were only a few cars, or, if there were more, they were buried in snow. What filled the lot were little camper trailers that all had stovepipes sticking up from their roofs. Some had smoke coming from them. No person was visible. The town looked deserted.

Across from the parking lot stood a clapboard, two-story bar and inn, the Fairview, and across from it a general store built of logs painted a rusty red. Down the main street between them were a gas station and a few old log homes.

At the end of the street, a city block or two away, was the river. In the other direction were a couple more buildings—a house, a metal Quonset hut—and then nothing except the road that led fifteen miles to the junction with the Anchorage-Fairbanks highway, the only other road in the area.

We walked to the end of the street, turned left, and went on into the Teepee Bar/Restaurant/Motel, from which I had first phoned Stanley. It was the only pay phone in town. The Teepee was a squat A-frame roofed with rotting tar paper the color of dried blood. There were two doors, one into the bar, one into the restaurant. At nine-thirty in the morning there were people in the bar. We went into the empty café.

A waitress brought us two cups filled with coffee after we seated ourselves in a corner at one of the six or eight tables. She was old and slow and so pale her skin seemed translucent. She was happy to see customers. "Hello, hello," she said. "Where'd you folks come in from?"

"Up the tracks," I said.

"I came from Texas by way of Oklahoma and Idaho," she said as if I hadn't responded at all. "After my husband died I drove my way north in bits and pieces until I ended up here. He was a terrible husband, always drinking, day after day. That's what killed him. I just wanted to get away and see something of the world. You know? I figured I couldn't go no more south because of Mexico and all. So I aimed north. This is a real nice town but not much happens in the winter. But that's okay 'cause it makes you feel safe. No one'll follow you *here*. Let me know when you're ready. I made the chili myself." She handed us the menus she had tucked under one arm, then shuffled back to the kitchen.

Melissa fidgeted with her menu. In her experience, waitresses suggested the fish of the day and then retreated discreetly.

As we sipped coffee to warm up, Marvin came in from the bar with a much shorter man who wore a stocking cap and a shirt torn at both elbows. They appeared preoccupied, and took no notice of us, seating themselves at a table next to the kitchen.

"Gotta sell something," said Marvin.

"Sell the dogs," said the other man.

"I'm not sellin' Daisy," said Marvin.

"Dog's a dog," said his companion.

"To *you*," said Marvin.

They fell silent. I hesitated a minute and then said, "Marvin!"

He looked up. "Hey!" he said. "What's happening?"

"*We* need some dogs," I said.

Marvin nodded. "Right on," he said.

"This is Melissa," I said. Then, to Melissa, "Marvin's our neighbor."

"Pleased to meet you," said Melissa.

"This's Teepee Joe," said Marvin. Joe rose slightly then sat back down.

"We really do need some dogs," I said.

Marvin glanced around, then said, "I got a felony rap to beat. It's gonna cost me some money."

"He's gotta beat a felony rap," said Teepee Joe.

"What did you do?" asked Melissa, her eyes growing wide.

Marvin waved a hand to brush aside the question. "I've got an appearance in Anchorage next week."

"He just got the summons," said Joe.

I thought, "He's killed a man!" I felt a rush of adrenaline. The last frontier!

"Are you going to be all right?" asked Melissa.

"I just need some money," said Marvin.

"How many dogs do we need to pull us into town?" I asked.

Marvin shrugged. "I got nine now," he said.

"When did you get *this* idea?" Melissa asked me.

"How much do you want?" I asked Marvin.

Marvin kept his eyes on me. "I can give you two," he said. "A hundred and twenty-five apiece. And if you want 'em I'll throw in one more for free."

I looked at Teepee Joe. "Is that a fair price?" I asked.

Teepee Joe blinked. "A fair price?" he said. He glanced at Marvin. Marvin didn't look at him. "Why . . . that's a *steal*. For Marvin's dogs? That's a *steal*."

"Are three enough to pull both of us and haul firewood?" I asked Marvin.

"Better than walking," he said.

I pulled out my wallet. I leafed through my bills. I had $475. I handed Marvin $250.

"Right on," repeated Marvin.

"But we need a sled, too," I said. "Do you know anyone who has a sled to sell?"

Marvin stood up to put the bills in his pocket. "I got an old sled buried in the snow behind my place. You're welcome to it if you want to dig for it."

"Where is it?" I asked.

Marvin closed his eyes for a moment. Then he said, "Go out behind the greenhouse about a hundred feet. Between two spruce there's a trail that's snowed over, but you'll see it. Off to the left I dumped the sled."

"Thanks," I said.

"You can take Garner and Bell," said Marvin. "Bell's a princess. I'll throw in Kobuk. He pulls."

"Bell's a princess," said Teepee Joe.

The waitress brought Melissa and me each a bowl of chili. "I made this myself," she said. "It's better'n pancakes. Mornin', Marvin. Mornin', Joe. You guys want to eat?"

"Later," said Marvin. "I have to get in touch with my lawyer." He went back toward the phone in the bar. "Anna's gonna feel better."

"You won't be sorry," said Teepee Joe as he followed Marvin. "Marvin's got great dogs."

When they'd left, Melissa said, "Why do we need *dogs*?"

I stirred my chili. "This is Alaska. Now we don't have to walk."

"But how do they *work*?" she insisted.

"They're already trained," I said. "You'll see."

Marvin and Joe must have gone out the barroom door. Melissa

and I waited a while for them to return and then said goodbye to the waitress.

"Stay warm!" she said. "Don't worry 'bout nothin'. Nobody will find you here!"

We walked back down Main Street. "Do you have the feeling that everything here is very *intense*?" said Melissa.

"Everything," I agreed. "The cold, the light, the people, the—"

"Yo!" called a giant of a man standing up the street outside the Fairview. "Yo!" He waved an arm at us like a wide receiver signaling for a pass.

If I had been on a New York street I would have immediately crossed to the other side feigning a businesslike preoccupation. In Talkeetna, on the only street, surrounded by river and forest, I had nowhere to escape.

The giant came toward us. "Out*standing*!" he cried. "Looking *good*!"

Melissa took my arm. I took hers.

"I'm Rosser," he said, sticking out a hand with a middle finger missing. "I hear you're mushers now. Outstanding! Welcome to the country."

I introduced Melissa and myself.

"Starvin' Marvin's my best friend," he said. "We have a straight trail between our places. Come visit! You'll be on the back trails soon. Micky and me and Nara live about five miles down the 231 trail, but from Marvin's it's a cruise. Stay the night! I've got sixteen dogs, all told. Three more won't bother anything."

"Thanks," I said. "But we have to dig our sled up first."

He hesitated momentarily, not quite sure what I meant, but decided to let it pass. "No problem," he said expansively. "We got a moose this year. Moose sausage for breakfast. Can I buy you a beer?"

"We just had coffee," said Melissa.

"You can get dog food in the B&K," he said, indicating the general store. "Three dogs will require about a bag every ten days to two weeks, depending on how well you care for them. It's amazing how little they can survive on, but if you feed them right, you'll see the difference."

"What did Marvin *do*?" said Melissa.

Rosser turned around to look at the Fairview. "It started in there," he said.

As he spoke a bareheaded man came out of the bar and grinned at us.

"One more time, Rocky!" Rosser called.

The man pointed his index finger, winked, and then went to a snowmachine. He yanked the starter cord, straddled the machine, and turned into a curve quickly enough to lift the front of the machine off the ground.

Rosser waved. Then he said, "Rocky's eighty-nine years old. No joke. He took a nap about four, but woke up in time to buy the next round." Rosser slapped me on the shoulder. "That guy's got more gold claims around here than the Feds would let us stake *now*. But fifty years ago . . . haw!" He lifted his sunglasses. His eyes were red around the edges but kindly. "Sometimes on winter mornings I think this *is* fifty years ago," he said, gesturing at the quiet, snowbound town.

He dropped his sunglasses back in place and stretched from his toes, arms high overhead, back arched. "*Oooraawohh!*" he bellowed.

Birds started from nearby trees.

Then, more pacifically, he said, "That's my bull moose mating call. I don't use it during rutting season anymore. A big cow moose once tried to rape me. Chased me for miles. I had to beat her off with a stick. You sure I can't buy you a beer?"

When he went back inside the Fairview we went on to the B&K. I felt the way I did when I was six, when most everything outside the house seemed so new and intriguing that I often skipped instead of walked.

We didn't skip. Faces through the window of the Fairview were turned our way. It was apparent that we were on display. I had once visited a friend in Harlem who instructed me on how to walk to the subway alone: "One hand behind your back," he said. "Go slow. That way they won't know until you're past that you're only holding your fist. Can't be too cool."

I put one arm around Melissa. The other I held behind my back. We went slow.

The clerk in the store told us to leave our two fifty-pound bags of dog food for the freight train to pick up at the station. The train was due that night. The bags would be dropped, we were told, near our trail.

The hike back up the tracks was romantic. To be alone together in such a large landscape aroused us both. When we came to a small open glade between trees I said, only half jokingly, "Should we dally in the snow for a while?"

Melissa laughed. "Forget it," she said. "I'm a good Catholic girl. Besides, this is already the strangest date I've been on in my life."

Then we noticed something coming up the tracks—too big for a snowmachine or dogsled and much too small for a train. We stepped away from the snow-covered ties.

A little box on train wheels, making a golf cart's putting noise, slowed to a stop beside us. The sole person in the car lifted a vinyl door flap and said, "How we doin'?"

He was a large man, an Indian, with a cigarette between his lips. He squinted. The squint made him look as if he were grinning.

"Outstanding," said Melissa.

"I used to give Stanley and his wife a ride every once in a while," he said. "But it's against the rules." He held open the flap.

"We won't tell anyone," I said as we stepped aboard.

Ted operated the gas car to check the tracks before trains came through. For twenty-eight years, he had worked for the railroad. "But I'm retiring soon," he added. "And then I'll stop smoking." He pulled another Marlboro from his shirt pocket and lit it off the one before. "But at least I'm not hooked on broccoli. Some people have big greenhouses in the woods. They grow pretty potent broccoli."

He throttled down as we neared our trail. "Personal use," he explained without taking his eyes from the tracks. "It's legal in Alaska."

When we'd climbed out, Ted didn't linger. "Got to chase the moose out of the way so the train don't make hamburger out of them," he said as he pulled away.

The next morning we went over to Marvin and Anna's. They weren't home. Their dogs were gone, too, except for three. They barked. They had the Oriental eyes of huskies and the long teeth of Dobermans. I tried to pet them but they raced in circles at the ends of their chains, barking.

I took a shovel from the side of the cabin and stepped off Marvin's directions to the sled. We found the old trail and the twin spruce. At the top of a low snow mound I began digging.

When I tired, three feet down, standing up to my waist, Melissa took over. When she tired I resumed shoveling.

Then we found a plank of wood that wasn't a branch. It was, I hoped, the runner of a sled.

I dug hurriedly around it. A half hour later I broke the revealed sled loose from where it had been frozen to the earth. I hauled it out of its hole.

"Look!" I said.

We looked. The sled listed heavily to one side. All the wood that would have formed a place to sit was gone. Its curved handlebar was broken in the middle, two protruding stumps indicating the arch. It was a skeleton. But it was ours.

We pushed and pulled it home. We took it inside the cabin. I was afraid that only ice held it together, and I needed to see it thawed so that I could rebuild the parts it lacked. In high school, I had been led to take French instead of woodshop. As I studied the sagging pile of wood in the lantern light, I regretted the deficiencies in my education.

I thought of how angry I was that so much of my institutional schooling had been in pursuit of grades and not insight. I thought of how aboriginal Eskimos who had never before seen a machine could stare inside a broken diesel generator on a stranded ship and see the problem that had stumped trained white mechanics, because the

Eskimos were aware of cause and effect in the world from firsthand experience—a generator being less complex in operation than the movements of sea ice. I thought of how much I wanted my children to know intimately the real world and not just French or long division.

I did a lot of thinking like this because it kept me from having to figure out how to rebuild the sled. That stumped me. I went to bed, to dream of swinging a hammer at a row of nails and either bending them or missing them completely.

In the morning the sled had thawed enough for puddles of water to encircle it. The sled looked sad and incontinent. I stoked the fire and set to work.

First I examined the sled from different angles. Then I took Stanley's toolbox from a corner and laid out a few tools. Then I remembered how my father, who had astutely purchased one of the first Magnavox hi-fis ever made, asked his children, twenty years later and some six months after buying a new stereo, "Now, which one of these knobs turns down the volume?" I was handicapped by education *and* genetics. What was left on which I could rely?

Nails.

By the end of the day I had pounded enough nails into the sled to hold it upright. It hadn't been easy. The wood was so hard that I first thought it was still frozen solid. Nails bent. But by dusk, with even the derelict puddles dried, I decided that the wood itself was so old it had petrified.

Our sled, standing tall beside the stove, was an archaeological relic.

We were in possession of a museum curator's prize, a work of historic art.

Melissa had a different perspective. "That's a piece of junk," she said.

I tried to make her see its beauty. The dark grains of the gray wood gleamed in the kerosene light. It didn't sag!

But it still lacked a place for a passenger to sit. In the course of stomping around outside the cabin I had found weathered planks of wood left over from roof or floor construction. I planned to saw a few pieces into lengths that I would lash down the middle of the sled to form the basket.

The next day, while digging through the planks, I found two long steel strips a few inches wide and about eight feet long. There were quarter-inch holes spaced a foot apart down the center of the steel. Sled runners! A sign!

I carried them into the cabin like Midas with his gold. "I can screw them to the wood runners!" I told Melissa. "They'll make the sled last forever!"

My back muscles were so tensed from the hours kneeling over the sled, from days of chopping wood and hauling water, that it was painful to move. I didn't complain. Providence was providing.

Providence, however, had not included any appropriately sized screws in Stanley's toolbox. I ended up pounding nails halfway into the screw holes and then bending the nails over to keep the metal attached to the wood. I filed the heads off the nails to ease the drag.

When I'd finished with the sled we went over to claim our dogs.

Marvin and Anna still weren't home. I assumed that the dogs remaining on their chains hadn't been fed for a few days. When I got close enough I saw that there was a piece of paper thumbtacked on the tree where each dog was chained. BELL, said one sign. KOBUK, said another. The third said, GARNER, LEADER.

Bell was a long-legged beauty. Kobuk was big. Garner ran in tight circles so frenetically I wondered if he was demented.

Three harnesses hung outside the cabin door. I assumed they were for us, and I was grateful for the ease with which I could make that assumption. Considerate neighbors!

Then I had to approach the dogs with the harnesses. I had been an active kid, and so had been bitten more than a few times by dogs that strayed where I did. To think of kneeling beside these manic slavering wolves was so unthinkable that I didn't think. I just did it. I grabbed Garner's chain and reeled him in so that I could pet him and harness him.

He suffered my petting hesitantly, but he didn't bristle. Then I spent fifteen minutes trying to figure out how to get the harness on.

I had such a difficult time holding him still that I abandoned my original plan to drive all three dogs down to get the dog food left by the freight train. One dog was strong; three would be uncontrollable.

Melissa went back to Stanley's for a little plastic child's toboggan. I was going to walk Garner on a leash to the tracks, load one bag atop the sled, and run Garner up the ridge.

When I got the leash on his collar he tugged toward the cabin, then down the trail, then around and around my legs. I crumpled to the ground, tied like a hog. Garner strained over me, barking.

I counted to ten and then began yelling. Garner immediately sat down. I untangled myself. When he started to jerk the leash again I yelled some more. He stopped.

I had expected the dogs to understand "Mush!" or "Whoa!" It hadn't occurred to me that they might know the command "Goddamn you stupid son of a bitch stop it!"

When I'd wrestled him down to the tracks in leaps and pauses, I met Melissa with the child's sled. I took the leash off Garner's collar, attached one end to the back of his harness and the other to the sled, on which I'd set a fifty-pound bag of food.

Garner seemed to know, finally, what was going on. He tugged against his load while I held on to the sled.

"He knows what to do!" I said to Melissa.

I released the sled. "Mush!" I cried. Garner bolted up the tracks. The bag of food immediately slid off. Garner raced around a bend and out of sight. The empty sled clattered behind him.

"Whoa!" I shouted, running after him. "Whoa!"

At first I was furious. Then I was discouraged. Finally I was resigned, walking up the tracks carrying my sweat-soaked hat and parka, calling, "Garner! Good dog! Here, Garner!"

In time I saw Garner loping toward me, the plastic toboggan bouncing noisily back and forth between the rails. He struck me as the kind of dog—bred to run—who had raced for an hour thinking, "Go! Go!" and then finally, dimly, "Why?"

I bent down to welcome him. He stepped right into my arms. He seemed proud.

I sat in the sled and gripped it tightly. He pulled me back toward our trailhead. "All right!" I said aloud. I was mushing! Sitting in a kid's toboggan, it's true. And pulled by only one dog. But no one could see me.

When I got back to our cabin with a bag of dog food on my shoulder and Garner walking behind me I saw the other two dogs chained beneath the trees. Melissa had walked them over. "They were so sweet," she said. "I think they're wonderful dogs."

We fed them as much as they could eat.

After breakfast the next day—pancakes, from our fifty-pound sack of flour—I dragged our rebuilt dogsled down the ridge to the tracks. Melissa ferried one dog at a time to me. I put on each dog's harness while she went back for the next. I had rigged a long line of manila rope to the sled and affixed shorter ropes to the back of each harness.

When we had three dogs in a row, Melissa sat in the sled and I stood on the back holding on to the stumps of the handlebar. "Mush!" I shouted.

Bell turned halfway around, tangling her line. Kobuk barked but didn't move. Garner tugged once, met resistance, and stopped.

"Let's go! Okay! Mush! Come on!" I tried.

Garner looked back at me and then, perhaps because he had heard "Come," took a few steps toward the sled.

Kobuk jumped him, snarling. Bell leaped into the sled.

Garner and Kobuk fell to the snow growling and biting.

"Oh, my God!" said Melissa.

"No!" I screamed. "No! No!"

"Stop them!" Melissa cried.

I waded into the fight, kicking. The dogs kept slashing at each other. I grabbed the line attached to Garner's harness and tried to pull him clear. The sled moved a few feet. Kobuk locked his teeth on Garner's ear and began gnawing.

"Stop!" shouted Melissa. "*Stop!*"

"You asshole!" I shouted, booting Kobuk under the jaw. "No!"

Kobuk let go. I yanked Garner clear. His ear dripped blood. Blood spattered the snow, my boot, Kobuk's muzzle.

Melissa began crying.

I stood between the two males panting. Kobuk wagged his tail. Garner tried to lick his ear.

"What horrible dogs," said Melissa, swabbing her eyes with her gloves.

"This is how a wolf pack establishes dominance," I said. "They weren't out to kill. They didn't go for the throat."

"There's blood everywhere!" said Melissa.

"It's all right!" I shouted.

Melissa was stunned at my outburst. I paced away from the sled and then returned. "I think it's all right," I apologized. "We'll try again."

What had unnerved me even more than the fight was the realization that I was way over my head. What did I know about dog teams, or medical emergencies if Melissa or I had been bitten? What would I do in a survival situation if a storm blew in? Or if an animal attacked us out of the woods? For the first time it occurred to me that there was danger *everywhere* in the boreal forest, and the danger was not latent but inevitable.

I untangled the lines without speaking. When I had the dogs straightened out, I walked a little way in front of them and said, "Okay."

They pulled toward me. I ran on ahead until they caught up, then ran some more beside them until the sled drew near. When the sled started to pass me I jumped on the back. The dogs kept going.

A half hour later they were still going. We were running a dog team. It seemed like a lifetime ago that we had run for the subway.

The breeze that our speed created made my face numb. Melissa pulled her legs up to her chest with one hand, held a glove over her nose with the other. She was smiling.

"Dashing through the snow, in a three-dog open sled," I sang. "O'er the tracks we go, laughing all the way, ho, ho, ho." Melissa chimed in on the "ho, ho, ho."

But my third "ho" became an unexpected grunt. I flew over the handlebars. I landed on my back atop the dog closest to the sled.

Melissa sprawled face-first against me. The sled had stopped as if it had hit a wall.

I leaped up clutching my crotch. "My future!" I cried. A stump of the handlebar had hit me as I sailed. I wasn't sure if it had dealt me an irreparable blow.

"I think I'm just winded," I gasped, dropping to one knee, feeling for damage. "Oh, *man*."

"But look at *that*," said Melissa. She pointed at one runner that was now bent up at a ninety-degree angle. It was wedged between the V of the tracks where a siding curved away.

The runner that wasn't bent was a foot longer in front than the runner that was gripped by the tracks. The whole sled was skewed. It was now a trapezoid instead of a rectangle. But it hadn't collapsed.

Melissa and I walked around for a while trying to get our balance. My breathing was shallow, as if from shock or, more likely, great anxiety. I glanced at the trees, to see if one was ready to fall on us, then at the sky, for meteorites.

For the first time it occurred to me that a constant awareness was our only hope, that luck was limited and angels often busy elsewhere. This life needed a constant awareness. At every step: *think*. With every blink of the eyes: *think*.

"I'll be more aware," I said aloud. "I *have* to be more aware." What we lacked in experience I'd counterbalance with attention. This was not Zen training. This was simple survival.

When I'd pried the sled free we proceeded toward town as if nothing had happened. That was the perspective the dogs seemed to have. They just kept pulling. Melissa and I, however, could see plainly that something had happened. The sled was like a parade exhibit: Bozos from the Woods.

Even with our synapses still jangled, the beauty of the day filtered through to us. Waves of small birds flew between the crests of birch like blown spume. The sun refracted from the countless tiny prisms of the snowscape. The sled runners scratched along where the nails were bent over the steel, but the sound wasn't coarse; it had its own steady lull. The rest was silence.

As we neared the town we crossed over a long steel-girder bridge that spanned the major tributary of the Susitna. The dogs stepped lightly from tie to tie, though there was fifty feet of air visible below them. Plainly they had done this often before. With the same familiarity, they curved down into the parking lot. Immediately, a howl went up from what seemed to be a hundred dogs nearby. Our dogs stopped, but began barking, too.

The door of a camper trailer burst open and a man peered out. He ran a hand over his face to help bring his eyes into focus. "Well, don't you look *good*!" said Rosser. He grinned at us.

Then he stared at our sled. "Ah . . . ," he amended.

He stood in the doorway for another moment, wearing nothing but a gray union suit. Then he said, "Hang on now," and shut the door.

I stood between Garner and Kobuk while Melissa held the sled to keep it from moving. From behind Rosser's trailer the wild barking continued.

Rosser came out of his trailer hurriedly dressed—boots unlaced, shirt unbuttoned. "Morning!" he said. Then he turned around toward the howling of the hundred dogs. "Shaddup!" he yelled. The noise stopped as if a plug had been pulled.

He bent to stroke Garner's head. Garner flinched. Rosser took a quick look at the chewed ear and said, "I guess Marvin forgot to tell you that Kobuk's a fighter. He's a pure-blood malemute. Malemutes tangle with their own *tails*. Garner, now, he's a normal crossbreed like most of us run." He hesitated. "Though I wouldn't call Garner exactly *normal*," he added.

"They all pulled us so beautifully," said Melissa. "After we got them to go. Until we stopped like crash dummies."

Rosser nodded without having heard. He was studying the sled. "You build this yourself?" he asked.

"Just repaired some parts," I said.

Rosser deliberated with himself and then said, carefully, "There are more dog teams in this part of Alaska than anywhere else. Some of us who live up the tracks have run the Iditarod. These are our trailers here for when we're in town. And, uh, I'd be glad to help you fix up your sled. It'd be my pleasure."

"That would be great," Melissa said quickly.

"Tourists sometimes pass by on the train," he explained. "And they wave at us, and take pictures, and . . . it'd be a pleasure if you came back to visit. I have a workshop attached to the cabin."

"It'd be *our* pleasure," said Melissa.

"Great!" he said. "I'm trying to finish a well. You could help me on it in return."

We then tried to memorize the route from Stanley's, past Marvin's, to Rosser's home. It seemed easy.

While Melissa watched our dogs, I ran to the general store for more dog food and some frozen orange juice and vegetables. I also bought a case of beer as a gift for our visit at Rosser's. After I'd loaded our supplies we turned the sled toward home.

"He said that he had twelve dogs here that he runs *all at once*," said Melissa when we had started back north.

More impressive than the realization that twelve dogs made a din like a hundred was the fact that anyone could commandeer twelve harnessed dogs. It seemed to me like driving a Formula One jet-fueled race car over ice.

The next day we rested. Was it the seventh day? I felt as if we were creating a world. Brilliant light! Dark fears. I couldn't yet quite keep the two divided.

Melissa cooked a fancy dinner atop the cookstove. "It's not like being a short-order cook with a hot griddle," she said as she stirred her sauce. "It's like . . . I'm not sure. I have to put thin pieces into the firebox to get a high heat and big chunks for medium, unless I just watch the color of the top plate, which sometimes glows red just on a bed of coals. I sure can't turn a dial. It keeps me hopping. Is this how people used to cook?"

"People used to cook with sticks stuck over a fire pit," I said.

She moved her pot off the stove with one hand and grabbed a skillet with the other. "But they liked their meat *rare*," she said.

As we sat down to eat at the table in front of the window that overlooked the mountains I confided that I wanted to climb Denali. I explained, almost shyly, that there was nothing else so compelling to me now that I'd been able to stare at the peaks.

Melissa didn't have a chance to respond. Our dogs began barking, and then we heard a knock on the door.

We looked at each other as if we were being invaded. "Come in!" I called.

Even before I spoke the door opened and a man with a full red beard and bright blue eyes stuck his head inside.

"Anyone home?" he said. "Oh, hi! I heard your lady had great legs. Hey! There you are. Aw, you *do* look good. If you're hard-core, too, I'll be real jealous. Can I come in?"

He came in. He didn't wear a parka. He wore only three wool shirts, one over the other, and blue jeans with heavy black motorcycle boots. He looked like a biker transplanted to the woods.

"Pleased to meet you," he said. "I'm Denny. Boy that smells good!"

Melissa stood up. "We have plenty," she said.

"Ooh, ooh, don't move so fast," he said as she went to the stove. "Let me savor this. You don't know how lonely it gets living in the woods with nothing so lovely to look at."

He winked at me. Melissa blushed.

"I'm one of your neighbors," he said. "You don't have many. I have a five-story cabin about five miles from here. The Professor is on Hidden Lake, a mile further. Mike and Amy live about a half mile down Dead Dog Ridge from you, but they're gone a lot. You know Marvin and Anna."

"Dead Dog Ridge?" asked Melissa.

Denny pantomimed horror. He hid his face behind his hands and shook his head. "I thought you knew," he said. "Marvin named it. He's not the aesthetic, environmentally sensitive kind." Then he brightened. "But I can tell right away that you're liberal, sort of left-wing leaning, probably Sierra Clubbers. Right?"

"I don't think so," I said hesitantly.

"But that's all right," he said. "We need more people who don't shoot first and ask questions later. You don't mind if I visit, do you?"

Melissa brought him a plate of brown rice with her sauce and some yogurt she'd made from powdered milk and dried culture.

"Oh, thanks. That looks so *organic*. I'll bet you're vegetarians, too. I'm against killing anything, myself. That makes me different from everyone else out here. I'll bet you guys didn't think there'd be so many rednecks in the aboriginal forest, did you?"

I hadn't noticed any rednecks. I tried to frame a response.

"Good!" said Denny, digging into his food. "That's good! Be discreet. Don't judge too quickly."

He smiled at us. He ate happily.

I couldn't remember the last time that anyone had barged through my door without a prior phone call or introduction to make himself so comfortably at home.

"How long have you lived here?" Melissa asked, pulling a chair close beside me.

"Sixteen years," he said. "I came right after Vietnam." He laid down his fork. "I was Special Forces, until they kicked me out of the corps for insubordination. But I was too familiar with operations to be cut completely loose, so they attached me to the 101st Airborne. I lay in my foxhole one night when the shells were screaming overhead, thinking what I'd do when I got out. I lay there for *five days*. I thought of *every*thing—the high life and the low life but mostly a life where there wouldn't be little slimy bugs crawling down my neck. I figured Alaska would be safe. *N*obody thought about Alaska in the sixties except miners and ex-cons. I started building my cabin in my head, but after five long days I ended up with a five-story place. You'll have to come see it. It's really impressive."

"I can't imagine a five-story cabin," I said.

He laughed. "I *know*! The imagining was hard. But the building was just a lot of grunt."

He shoveled food into his mouth like a Hong Kong Chinese dishing rice from a small bowl.

"But enough about me," he said. "I came to find out about *you*."

"I'm mostly overwhelmed by practically everything," I said.

He chuckled. "That's the right perspective. *Ancora imparo:* 'I still learn.' That's what Michelangelo said on his deathbed. I'll bet you didn't know that."

"Are you still hungry?" asked Melissa.

"Oh, no, no. I'm stuffed. That was *excellent*," he said. "Unless you have some more."

Melissa went back to the stove with his plate.

Denny turned to me. He dropped his act of eccentric mountain man. With an intensity that startled me he said, "How far out are you going?"

"I don't know," I said. "This is just our first home. I don't know what's out there."

He nodded. He leaned closer. "Everything's out there," he said. "Everything. I'm tied to town by my lust. It's my pleasure and my regret. But I've driven dogs through the Mackenzie Mountains in the Yukon with my lady and little boy and then canoed out six months later. We saw *no one* else. I've explored enough of this area to see that it's part of the last mapped lands on earth. There's nowhere further anywhere to go." I was alarmed to find my head six inches from his. "Go!" he said softly. "Don't get trapped. Go further."

I pulled back abruptly. Melissa set his replenished plate in front of him. "Oh, gee, thanks!" said Denny, straightening up. "I'll bet you have some tamari, too. I don't mean that your cooking isn't spiced enough but I really like tamari."

Melissa looked at him curiously. "Rick bought five gallons," she said.

"I knew it!" he said. "Ex-urban natural foods people. But if you're going to be hard-core you'll have to live with dried berries and rabbit meat."

Melissa stared at him. "What do you mean about going 'further'?" she asked.

Denny grinned. "Aw, that's just what we say around here. Talkeetna is like a halfway house. It isn't Anchorage or El Paso or Schenectady, but we've all come from places like that. We go up and down the tracks. We talk about going over the Range or out toward the glacial canyons. But it's just talk. We're mainstream Americans who stumbled into the edge of wilderness. Look!" He unbuttoned his shirts like Clark Kent tearing open his suit. He held his arms wide and stuck out his barrel chest. His T-shirt was emblazoned with the Harley-Davidson logo. "Made in America," he said.

He began buttoning up. "I keep thinking I'll meet some people who have come here to build a whole new world and not just escape from an old one. Wouldn't it be great to be self-sufficient with the best of Eskimo and Indian culture *and* good ol' American know-how? You can create *anything* out there."

He glanced up to see if we were still attentive. When he saw that we weren't fidgeting he plunged on. "Even if this civilization isn't doomed by its own greed, which it probably is, there's still an unnamed salmon creek out there that'll sustain the wildest dreams."

"We're not staying here," I said impulsively.

He burst out laughing. "I've met only two people in sixteen years who've cut the cultural umbilical cord and gone out for good. And they're both dead."

"What do you mean we're not staying here?" said Melissa, turning to me.

"I just mean that we're still looking for our own land," I said, avoiding her eyes.

"Where else do you want to *go*?" she said.

"I only mean—," I began.

Denny broke in. "Hey, oh, listen. I don't want to start a domestic quarrel. I lost my woman ten years ago. If you two don't stay together you'll both end up back in town."

He leaned toward me and said conspiratorially, "If you push 'em too hard you'll lose 'em."

"What are you *talking* about!" cried Melissa. She was upset.

"Nothing! Nothing!" said Denny. "Oh *boy*, this is the best food I've had since I met a little hippie girl at the Bread Factory. That's Anchorage's health food restaurant. They have tamari on the table instead of salt. We spent the most romantic week at my place. But then she fell through the ice."

"*What* ice?" shouted Melissa.

"Ooh, I think I better go," said Denny, grabbing a last forkful.

"Now, don't you two worry. I won't get lost. It was great getting to know you. Just take it easy and go slow."

He backed toward the door. "You're going to do *wonderful*. I can tell. Thanks for dinner. See you!"

He shut the door gently.

"Will you please tell me what is going on?" said Melissa, standing very straight.

"He was just trying to be encouraging," I said.

"He was making me crazy!"

"But now we know what's out there," I said.

"I don't even know what's *here*!" she said.

"There's people like us here. Normal people who were curious about Alaska."

"*He* was *normal*?" said Melissa.

I thought of Rosser with his sunglasses at dawn. I thought of Marvin's felony rap. I thought of the abused waitress from Texas.

"Well, at least he appreciated your cooking."

Melissa took a deep breath. "Are you going to climb that mountain?" she asked.

I was caught off guard. "Oh boy," I said, buying time. "I thought we'd visit Rosser first."

"Listen to me," she said. "I don't care what's 'out there.' We *are* 'out there.' I can't even write to my friends because anything I'd say would be incomprehensible. *Wolves* pulling us through the forest. *Rabbit* meat? And *you're* going to climb the tallest mountain on the *planet*? You've only climbed the Empire State Building!"

"Now wait a minute," I said.

An hour later we resolved our argument in passionate love. With the moonlight flooding through the window, everything seemed as it should be: vivid, powerful, intense. As I fell asleep I wondered, "Is that normal?"

The next day we harnessed the dogs to go to Rosser's. Melissa sat atop the beer. The day was warm, the snow soft. Spring seemed in the air.

I expected to get lost. I had brought a pen and paper to map the route we followed, which I feared would bring us back to our doorstep, as Einstein's theory of random excursion predicts.

But a few hours later, after a pastoral journey through dense forest marked only by small-game tracks that we couldn't identify, we came upon a little cabin. Rosser stood under the porch, leaning against a log pole, as if he were expecting us.

Instead of shouting a greeting he nodded his welcome and came out to help us with our dogs. He seemed serene. I thought, "Of course: he's home."

The cabin was crammed with utensils of daily life: shelves of cookware and books, rafters hung with snowsuits and gloves, the corners of the floor packed with rows of boots or boxes of children's toys. All of it seemed *organized*.

We were welcomed by his wife, Micky, and his five-year-old girl, Nara. They were gracious. Micky dished out moose steaks that Nara served on china plates.

The three of them gave us a tour of the cavernous root cellar beneath a trapdoor in the floor, then through the shop where a set of serious craftsman's tools was ordered along the walls, then up to the brink of a circular pit at the end of the shop—the hoped-for well— and finally out to a woodshed where a haunch of moose hung frozen. We were introduced to each dog by name. It was a conventional suburban afternoon visit in the northern forest.

But by dusk, Rosser—"Mark" to his wife—and I were drinking beer, and the women were in the upstairs sleeping loft, whispering and laughing.

We were still drinking beer long after they had gone to sleep.

What made it different from hanging out in a Formica kitchen beneath fluorescent lights was not the lantern-lit log walls chinked with moss or the sled dogs singing in the night. It was the conversation.

Rosser did most of the talking. And most of the drinking. He told me how it had taken him two years to acquire the skills to live comfortably in rural Alaska even though he'd been raised in rural

Michigan. The hunting was different: game at latitude 62 traveled across enormous areas instead of across farm fields. Building was different, in order to accommodate huge snow loads. The garden season was short and difficult: there were frosts in June and late August, and the acid soil was only a foot deep atop the remains of glaciers. And the isolation, even this close to the only community center within five thousand square miles, made Michigan's Upper Peninsula look urban by comparison.

He told me Talkeetna had been a gold-mining supply point along the railroad until the mid-fifties, when scattered homestead land was made available. He described the requirements of a dog team ("Lots of food and a big stick") and explained his cabin's foundation, constructed from dried spruce logs coated with creosote against ground rot.

I felt like an anthropologist learning the structure of an exotic life, and Rosser knew it. He leaned back against the frosted kitchen window, feet up on a hand-hewn log table, head framed by starlit spruce, and offered information casually but directly. He told about a friend who had fallen through overflow on the winter Susitna into waist-deep water and survived by drying his clothes over a fire of cottonwood bark and dead willow branches. He confided that he had not yet learned how to make beaver mitts or any other fur clothing though gas-car Ted and his wife—the only Athabaskan Indians remaining in the area—tanned their skins with moose brains. "And you can't get softer skins than that."

He wasn't trying to be an instant encyclopedia of Alaskan bush life, but the knowledge was marvelous to him, not least because it made good listening.

I learned that birch bark makes the best kindling. Rosser knew because he had once stripped a birch tree of its bark so that the tree would dry standing, and had then, a few months later, dropped a cigarette into the bark pile at its base. I learned that spring is the best time to haul firewood because the warm days and freezing nights create a concrete snow crust as hard as pavement atop which the dogs can haul heavy loads. I also found out that no one said "Mush" to his dogs. A low whistle to start the team was particularly cool. "Mush" was for cartoonists.

In response to his stories gleaned from six years in Alaska I offered my week's worth of slapstick. He laughed dutifully, but then returned to tales full of color and of information that was essential for a novice in one of the most extreme environments on earth.

In time, he drained a last beer and said, "But I don't know anything. My brother's a doctor. He's smart. I'm just the black sheep of the family."

Before I could assure him that he was competent—which to me surpassed "smart" by a long shot—he stuck his can into the empties case and said, "I hope you're ready to climb fifteen feet down into the well in the morning. We're gonna have us some *fun*."

"Go to sleep!" called his wife from upstairs.

"So what did Marvin *do*?" I asked suddenly.

Rosser paused. He shrugged. "He tore down the Christmas sign on the Fairview because the owner wouldn't serve Anna. The old redneck asshole put a sign up that said HIPPIES USE SIDE DOOR. Marvin got pissed."

"That was a *felony*?"

"The damage was more than five hundred dollars."

In the morning, Micky cooked an enormous breakfast of eggs and potatoes from the root cellar, with moose sausage and home-canned blueberry jam. Before we ate, Rosser drank a pot of coffee. When he extended the pot to my cup his hand shook.

After breakfast Rosser lowered a five-gallon bucket into the well and I slid down the rope attached to its handle. I used a small shovel to dig earth into the bucket. He hauled it up. The bucket was a foot and a half wide. The shaft was three feet wide. Each bucket of dirt and rocks weighed at least fifty pounds.

Yet I didn't worry that he might drop it. When I struck moist earth, he lowered a long metal pipe with a well point attached to the end. I jammed a log horizontally into the shaft six feet from the lip. Then I climbed up to stand atop the log, holding the pipe a few feet from its top. Rosser banged on the pipe's three-inch head with a twelve-pound sledgehammer. My hands were very close to where the hammer rang on the pipe. If he missed a blow I'd lose an arm or part of my cranium.

But he had become a John Henry to me, even though he had the shakes in the morning. It didn't occur to me that he might miss. And he didn't.

When the well point had been driven deep into the subterranean stream that would supply their water, I climbed out and Rosser lowered lengths of three-foot-wide corrugated steel tubing into the well, then filled in dirt around it.

Afterwards we spent a few hours in the shop, where I watched Rosser swiftly lash and screw and hammer our sled into a shape that resembled his own sled's. "This kiln-dried oak is hard wood to pound a nail into," he explained tactfully, as he yanked out my handiwork.

When we had harnessed our dogs for the run home and headed off amidst waves and goodbyes, Melissa offered her perspective. "Do you know how scary it is to live out here?" she asked as we followed our tracks.

I was driving a beautiful dogsled on a familiar trail in late-afternoon sunlight. "No!" I said happily.

"Micky said that every other family except Marvin and Anna who have tried to make a home here have either split up or gone back to where they came from. She said that the only people left are loners or crazies. She told me that *she* has to drive *seven* dogs a half mile to the creek every day to fill cans of water for them."

I laughed. "But they have a well now!"

"You're missing the point," she said.

"Well, what was so amusing that kept you giggling upstairs?" I asked.

She turned around to smile at me. "We were talking about how funny you boys are when you try to be on top of things."

We drove along in silence for a while.

"Like what do you mean?" I asked, a little perturbed.

She gestured at our sleek sled. "When we get a camera, I'll take a picture to send back to New York," she said. "Now that we have a *real* sled."

For the next few weeks we busied ourselves with felling spruce that had died and dried while still standing. I discovered that live trees were, even in winter, saturated with moisture, so that they burned with a cool hiss instead of a hot crackle. We tried to fix up Stanley's cabin by jamming old pieces of fiberglass insulation between gaps in the log walls. We went over to thank our neighbors for the sled and harnesses. We stared at the mountains by day and the aurora by night.

The aurora kept us up late. It lit the sky in spectral curtains that rippled and curled and set the dogs to howling.

We wrote letters back home, but it was as futile an exercise as astronauts trying to describe the landscape of the moon: "Real pretty." "Awful different."

The snow melted rapidly as the days lengthened. The days lengthened radically. The sun rose six minutes earlier every morning. It appeared increasingly to the north, not the east. It was strange and fantastical, like an eclipse.

Then Denny reappeared as suddenly as he had before.

"I've been expecting you!" he said as he marched through the door. He wore only two wool shirts now, and a red bandanna to hold back his longer hair. "I thought you were the kind who would *want* to explore. Come on! You won't get anywhere hanging around here."

"We've gotten to the limits of our abilities," I said.

He sighed. "Well, at least you're not dead," he said. "Now come on. Follow me!"

We fed the dogs and followed him.

Two hours later we crossed a frozen lake to stand before his five-story palace. He didn't let us spend more than a minute gazing up at it. "It needs too much work to be a showcase," he said, hurrying us on. "It's big, I know, but I built it without knowing how to use logs. Let me show you a place that's *professional*."

He started to escort us farther into the forest but paused. He turned back to look at his home. "But it *is* big, isn't it?"

The peak reached the tops of the trees. The gaps between the logs indicated a rather slapdash construction, but it was a monument to human possibility.

"It gives me hope," said Melissa.

"Good!" said Denny. "Good enough."

We hiked on through the woods. When we came to the shore of another lake he pointed and said, "That's the Professor's home. It burned to the ground five years ago. Or the old place did. I designed this cabin when he was so despondent I thought he might actually leave the country. Doesn't it look aesthetic nestled back in the trees?"

The cabin was spacious, as picturesque as a ranch house in *Town & Country*.

"We all got together to help him rebuild. It was a month-long party. The Professor's a natural resource. Before he left his university he was an authority on altered states of consciousness and even wrote a textbook that was used in colleges *across the country*."

Denny hurried us closer, then paused. "But that stuff's past for us now." He looked carefully at Melissa and then me. "Right?"

"I've tasted every drink once," I said.

"Right," said Melissa, more diplomatically.

Denny picked up the pace. "I used to have moral qualms even about marijuana," he said, "but after I saw how destructive alcohol is in this state I started thinking different. The Native population is a tragedy. What's happening here is no different at *all* from what happened to the Plains tribes during the Westward Expansion. And many of the whites here are aggressive, rapacious, sugar-junky, marginally psychotic episodic drunks. Just like on the frontier!"

He ushered us to the porch of the cabin. "Hello! Hello!" he called, cupping his hands to his mouth.

"I guess he's gone to town for supplies on his snowmachine," he said quickly. "Well, we can still take a sauna."

He went over to a small building beside the cabin. "Look! There's plenty of wood already split!"

He disappeared into the sauna with an armful of wood.

Melissa and I exchanged glances. "I want a towel," she said. "A big, wraparound towel."

Smoke began to lift from the chimney pipe. Denny came out to get some more wood. "This is the only way to bathe in the woods," he said. "It's better than peyote. You'll see. After we soak in two-hundred-degree heat we'll plunge in the lake. It's mind-boggling!"

We found a towel for Melissa. Denny was disappointed. "No one can see you," he said.

Melissa changed behind the sauna and entered wrapped to her knees.

Denny stoked the fire until the metal thermometer near the ceiling topped out past two hundred. We all turned bright red.

The conversation hung as limp as Denny's muscles.

Then he splashed water from a wooden bucket onto the rocks that covered the stove. It made the heat unbearable. "Now!" he shouted as he rushed outside.

He ran wide-legged to the lake and dropped through a hole in the ice. At once he was up and racing back.

"Hoo!" he said. "Haw!"

He shook himself like a dog. "Go on!" he insisted. "All circumpolar people know about this."

Melissa and I stood steaming like overheated radiators. "I think I'll pass," said Melissa.

We all went back inside. "Three times!" said Denny as he fired the stove back up. "Three times into the lake and you won't *believe* what happens."

After the second splash of water onto the rocks I followed him into the lake. It was like being hit in the head with a mallet by the most beautiful woman in the world: stunning but exciting. Even after I'd jumped out of the water my head continued to swim.

After the third blast of steam we all jumped into the lake. We whooped. We splashed. The trees overhead whirled. I couldn't remember a time when I was so pleasantly dazed. I couldn't remember much of anything.

I did note, however, that the ritual of a sauna lacked eroticism, once the plunge had been taken. Denny didn't even glance at

Melissa. He stared at his own feet as they beat the path back into the sauna.

When we'd dressed, still wobbly, Denny pointed across the lake and said, "Your place is only two miles away. Can you tell we walked almost *ten* getting here?"

"Yes," said Melissa, sitting on a tree stump.

"There's a trail right across the lake," said Denny. "You'll be home in a half hour."

He walked us across the lake and showed us the trail. "The real wilderness is still a distance away," he said. "We have trails here. There aren't any trails where you hope to be. I mean, where *I'd* hope you to be. But a trail sure makes life easy!"

Then he repeated that in a half hour we'd come upon Dead Dog Ridge and invited us to spend a day at his place sometime soon. "After a little honey coming up this weekend helps me clean inside." We said our goodbyes and Melissa and I walked off contentedly along the trail.

Within a few minutes the lake's white expanse was hidden by the forest. We felt adventurously alone. We tried to hold hands as we went, but the snowmachine track that defined the trail was too narrow. We talked about how we would build our own sauna—me, in front, calling over my shoulder. We debated whether a sauna or a root cellar was more important to build first.

Fifteen minutes later we lost the trail. I found myself standing amidst the discarded branches of a birch that had been carried away for firewood, the top six inches of a saw-cut trunk remaining above the snow.

"I guess we veered off onto a wood-cutting trail," I said. We backtracked. We found where I'd taken the wrong fork.

Though we'd seen fewer than a half-dozen cabins in the entire area up the tracks from Talkeetna, I had adopted Denny's perspective: that there were *lots* of people here amidst the connecting trails, and a trail always leads somewhere. Even when the trail we were walking ended at another wood site, I wasn't concerned. We followed our own footprints again, and returned to where the wood trail diverged from the main trail. We could see, however, that the wood trail we'd just followed *was* the main trail. Continuing on from the fork was an indentation in the snow, drifted over but plainly a trail because when I stepped on it my weight was supported.

"Are we lost?" asked Melissa.

I laughed. "We can't be lost. According to the sun we're still headed in the direction we started, and if we try to get off the trail we'll sink a little into the unpacked snow."

A few minutes later we started sinking a little into the unpacked snow. I stomped around, feeling with my feet for the trail. I furiously tried to remember where along the westward horizon the sun did set at this extreme latitude. I'd checked it with my compass out of curiosity a week ago, but even in a week it had shifted substantially in the sky.

"Now I'm getting a little worried," said Melissa. "It won't stay light for long."

I couldn't find the trail at all. "We'll climb this ridge," I announced. "And get our bearings."

We struggled up to the crest of a low sloping rise that flanked where we'd been hiking. A hundred feet or so higher than its base, the ridge offered a panoramic view.

We saw forest rolling up to horizons of white mountains. We saw only forest and mountain. No smoke from chimneys. No lake with a cabin and sauna. No sign of human life *at all*.

"Oh boy," I said.

"I'm very worried now," said Melissa.

I struggled with panic. The world around us was much vaster than I had imagined. And there was no indication anywhere that people were present amidst the landscape. We couldn't see Talkeetna or the railroad tracks. It was like being the only fire lookout in the world's largest national forest.

I took a deep breath. The sudden surprise that we were *on our own* in a land we couldn't chart began to give way to calmer thought. What would we lose by trying to make our own way home? At worst we'd have to follow the confused tracks of our own feet back to the Professor's. It seemed to be logically impossible to walk toward Denali and not run into the Susitna River.

From the time I was a kid I'd prided myself on my sense of time and my sense of direction. After the sauna, in the perplexing skies of the far north, I hadn't any idea if it was five o'clock or eight. But our direction seemed obvious.

We had no matches, no compass, not enough clothes to keep from freezing in the March night that would drop ten or twenty degrees from the low thirties of the day. "This way," I said.

We hiked for another hour. The light grew blue. The air was cold when we paused to catch our breath. Melissa didn't express whatever anxieties she might have had, and I didn't offer false hopes. We were together, and together we'd make it.

When the sky became filled with stars and the green glow of the aurora, we stumbled into a clearing. There was a cabin at the far end. It was our cabin.

We went a few steps closer.

"It really is," whispered Melissa.

We drew closer to each other. I took her hand. "When we stick by each other," I said, "there's nothing we can't do."

We looked at the cabin in the starlight. It was beautiful.

I kissed her slowly. The wild luck of coming right up to our cabin seemed no more coincidental than a chance meeting that leads to marriage: fate is at work, too, and the stars.

"I love you so much," I said. "And I do know that we can do anything."

She smoothed back the hair from my temples. "Is that like a vow?" she asked, smiling.

"For better or worse," I said. "And this is definitely better."

For the rest of the spring we practiced everything. We studied the tracks of animals in the woods behind the cabin and discovered that the amount of wildlife was as large as the landscape. We tried to discern marten from fox from coyote from wolf from wolverine, using a book on tracking from Stanley's bookshelf. We started ten different kinds of vegetables inside the house awaiting June, when the ground would be thawed enough to plant. We even found a bit of ease from the demand of chores by working together concentratedly and then just quitting when we got tired. How different from urban life!

We had no electricity, no plumbing, no phone, no gas, and we washed our dishes in a pan on the wood stove, lacking a kitchen sink. But we were comfortable.

When my unemployment checks started coming, I couldn't think of anything else we might need.

Marvin made me change my mind.

On a day when I utilized the last of the snow on the tracks to make a supply run into town, Marvin came over to check on us. He found Melissa kneeling over a trunk of birch, laboriously cutting it up with our little band saw.

"What's wrong with your chain saw?" Marvin asked.

Melissa said that we didn't have one.

What's wrong with Stanley's?" Marvin asked.

Melissa said she didn't know if he had one.

"Does Rick know?" said Marvin carefully.

"Rick doesn't know about mechanical things," said Melissa.

Marvin was quiet. He bent down and took the saw from Melissa. He turned it over in his hands. "You're not kidding me now, are you?" he said.

When I returned that afternoon there was a tremendous pile of wood outside the cabin door.

"We just learned about chain saws," explained Melissa.

"But where did all this *come* from?" I said.

"Marvin cut down a tree for us. It nearly hit the house. He said, 'Why go further than you have to?' I liked that."

The next day I went back to town and found a used chain saw for sale. Within a week, we had a summer's supply of wood. The roar and bite of the chain saw made me feel particularly gruesome when I placed its teeth on the flank of a birch, but I went far enough into the forest to be in seclusion with the mystery of death. Before starting the saw I touched the tree I'd selected and said a prayer.

. . .

On the last day of May Melissa came up beside me as I sat at the front window staring at the mountains. She took my hand and placed it on her belly.

"Six weeks already," she said.

I turned from my study and took her in my lap. "How do you feel today?"

"I feel fine," she said.

"No sickness?"

She smiled. "Not when I take my vitamins and get lots of love."

We hugged each other.

Then I gestured at the Range. "I can't get over how close it is," I said.

"January's close, too," she said. "I dreamed last night that it's a boy."

I grinned. "Lightning if it's a boy, Lassie if it's a girl."

We were silent for a minute. Then she looked out the window and said, "I really hope you don't try it."

"But then I'll be ready to settle down," I answered at once. "Then I won't have to sit here and study the routes."

"I found the ice axe and cleats you tried to hide outside," she said.

I was embarrassed. "I got the axe used and the crampons were on sale," I said.

She stood up. "Those people coming into town are *professionals*, you know. They *look* like professionals in their expensive gear. They've probably all climbed *Everest*."

We both had been intrigued with the climbers who came to Talkeetna in increasing numbers as summer approached. They got off the train with piles of shiny equipment and faraway looks in their eyes. They clomped around town in heavy climbing boots and colored plastic jumpsuits for a day or two and then disappeared. When they returned they were sunburned and shrunken inside their clothes, but ecstatic.

Talkeetna, we learned, was the center of mountaineering in Alaska and one of the four major climbing bases in the world, along with Yosemite, Chamonix, and Kathmandu. During the April-to-July climbing season single-engine bush planes went from the grass airstrip downtown to the Southeast Fork of the Kahiltna Glacier, where they landed on hydraulic skis and deposited expeditions underneath Denali.

"The first ascent of the mountain was made by an archdeacon in a wool coat accompanied by a twenty-one-year-old Athabaskan from the Interior who had never seen Denali up close before," I told Melissa. "They got to the base of the mountain in 1912 by dog team from near Fairbanks."

"And how many of their expedition died?" she said.

"None! They didn't even get frostbit!"

Melissa paced beside me. She kept looking at me.

"But a few people do get killed every year now," I admitted.

"You're going to be a *father*," she said.

"But I want my kid to be competent at all this, too! I want him, or her, to know how to drive dogs and run rivers and climb the snow peaks. I've got to know what's in this world."

"But what if you *die*?"

I started to say, "Then he'll know that I didn't just sit around wondering. He'll know that I *tried*. And he'll keep on trying." But instead I said, "I won't die. There are dozens of different routes up Denali, and the West Buttress is the easiest."

Melissa wasn't convinced.

"This is the best time to go," I continued. "We're set up now. We have lots of wood. We have a safe house. You don't have to haul water because I'll get a couple of garbage barrels from town to catch rainwater off the roof. Later we'll be building our own place and caring for the baby and besides, I could get killed then as easily as now."

"But I'm *pregnant*!" said Melissa.

"Now, now," I said. "It's all right."

"Don't you use that patronizing tone on me," she said.

"I'm not using a patronizing tone," I said.

We had a big fight that night. In the morning I got up and ran fourteen miles up and down the tracks. I was blowing off steam. I was also training.

I wanted to climb the mountain because I couldn't not climb. I had come into a land that I felt to be holy. It was barely touched by men. At its edges it was as virgin as it had remained from the time the ice receded and the first seeds took hold. And above it all like the minarets of Mecca were the snow summits. I was a pilgrim. Until I reached the peaks I wouldn't know the heart of this world. I *had* to know the heart.

Of course my desires were obsessive and compulsive. Of course it was irresponsible to abandon security, to bring risk to the mother of my child. But it was the same impulse that had carried us to Alaska. I had a pilgrim's faith that any journey up into light was blessed.

I didn't worry that I would die. I only worried about Melissa's understanding.

A week later Melissa packed special foods she had baked: oil-rich bread, coconut cookies. She put them into my gear bag alongside the freeze-dried packaged dinners some Japanese had given me after they returned from their climb. She'd patched my army-surplus wool pants where I'd ripped them hauling wood. "No more than two weeks, right?" she said.

"No longer than two weeks," I agreed. "I don't have to reach the summit. The summit isn't the point."

"Ray *died* because he reached the top," she said. "And look at Kathy now."

Ray Genet, the country's most famous mountain guide, had frozen to death descending from Everest a few years before. He had successfully taken a hundred people, including Bobby Kennedy, up Denali, but his motto—"To the summit!"—had killed him on Everest. The mother of his son, pregnant with his second boy, had flown from Talkeetna to Nepal to try to retrieve his body. She was still grieving.

"Mountains should be climbed with as little effort as possible, and without desire. That's my climbing philosophy," I said.

"Two weeks," she said.

When we had finished packing we went down to the tracks. On my back I carried an old pack in which I'd stuffed my sleeping bag and tent and winter clothes. Hanging off the outside were two pots, Stanley's snowshoes, the ice axe and crampons, and a rolled-up foam pad that I'd borrowed from Denny. On the little plastic kid's sled I'd lashed the food bag.

The trees had all become greened with their first budding leaves or, on the spruce, needles. The color was the same. It was a goldish greenish *radiance*—there was no word for it in the language. The edges of the spruce where the new needles grew, the entire birch that held, I'd read, almost one million leaves per tree, were all lit up. We stood on the tracks watching the spring, hoping Ted would come by with the gas car, until I realized that I was going to be carrying all my stuff up a mountain (it was *there*, visible even through the foliage). We walked into town.

"Can you understand why I have to go?" I asked as we walked.

"Does it matter?" answered Melissa behind me, nudging the sled every once in a while with her foot.

"Sure it does," I said.

She was silent for a while. A pair of ravens flapped lazily toward us, then suddenly, right overhead, executed a full barrel roll. It was a gesture of such ease and freedom that I started to laugh aloud, but Melissa said, "I don't feel like you're trying to *prove* anything. Which is good. But I wish I felt like your first priority was *us*. I—"

"But it *is*," I interrupted. "I'm exploring for *us*. One day you and me and Spot—or Spotette—will be able to travel *all* this world, together, because we'll know what's there. If we've—"

"I'm not finished," she said.

I was silent.

"I know your heart is in the right place," she continued. "But I don't like the sense I have that I'm just tagging along like a good squaw. I want to feel like we're a part of things, together. We came here because it was *your* dream, and being a monk away from the world is appealing to *you*, but *I'm* not climbing with you. I'm just *here*."

For a while I didn't answer. We walked along.

"I promise you that one day we'll go back up to the mountain together. We might not climb, but we'll be there. I *know* we will. I scouted for us once alone and, well, it's certainly brought us together. That's what I'd like more than anything else."

I stopped. The sled banged against my leg. I dropped my pack. I stepped over the gear to where Melissa stood. I bent down and put both hands against her belly. "Yo, buddy," I said. "I know you can hear me. This is your daddy. I'm not leaving you, buddy. You are more important to me than anything else. I'm just going to look around to see what's possible for us. Your daddy would *never* leave you. *Capisce?*"

I looked at Melissa. "You sure it's a boy?" I asked.

She shrugged, then nodded.

"How about Trigger?"

She smiled and shook her head.

I stood up. "Just being here should be sustaining," I said. I kept one hand on her belly. "Whether we're next to each other or apart. Just here. That's what we left New York to find: a sustaining home. For all three of us." I waved one hand to include the world. "Here."

Melissa looked past me. "If we stay *here*," she said, "Ted'll turn us to hamburger."

We pulled the sled off the tracks as the gas car drew up. "How we doin'?" asked Ted.

"Better," said Melissa.

"At least if he smoked," Ted said to her, taking a cigarette from his vest pocket, "he'd linger a little before passing on."

"Not funny!" I said.

Ted still wore his grin, but his eyes looked hurt. I had the sense that he'd been rehearsing his line for days.

"It's all right," said Melissa. "We'll be back together in two weeks."

When we got to Talkeetna I went to the trailer that housed the seasonal Denali National Park mountaineering ranger station to register my climb.

The rangers were dressed in khaki uniforms and had the air of people who know exactly what they're doing. "Do *you* know what you're doing?" they asked me.

"I know where I'm going," I said.

They studied my secondhand gear and tried to talk me out of going. I told them that I had climbed in the Himalayas, which was true. I hadn't climbed to any summits, though, only through high passes until I reached Tibet, where Chinese border guards marched me back into Nepal over my protestations that I was a mendicant headed to Lhasa.

Finally they complained about the new park regulation that allowed anyone to climb without restrictions. I went to the airstrip.

Melissa watched me go like a mother watching her only son march off to war.

I curled in the back of the small plane, wedged against my gear, staring out the plastic window. The plane banked over the Susitna. Immediately I began laughing. The town quickly disappeared amidst the spring forest that rose to blue mountains. I laughed until I was weeping. The town was incidental, I was incidental. The new forest was vibrant, I was vibrant. I couldn't stop laughing and crying until the plane sliced between snow peaks. Then there was only rock and ice and such light as was blinding.

The plane landed on the Southeast Fork of the forty-three-mile-long Kahiltna Glacier. A canvas Quonset-like tent stood at the northern edge, where a radio operator helped coordinate flights in and out. This was Base Camp, triangulated by Denali, 17,400-foot Mount Foraker, and 14,500-foot Mount Hunter. It was like being in the center of the Great Pyramid.

After I dumped my gear in the snow, the plane took off down-glacier, looking and sounding in that vast arena like a mosquito. When its tiny drone had faded, there was only wind and silence.

I set up my tent wearing just Alexander's shirt and wool pants. The sun, reflected from all sides, was intense. When it passed behind a peak the temperature dropped forty degrees.

I slept until midnight. In pastel radiance I packed up and began walking. The color was less pink or gold or indigo than a diffused glow made up of the cosmic wavelengths that, at northern latitudes, are not deflected by the Van Allen belt. The mountains around me were veined with quartz and silicon. It seemed less poetic than a matter of fact that the radiation bombarding them made the mountains resonate. I listened for celestial harmonies, but ended up singing old songs.

Each time I stopped to sleep I dug into the snow for protection from storms before setting up my tent. There was only one storm. I sat in my tent, then, just sitting.

The rest of the time there was sun, occasionally streaked by local wind-roiled clouds. As I climbed, I thought of my love for Melissa and our family. I thought of Denny's pronouncement that we could create *any*thing in the wilderness—a new culture, a better world, a life unimpeded by the vagaries of human economics. I thought of a line from Nabokov, "a slow suffusion of inutile loveliness," and repeated it over and over.

I decided that people who went into the wilderness alone did so for regret and revelation. I regretted much—loving words unspoken and too many words angrily announced, charitable gestures stillborn and numbing years of dismal routine. When I was able to quiet my thoughts, each breath was a revelation.

Twelve days later, alone, I looked down from the summit on more of the world than seemed possible without having wings. I had only fallen in one small crevasse, just up to my waist, and felt no effect at all from the altitude. I hadn't cared if I got to the top. Just being in the heart of the mountains was unearthly. It was enough. It was complete. I was filled with an acceptance of things just as they are, which is grace.

I looked out at silver rivers and ocher tundra and dark forest. From four miles up, I found the perspective I had courted. That land was, without any doubt, home. I didn't need to explore any farther. I couldn't tell where in such an enormous landscape we'd build, but it didn't matter. I turned to the four directions and saw the same thing everywhere. I clasped my hands against my chest and smiled.

A half hour later I was joined by a professional Talkeetna guide. I had passed his group earlier. His three roped-together clients collapsed around us to lie as if dead. He offered me a candy bar.

"You realize you're just incredibly lucky," he said.

At first I thought he meant because the day was so windless and clear and relatively warm—just zero Fahrenheit—on a mountain notorious for its severe weather. Then I wondered if he meant because I had no altitude sickness. Finally I admitted that he probably meant because I hadn't died.

I was too happy to speak.

He pointed out the five massive glaciers encircling us below that buttressed the peak in concentric pinwheel geometry. He named the mountains plainly visible on the horizon 250 miles away. "This kind of summit day only happens once every few years," he said.

Any confusion that I might have had about my luck vanished. The root of *luck* means "to allure."

We stood silently until one of his clients groaned. "I'm going to have to carry that one," the guide said. "Can you rope into the other two and help them down?"

When we got back to their high camp I kept going. "My wife's pregnant back in town," I explained.

"Oh, so *you're* the one," he said. "You'd better step on it."

The next day, with storm clouds gathering, I dropped onto the Southeast Fork, face-first. I was sunburned, shrunken inside my clothes, but my arms were outstretched. I radioed for a plane. It slipped in under weather that would sock in the mountains for a week.

I landed in Talkeetna amidst a driving hailstorm. I dashed over to the B&K to huddle under the eaves and adjust to the *green* in the world, the balm, the smells of organic life. A local whose name I didn't know came up to me and said, "Man, I'm glad *you're* back!"

I was still having a hard time speaking.

"You know how colorful your lady is?" he explained. "Well, she's been more colorful."

I found Melissa camped in a tent by the river. She had not been back to the cabin since I had left. She had lived in town on the kindness of strangers, who were now her friends. When I stuck my head inside the tent door she turned slowly from where she had been kneeling, staring out a mosquito-net window across the river to the mountains. There were tears in her eyes.

"Don't leave me like that again," she whispered. "Please."

For the rest of the summer we tried to make things as simple as they seemed to have been before my climb. But we had both seen how profoundly alone we could be in such a landscape—not wandering the woods in search of a trail or standing beside the tracks after the train had gone, but *alone*, in a tent beneath the peaks with only faith and dread for company.

I had been overjoyed. She had been terrified. And we had a baby on the way.

5.

UNTO US A LIFE IS BORN

I stepped outside into dazzling light. Winds from the polar ice pack had blown the sky clear of blanketing haze. The earth's warmth had lifted into the stratosphere.

Serious cold. Severe clear.

I hunched my shoulders and walked out onto the ice. The morning sun reflected up to burnish the underside of my hat's brim. The glare around my feet was so intense tears came to my eyes. So I turned around and looked up to the fourteenth floor.

The brick and brownstone were lacquered with a luminous and intoxicating splendor. Chicago had never been so beautiful. Somewhere inside the old apartment building Melissa lay with our just-born boy.

"*Nobody* should go outside unless it's *absolutely necessary!*" the TV weatherman had insisted the night before. "This is a record cold to beat *all* records!"

At dawn, in my father's great wool overcoat and black fedora, I was going out to buy breakfast for the midwife.

Fifty-fourth Street on the Southside was normally a furtive street, part of the Black P-Stone Nation's turf, gangland territory. Normally it was not a place to loiter, especially on New Year's morning, a few hours after God only knew what kind of excess had spilled into the street.

But this New Year it was as desolate as a glacier on the upper slopes of Denali. "Eighty! Eight-oh! That's *eighty below zero* wind-chill!" the newscasters had sputtered.

I slid to the middle of the sidewalk and stood for a while grinning. If a black sedan spraying bullets from a machine gun had careened around the corner, I would have stood grinning.

I walked down the block of concrete-collared trees and iron-barred windows. I played "crevasse" with the verglas-filled cracks in the sidewalk, stepping only on the "snow bridges."

At the next intersection, a squad car idled, banners of exhaust rising from its tailpipe. I went up and tapped on the driver's-side window, behind which a cop dozed. He opened one eye and then bolted erect. He grabbed for the shotgun between the seats.

I remembered that I was wearing a 1940s Chicago mafioso costume: long dark overcoat, black fedora. I had recently shaved my beard. I probably looked, to a beat cop on overtime, like Uncle Louie, the hit man.

But I couldn't stop grinning. "I just had a son," I said.

The cop studied me with a professional once-over. With the hand that wasn't clutching the gun he cracked the window an inch.

"I just had a son," I repeated. The bright-light tears sprang back to my eyes.

We stared at each other for a moment, me in my goofy happiness, the cop in his all-night wariness. Then I noticed how tense he really was. I took my hands from my pockets and rested them on the car. He relaxed. He rolled down the window.

"We live in Alaska," I said, "but we came back to be near my parents for the birth. I'm looking for a place that's open to buy breakfast. I just had a son, in the midwife's apartment, right back there."

"Yeah. Okay. I believe you already," he said. He stuck out his hand to shake. "But they won't believe this back at the precinct."

The midwife had been exceptional. Melissa and I had driven her to her Southside home after a routine prenatal appointment followed by an impromptu New Year's Eve celebration. Then, instead of returning to my parents' place on the Northside, where we'd planned to have the baby in three more weeks, we had deferred to the weather and stayed the night.

At 3:00 A.M., Melissa's water broke. At 8:00, the midwife's two-year-old had wandered sleepily into the bedroom where I was holding the newborn and, for no identifiable reason, had begun singing, "Happy birt'day to yoooo."

The intensity of Melissa's labor, during those intermediate hours, made solo climbs of great snow peaks seem a comparatively puny excursion into the upper realms of human experience.

Melissa shrieked, "Oh, *God*!" during the most powerful contractions, and I held her, futilely. The midwife reminded her, during the moments of clarity that followed the pain, that first-time mothers with fast labors have some of the most difficult births. But no one banged on the apartment door demanding that we keep it down. It was, after all, New Year's Eve.

When the moment of birth arrived, it lasted as long as death. I was kneeling beside Melissa, hugging her in a tight embrace, staring over her bare shoulder at the midwife's long, slender hands cupped to receive the child.

The baby's head appeared covered in the white creamlike vernix that protects the premature fetus in utero. I could see at once that a tremendous hideous growth covered half its face.

Time slowed and stopped, like my heart.

"Ah," I thought.

This was the eternity between the instant the bullet enters

the cranium and the moment the spatter of gray matter exits the other side.

"My fears were true. Life has been full of great ease! I've been grateful! But sorrow is as common as happiness, and both are inescapable. And I always did wonder from the time I was eighteen if it was a good idea to have done that chromosome-altering mescaline."

Then the tiny fist that had lain against the cheek pulled away, and the perfect head of my perfect boy opened its mouth and cried, "Hah! Don't you ever take *me* for granted."

The pulse that returned in a roar blinded me while the newborn was handed to Melissa. When I finally returned to the planet it was my turn to lift the child and look at him.

He stared up at me. I stared down at him. Every time we ever gazed at each other from that moment on was an echo of that first long look.

Pediatric literature calls this "bonding." That's like calling the Buddha's moment of enlightenment under the bodhi tree "neat."

Melissa's face was mottled by capillaries that had burst during labor. When I turned to her, still cradling our son, she looked like the thirteenth-century statue of the pietà in the Cloisters museum on the northern tip of Manhattan Island. From one angle there was pain so apparent it made my eyes fill. From just a step to one side there was, too, in the same face, such serenity and such grace that I couldn't then focus on much of anything.

I was aware of the dawn light through the frost-stained bedroom window. I was aware of our isolation on the fourteenth floor of an old apartment house on the Southside of Chicago. The rest of the world was out there somewhere, but it was as far away as if we'd been in the heart of the Alaskan forest.

We had had, by coincidence, a log cabin birth, on a foam mattress bed, in solitude, with the winds of the polar ice pack waiting to greet me when I stepped outside the door.

Two days later I was back at my job. Six weeks ago we had arrived in Chicago just about broke: my unemployment compensation had ended. Luckily, we had cared for some distant neighbors' dogs during the summer while they worked seasonal jobs, and so they were feeding our dogs for our months in Chicago. But even with free rent in the spare bedroom of my parents' apartment, city living was alarmingly expensive. Melissa had a marketable trade, but was frankly and hugely pregnant. Jobs for "middle manager, short term" were not listed in the *Tribune*'s want ads, so I was stymied. I could neither cook nor pound nails nor wire a house. And we needed more bucks than I could make serving burgers.

Melissa had been looking forward to shopping for *her* contribution to our future house: pink and black coffee mugs with matching place mats, fabric with which to sew curtains for the kitchen windows. She also planned to buy enough material to make kimonos as Christmas gifts for her women friends.

I got a job setting type. I worked the graveyard shift, 11:00 P.M. to dawn, at a computerized console that sported more buttons than the cockpit of a 747. I had worked with computers before. Sort of. And I could type. With two fingers—my legacy as a newspaperman's son. I remembered a Three Stooges movie in which Curly turns helplessly to Moe after they've been launched toward Mars in a rocket. "Push buttons," counsels Moe.

I kept the typesetting machine's 150-page manual under my chair, and was saved from being fired by bringing a dozen Dunkin' Donuts to the foreman each night. I'd grown up with Chicago politics and knew how to bribe discreetly.

After the first week, when I'd read the manual most of the night, I began reading other stuff. There wasn't much else to do, and at 2:00 A.M. my donut-happy foreman didn't care about anyone having to look busy.

I read John Muir: "I wish I knew where I was going. Doomed to be carried into the spirit of the wilderness, I guess." I read William Blake: "Great things are done when men and mountains meet."

On the day I returned to work after the birth, however, I set my own type.

"Janus, the most ancient of the Roman deities, was originally the

god of light," I copied from my father's second-edition *Reader's Encyclopedia*, "who opened the sky each daybreak and closed it at sunset.
January 1st is his special day."

Melissa wanted birth announcements.

"Janus Leo was born on New Year's Day, on a morning of bright
sunshine, healthy and wide-eyed."

Soon I'd be typing, as part of my nightly work, "In the world of
adventure there is no greater discovery than Mercedes."

Two things kept me going at work. One was the opening of
federal homestead land, due to start at the end of the month, two
hundred air miles from Fairbanks. I had heard rumors about it in the
Fairview before we left Alaska. It was supposed to be the last great
American homesteading, the same program that had sent covered
wagons racing into Oklahoma a hundred years ago. A hundred and
sixty acres at $2.50 per acre to each pioneer. I had called the Federal
Building offices in Anchorage to confirm the rumor. "After this, the
United States government has no more land available for homesteading," they had said.

The other thing that kept me going was *Big Bob's Blues Before
Breakfast Showcase*. On a radio station that had been, until 4:00 A.M.,
classical music, Big Bob played Chicago blues: up-tempo, electric,
no-stoppin'-me-now blues. "Ain't gonna worry my life anymore,"
Muddy Waters sang just for me.

I was, however, a little worried about the city. For most of my
adult life I had been a city boy. But eleven months in Alaska had
blown my urban confidence apart.

It wasn't the muggers and psychos and punks and other marginal
types who worried me. We respected each other's eccentricities.

On one lunch hour, at 3:00 A.M., as I stood on a desolate industrial
corner staring up at the dark edifice of the Merchandise Mart, a
Pentagon-sized building of moldering stone where ten thousand pi-
geons squatted on small window ledges, a slender man stepped from a
doorway down the block, immediately withdrew when he saw me,
then hesitantly came near to demand, "Gimme your money, man!"

He almost added, "Please."

I nearly laughed, but then felt sort of sad for him. No wonder he was wandering the back streets in the middle of the night: no one had *ever* taken him seriously.

"I'd like to climb that," I said, pointing to the looming Mart.

He took a step back before rallying. "I said, gimme your money!"

"I'd do it at night and write something on every window in bird crap, so in the morning when everyone came to work they'd see YES! or HIGHER! or something."

He visibly sagged. "You even got any money?"

"Standing here at three in the morning? Come on. But if I had a rope I'd swing up like Batman."

He shuffled around. "Why'd you want to do that?"

"Just to do something different."

"Yeah, well, you different all right."

What did worry me was everybody else. I couldn't figure out what sustained three and a half million people in such a concentrated area. I was acutely conscious that all the food and all the fuel came from somewhere else, usually far away. When the lights had all gone out in New York City in the summer of '76, I just lit candles until I looked out of my window at the 181st Street promenade. *That's* where the weird sounds were coming from. Howls and shouts from the assembled mob, as in any primitive society during solar eclipse. Just because the electricity had stopped.

What if the refrigerator trucks quit rolling into town with Melissa's California celery for her new juicer? What if the 7-Eleven on the corner ran out of milk? What if an international oil embargo jacked up jet fuel cost so high we couldn't get back to Alaska?

I didn't feel safe being at the mercy of a Strong Economic System that, by definition, went through cyclical periods of severe depression and deprivation. The great westward migration of the late 1800s was precipitated by a national economic depression. Why starve in Philly when Oregon was the Promised Land? And so what if Reagan was making America richer? Sooner or later the electricity would go out again, and when it did, I didn't want to be on the subway returning from work.

Of course, nobody who passed me on his way *to* work at morning rush hour seemed to share my concern.

The utter difference of living in a log cabin in the boreal forest had given me the same disorientation that powerful movies had produced when I was a teen. I had stumbled out of *Easy Rider* and *Romeo and Juliet* blown away, unable to fit the inescapable reality of the familiar street into the equally inescapable reality that good guys *died* and that dreams didn't last.

When I walked back to my parents' place after a night setting type, I felt out of sync with the world jostling me. I was blasted from another all-nighter, alert but bemused. I felt like an anthropologist on Mars. What sustained these people pushing toward the public transport? How could they not be anxious in such a precarious world?

Certainly they seemed to *act* skittish: Don't look at anyone! Keep moving! Take a deep breath only after making the train!

Then one of the suit-and-tie commuters I seemed to pass almost every morning stuffed a dollar bill into my hand as I leaned against a window of the Jewel Food Store to let him pass.

"Okay," I thought. "So *I'm* the Martian."

I relaxed.

It was time to go home.

I crept as silently as I could into my parents' apartment and opened the door of the bedroom where Melissa slept with Janus curled like a little monkey against her breast. The rolled-down window shades were like parchment against the morning sun. A candle burned low, Melissa's lovely reminder of the winter night.

I knelt beside the bed and stared. Her mouth was open. A small stain of spittle saturated her pillow. The baby, who had rolled away from her nipple, was making sucking noises in his sleep. It was an exquisite portrait of common beauty.

Melissa opened her eyes, like a lighthouse blinking on.

"I think I'll go back to stake our land," I said.

She nodded.

"The homestead land is getting ready to open," I said.

She drew the baby closer to her. "S'okay," she said.

"It'll be good," I said. "It'll be right. It'll be *beautiful*."

"I love you," she said.

I picked up the candle to blow it out. I smelled chemical type and donuts on my fingers.

"I've been thinking about the house," Melissa said. She sat up and propped herself against her pillow. "I'd like to have an oak butcher's block in the kitchen, at the end of the counter, and I'd like the counter to be black lacquer, to match the dining room table."

I could not possibly visualize the house that was becoming increasingly definite to her. I could only see mountains and forest. But I loved her enthusiasm. "You bet," I said.

"And I'm going to grow herbs in the greenhouse. That way the house will fill with the smell of basil and dill and coriander when we open the connecting door."

I lifted Janus and held him under my chin. "With French doors between the house and greenhouse?" I asked, jesting.

"Eventually," she said.

I kissed the baby and said, "I'm glad you're excited, too. Most pioneer women just followed their men because they had no choice."

"Oh, I can be pretty strong willed," she said. "I *choose* this, now."

I laughed. "Black lacquer counter and all."

"Because if we're going to live in the middle of nowhere, we're going to live *well*."

"So is it all right with you if I quit my job and go find our land?"

"If you think you're ready to stop working then it's all right by me."

"Now I *start* working," I said.

Three days later, I hiked up the tracks to Stanley's cabin to get the snowshoes. It was twenty below zero, a late-January clear. I didn't see anyone. I was glad to have no distractions. I was on a tight schedule.

I grabbed the snowshoes and hurried back down the tracks. No birds sang, so I did. I sang an Alvin Lee song from Woodstock. All I could remember was the chorus: "Goin' home. Goin' home. Goin' home. Goin' home." When I stopped to admit that I sounded like an imbecile, I sang louder. "Goin' home, home, home, home, home."

By the time I reached the junction of the Talkeetna spur road and the Anchorage-Fairbanks highway it was midday, and already beginning to get dark. Sunrise at 10:00 A.M., sunset at 4:00. I stood under the only streetlamp for three hundred miles and waited. I was hoping to get a ride before the light flickered on. Almost no one drove the road in winter except for local traffic.

I wanted one long ride, through the night, so that I could get my staking materials from the government offices the next day. Then I'd charter a bush plane, in lieu of horses, and join the land rush.

In time, as I hopped around like a cirrhotic street preacher to keep warm ("Oh yes, heaven is just up the road!" I shouted to myself), a little passenger car came up the highway, slowed, and stopped.

"I'm headed to Fairbanks," I said.

"Come in! Come in!" said the driver, an older man wearing an oversized beaver hat.

I demurred. "How far you going?" I asked.

"Come in!" he repeated. "I'm just going fifteen miles up, but the car's warm!"

I backed off. "I think I'd rather wait for a longer ride," I said. "If it gets dark cars'll be able to see me in the streetlight."

He waved me in. "Take the chill off! I'll be crossing the wide Susitna River bridge, on across the valley to the other side."

"I don't want to get stuck in the dark," I said.

"Come on!" he insisted. "Toss your gear in back."

I gave up. I climbed in. He stuck out a hand. "I'm Mel Anderson," he said. "I'm a Christian."

"Oh Christ," I said.

"Fairbanks, eh? I can tell by the 'shoes that you're going to homestead."

I didn't bother to respond. I figured that I'd have to suffer twenty minutes of intense proselytizing and then get out in the middle of nowhere to stare at a black highway at twenty below.

"Do you know Jesus?" he asked.

I sank lower in my seat. "Can you hum a few bars?"

He laughed. He wasn't offended. "Oh yes, it's beautiful country we have. God's country. 'He hath made everything beautiful in His time.' Ecclesiastes 3:11."

I concentrated on my fingers. They *were* getting warm.

"It's the richest land left on earth out there," he said, brushing the frosted windshield with his hand. "Everything a man could want before heaven. I guess that's why they opened homestead land down the Petersville Road."

I froze.

"Salmon creeks, mountains, clean water. Praise God! The Lord wouldn't let the world exist without these places."

Weakly, I asked, "Homestead land down the Petersville Road?"

"Oh, sure. Don't you know? State land. Only forty acres tops. It's a new program. Not like the federal land. What would you *do* with more? Start a moose ranch?" He chuckled to himself.

"How far down the Petersville Road?"

"Near the mountains. But there's griz out there. Known denning areas. I sort of like having griz around, myself. Makes me feel closer to God. 'The Lord by his wisdom hath founded the earth.' Proverbs 3:19."

I massaged my eyes. I could see the leather-bound maps that I'd memorized a year ago in Fairbanks. I could see the shaded panda eyes of the denning areas and the topographic relief of the mountains rising like a wall from the lowlands.

"A man doesn't need much land for his own out here," he said. "Because the land keeps going. And it's all ours. As the Bible says—"

"How do you know about the Petersville homestead land?" I interrupted.

He shrugged. His beaver hat slipped lower over his forehead. "Word of mouth, I guess. The state isn't much for organization. But no government is. If you know what I mean."

I didn't care about politics at the moment. I suddenly wanted to study a real live angel. I leaned back in my seat and glanced over at him. I checked for wings, or a halo. He looked like . . . anybody. Chin, nose, goofy hat. I tried to fix his profile in memory, but it was futile.

When I hiked into Tibet I had passed through the holy site of Muktinath, where a blue flame jetted from the side of a mountain. I had secretly shot a dozen pictures of the scene: monks in saffron dress, mendicants on their knees, natural flame flaring amidst snow peaks. A month later, when I developed the film, the first ten and the last fourteen slides had been excellent, but the middle twelve—of Muktinath—were blank. At the time I had laughed. "Aw, come on," I had said aloud, looking around just a little warily.

Even as I stared at Mel Anderson there was nothing to see. A nice guy in an old car hunched over the steering wheel squinting through his frosty windshield.

We rode in silence for a few minutes. I tried to think of the Ah-Ha thing to say, like a crafty Pooh bear catching a Heffalump: "So, have you ever seen *It's a Wonderful Life*?" Or, "Actually, I believe in *everything* myself, like Aram: up, down, good, bad, city, country, even *angels*."

But Mel spoke first. "Well, this is where I turn. Petersville Road. From here to Fairbanks you're just about six hours, with good roads." He slowed to a stop.

"Uh, just a minute," I said.

"No, no, don't thank me. I was once young and adventurous myself. Glad to help. Hope you find what you're looking for." He shoved my gear at me. "God be with you! Praise the Lord!"

I didn't struggle. He rolled away. I stood on the side of the highway at twenty below in the middle of nowhere. I watched his car to see if it would just—poof!—vanish, but it didn't. The unpaved Petersville Road rose up into forest and gradually melted into trees, as Mel Anderson had.

I immediately crossed to the other side of the highway. I was going to hitch back into Anchorage—120 miles south—to get maps for this new homestead land. I wasn't about to ignore the most obvious sign I'd ever had in my life.

There was a boarded-up gas station at the intersection. Down the road from it was a plywood shack, and beyond that a bullet-pocked sign: FAIRBANKS, 260. The rest was forest.

I *was* in the middle of nowhere. I paced back and forth and

slowly began to reason. I knew that the Fairbanks land would officially open at midnight the following day. It was the last great land
rush in American history! Thousands of people might stake land.
Imminently! How long had the Petersville land been open? How
long would it *stay* open? What if old Mel Anderson just had a screw
loose? Could I risk losing a sure thing for a dream?

I crossed back to the Fairbanks side of the road.

But no! Jesus! Was I crazy? How could I *not* explore the Petersville Road? "Habitation: widely scattered." "Known deposits of
gold veined through Cambrian granite." I had to go look. I lugged
my gear back across the blacktop again.

Ah, but how could I gamble on something so important? If I
explored the Fairbanks land first, *then* I could return here, with the
necessary maps that surely I could get from the Fairbanks state
offices. That was logical. I could perhaps be in Fairbanks as quickly
as Anchorage, and then I'd be able to see *both* lands. Right. Good
thinking. I went back to the Fairbanks side.

A car came up from the south, toward Fairbanks. I was pleased.
Another sign! Go north first! I stuck out my thumb and waited.

When the car got close enough for me to see through the windshield it suddenly turned on its turn signal, left, toward the mountains, down the narrow Petersville Road.

Impulsively, I leaped into the middle of the highway, waving
my arms.

The car swerved and stopped.

"I've got to go down that road but I don't know where I'm going
and I don't have any maps!" I shouted at the driver through his
window.

He opened the door. He stretched his legs. "I'm going to check
out the state homestead land," he said. "I've got *those* maps. Is that
what you mean?"

His name was Russ. He was from Anchorage, by way of rural
Minnesota, Yellowstone Park, and the scientific station at the South
Pole. He had a young son, and his wife was pregnant. He was tall
and powerful and Nordic.

He had been a solitary fire lookout in Yellowstone, a recluse in

Antarctica, and he lived in Anchorage as a compromise between living remote and keeping his family. He was just the sort of person I imagined would want to homestead in Alaska.

I blathered away about how I had gotten to this narrow road headed toward the snow peaks. He said only what was requisite, only after my prompting. I was overjoyed to think that this was the sort of person who might end up being my neighbor. He'd be self-sufficient, self-contained, and distant.

Denny would appreciate his apparent competence. Marvin wouldn't be able to stare him down.

We reached the end of the plowed road, where huge walls of snow had been piled up to create a turnaround. We were just ten miles short of the point where the first prospectors in the twenties, after crossing the Susitna River from Talkeetna, had reached gold in the foothills. We continued on by skis and snowshoes.

There was no trail. The forest grew denser and the snow deeper as we went. Every once in a while we consulted Russ's maps and agreed: farther.

When we stopped for the night, Russ rolled out a bag atop spruce boughs and went silently to sleep. I struggled with my tent, flash-light in my mouth, tent poles bumbling in the cold. Finally, in great frustration, a little afraid of what it would be like to just sleep out in the open, I crawled into my bag atop the flaccid tent. It was then I saw the aurora through the trees. I felt very small, and very incompe-tent, but blessed.

In the morning Russ woke me with a pot of oatmeal he'd cooked on his gas stove. It was too cold to chat. We quickly headed on north.

I tried to keep up with his long strides so I could pump him for information. "Remote Parcel" was the official name of the state program, he explained. One percent of Alaska's lands were privately owned. Federal litigation had "locked up" the rest of the state in '72 pending a resolution of the conflicting claims of Natives and oil pipeline interests. Alaskan residents had been clamoring, loudly, for land they could own. This, now, was the beginning of the resolution: state land made available for state residents. The federal land was for anybody. Only *Alaskans* could legally live where we were headed.

Russ's maps showed where others before us, in the month the land was open to staking, had claimed their acreage. There weren't many.

We broke out of the forest onto a long tundra meadow, a narrow treeless expanse that extended up to a forested ridgeline. The maps said, "Long tundra, forested ridge, no people."

We eventually surmounted the ridge. The Alaska Range was just where it should have been: overhead. We stopped.

Beside us was an enormous boulder, left behind by the receding glaciers, atop which tall spruce grew. One sheer face was covered with moss that glowed a dark green even in the dead of winter. There were animal tracks everywhere around us.

"Feels like home," said Russ, grinning.

"Feels like home," I echoed. It felt so much like home that I ached, unless it was just my lungs burning from the exertion of panting in subzero air.

We stomped around. I discovered a spring flowing from beneath the snow on the side of the ridge. I was startled by the sight of running water at such temperatures.

"Look at that!" said Russ. He hadn't stopped grinning.

I looked from the spring to the mountains. I began to feel possessive. "This is yours," I said suddenly. "Really. I won't impose. You took me here. I'll find my own ridge."

Russ nodded as if he hadn't heard me and skied away. I remained. I didn't want to leave that spot. I remembered how Castaneda's Don Juan had kept to his place of power in times of duress. It was hard to imagine going any farther without climbing the foothills to glaciers.

In time Russ returned. He took off one ski and used it as a shovel to spray snow from beneath a spruce. He bent down and dug deeper to bring up a handful of dried grass and moss. "It's just such poor land for farming," he said, crumbling the frozen vegetation between his fingers. "It's all glacial till. It's probably got six inches of topsoil above the rocks." He sighed.

I knew nothing about farming, only that I wasn't a farmer. Goats and chickens in the attic! We'd manage.

He tossed the brush aside and smiled at me. He looked like a man who had reached just the point he'd wanted to reach. My heart sank.

"It's beautiful land, though," he said. "But I just don't think we're ready."

My heart soared.

"I'm just not sure we're ready for what it'll take," he said. "But it's so good to know it's here."

"But it's even got water in the winter!" I blurted. "And you found it!"

He nodded. He looked resigned. I wanted him to look resigned. But I was embarrassed that I wanted him to look so sure. I glanced away.

I saw a large feather atop the snow. Eagle? Owl? Raven? I didn't know. But it was a sign. It was a sign of freedom and fecundity. And I hadn't noticed it before.

"It's a big step," Russ continued. "To do it right takes a lot of planning. It's going to take us a few more years."

I didn't stoop to pick up the feather. I wanted it to remain just where it was. I wanted everything to remain just as it was.

"How about you?" he asked, the first question he'd addressed to me since we met.

I was unsure just how to reply, for fear I'd start jumping up and down. "Look at that," I said, indicating the feather.

He glanced where I pointed and said at once, "A bald eagle. Way out here. Isn't that something?"

We got lost on the way back south. We went right past our own trail. It didn't seem to matter. We were following the pathless way, and eventually did end up back at Russ's car.

I went with him to Anchorage and bedded down on the floor of his house, sleeping little, getting up every half hour to look at the clock on the gas range. At 7:00 A.M. I stole out the door to walk downtown to the state office building. When the doors opened at 8:30 I went up to the Remote Parcel office and claimed my land.

I located it accurately on a map, and defined its boundaries, even though I hadn't first gotten my own complicated staking package.

Then I called Alexander, collect. "I found it," I said. "I found the land. Remember how we used to joke that there was nowhere farther to go, that every place was known? Remember how we didn't laugh? What if we *were* trapped in a world that only got smaller? What if the Cherokee and Cheyenne and Sioux were *us, too*? Even Tibet shrank after the Chinese squeezed out the Dalai Lama. Remember how we worried that *we* were *it*, drinking Kirin beer in front of the VCR in a decorated New York loft in the last populous decade of the millennium?"

Alexander, who knew me, didn't interrupt.

"Well, it wasn't true! There *is* more! I found it!"

State officials around me in the office glanced at me the way anybody would look, briefly, at a shopping bag person who laughed at his own jokes.

"So," I concluded, "can you wire me a plane ticket so I can explore the other land near Fairbanks?"

Alexander had taken a breath to respond, then suddenly let it out. "What?" he said.

"I need to get north for the *federal* homestead opening, but I've got to take the jet from Anchorage or I'll be even later."

Alexander, who was very quick, didn't even try to keep up with my mania. "But you've already found it," he said after a pause.

"I did! There's enough for you *and* me. It goes on forever, and it's all wilderness. But I haven't seen the land that's three hundred miles farther north. How can I be *sure* until I've seen *all* the possibilities?"

Then Alexander laughed. It was a laugh so pure and so natural that I was immediately offended. "But you *are* sure," he said.

"How do *you* know?" I shot back.

"Quick!" he said. "Flash quiz. What's the difference between yes and yes? No fair looking at your notes."

"Three hundred miles!" I shouted, ignoring the people around me.

"Can I tell you what Dōgen said about people like you?" he

asked. I could tell that he was having a good time, and it made me even more annoyed.

"No! Not now! There isn't time. The plane leaves in an hour."

"How about Burt? Remember Burt, the super of our apartment building in our senior year when you furnished your room in Early Modern Dump? 'Even more fruits than fools,' Burt would say when—"

"Come *on*! I'm not screwing around. I need a ticket now! This is the last time in American history we'll be able to do this!"

"Well, *that's* a relief."

"Hurry! Alaska Airlines. Anchorage to Fairbanks. Next available flight."

The plane took off at 10:00 A.M. At 10:10 the liquor cart started down the aisle. One stewardess held it back from dropping along the slope created by the plane's continued ascent. Two other stewardesses dished drinks. They worked like Vegas croupiers dealing chips.

The flight was only fifty-five minutes in duration, at almost six hundred miles per hour. My two seatmates were headed on to the Slope, to Prudhoe Bay, to the oil fields on the Arctic Ocean coast where they would work, after the last two weeks off, for fourteen straight days of twelve- to sixteen-hour shifts in subzero weather for wages approximating the GNP of Ghana. They had jobs that most time-card punchers would kill to get. They slugged doubles. They looked grim.

I stared out the window. Just when the plane reached a plateau and the liquor cart leveled out to begin its return trip up the aisle, the Alaska Range came into view ahead. I bounced around in my seat trying to spot my homestead from four miles up. In less than a minute I involuntarily drew back as Denali passed below the wing tip.

It was that close to the plane. The land was that close to the mountain.

"I live down there," I lied to my companions. I sounded, even to myself, like a child.

I had interrupted their discussion of the relative merits of a Ford Bronco and a Chevy Blazer. They had one of each. They looked at me as if I were a twit. I grinned. The closest guy handed me his peanuts.

Then the plane began its descent to Fairbanks. I was even more intent on looking at the land north of the Range. Somewhere amidst the serpentine geometry of oxbowed rivers, white ribbons of tundra, and dark stands of trees was my *other* land. It all looked flat. I twisted around in my seat to spot the mountains, but they were already long past.

I was aware of the crescendo and decrescendo of my heart as we had approached the Range and then left it behind. I didn't *want* to live so far from the peaks.

But maybe I did. Maybe it would look different from the ground. I'd be damned if I'd admit that I was a greedhead who had walked right past the one true source of sustenance in hopes of getting two.

"More! Yeah. Dat's what I want. More!" I said aloud, impersonating Edward G. Robinson in *Key Largo*. I didn't care if my Prudhoe mates thought I was a twit *and* a loony.

But then I had to admit that *I* cared about my inflated desires, and was embarrassed for myself.

I still wasn't about to turn back.

I took a cab from the airport to the Federal Building and carried my snowshoes and pack to the land offices.

"I'd like a staking package for the homestead land," I said to a receptionist.

"We don't have staking packages," she said.

"Then who does?"

"Well, I don't know."

I was huffy. "What do you mean you 'don't know'?"

She was flustered. "We don't have staking packages," she repeated.

I slipped into the arrogance that I reserve for telephone operators who insist that there's no number for Pastafazool Company, only Pastafazool, Inc.

"May I please speak with your superior?" I said curtly.

She managed to say, "The *federal* land requires participants to build a habitable dwelling before a claim can be accepted. It's only the *state* program that lets you just mark your corners."

I was silent.

"Do you want the *state* program?" she asked.

"They told me when I called the Federal Building in Anchorage a few months ago that I needed an envelope of rules and boundary-marking requirements and maps and . . . a *staking package*," I said.

She shrugged. "Well, they were wrong. We handle the home-steading from here. It's in our region. Anchorage doesn't really know."

I left my snowshoes at the desk and went further into the offices to talk with higher officials. The result was the same.

"Do you mean to tell me that I have to spend a month out there building a house so that I can claim this land?" I asked after a few rounds of talk.

The man whom I had flushed from his glass-and-plasterboard cubicle wore a nameplate with DIRECTOR on it. He also wore the zombie-at-a-poker-game expression of a lifelong bureaucrat. "Well, no," he answered, standing behind a Formica counter. "Not unless you want your claim to be valid."

I felt ready to begin screaming. Three days ago, in Chicago, I had stopped by the bank where I had kept an eighty-dollar savings account from a newspaper route I'd had when I was a kid. I wanted to close the account. My mother circled the block in the car, waiting to drive me to O'Hare Airport. For almost an hour I was shuttled from desk to desk while the bank tried to track down my moldering account. When it looked as if I might miss my flight, I suddenly shouted, in response to one more buck-passing, "I want that money *now*!" Everybody in the bank hit the floor—tellers, executives, people in line. Three uniformed guards with guns drawn surrounded me. For a long tense moment no one moved. Within five minutes I had my money, and I made the plane.

In Fairbanks, in my parka and stubble beard, I burst into laughter.

The director suffered me patiently.

What was I going to do? Demand a bagful of dirt in compensation for an administrative screwup?

"How many people do you think *have* gone out to build?" I asked when I'd calmed down.

"We don't have those records," he said.

"Okay, so how many inquiries *about* the land have you had?"

"Very few. The land is quite remote."

"So if I spend three hundred dollars to charter a plane to fly me out and then I blaze a few trees to mark my corners and then return here to register the land I'll have no right to it whatsoever?" I asked to be sure, to be very sure.

"United States homestead programs require habitable dwellings to be erected before ownership can be considered."

"Then I've flown up here for nothing."

"I'm not qualified to address that."

I rested my head on the counter. Fluorescence reflected up into my eyes. "Good land out there though, eh?"

"It's riverine lowland interspersed with muskeg swamp," he said.

"Lots of bugs in summer, rotten firewood in winter. Does that sound close?"

"Native villages and the state of Alaska were entitled to first choice of Alaskan lands after statehood," he recited. "The Department of the Interior retained only national parkland, land with oil potential, and such areas as we're now offering for public disposal."

I began to feel a slow contentment growing. "Public disposal." I liked that.

"So what do you think of the Petersville Road," I asked carelessly.

"It borders Denali National Park and Preserve," he said.

"Thanks," I said.

"Have a nice day," he said.

I went outside into the familiar sulfurous gloom of ice fog, but this time I felt light. I'd landed back in Hieronymous Bosch land, but I wasn't fixed to the canvas. Bus exhaust hung like cumulus clouds ten feet above the street. Clods of gray ice clung at unlikely angles to the curb. Black stalagmites of frozen tailpipe crud looked like spoor of forest animals. And I marched right on through it, jaywalking, to reach Melissa, by phone.

I ducked into the bar beneath my Hotel of First Frustrations. It was even darker than the street. But the music was better: Merle Haggard instead of troll squeaks.

I aimed toward the blue and white glow of the telephone sign at the back of the room. When Melissa answered the phone I said, "We've got enough giant spruce on our land to build a palace!"

"Where *are* you?" she said.

"Fairbanks. But our land's closer to Talkeetna, out toward the mountains. For *real*! I've given up trying to fight it."

"Isn't Fairbanks a long way from Talkeetna?" She sounded distracted.

"Sure! But . . . well, it's a long story. But your kitchen's going to have pure spring water in the sink."

"It seems like *ages* since you left," she said.

"Melissa! Did you hear me? I staked forty acres under Denali!"

"I *heard* you. That's great." She didn't sound very excited.

"Are you okay?"

She dropped her voice to say, almost in a whisper, but firmly, "I've been having a hard time."

"Is Janus all right?"

"Oh, he's what keeps me going."

"So what's going on?" I began to feel adrift, no longer grounded in my happy little dreams.

"Nothing particular. I mean, I'm fine. But I just don't know." She hesitated and then said, "What do you think we'll *do*?"

"Build!" I said at once. "Peel logs! Design the house!"

"But are we going back to Stanley's?"

I was suddenly aware of a commotion at the bar that I'd ignored at first. Two men, still on their stools, were pushing against each other while the bartender shouted, "Outta here! Outta here! Take it into the street!"

I put a finger in my ear. "We'll go back to Stanley's," I said. "But maybe we'll stay in Anchorage first so I can get some more money. I don't know for sure. What's *wrong*?"

"Nothing!" she said. "I only want to *know*—"

There was a loud thud and a cheer from the bar that made me turn to look.

"Where *are* you?" Melissa cried. With the receiver a few inches from my ear her voice sounded tinny and weird. I felt too warm, and very confused.

We tried to talk for a couple more minutes. I decided, suddenly, more to give myself a direction than to answer Melissa's hesitations, that we'd live in Anchorage for a few weeks so that I could earn enough money to begin building our home. I hadn't until that moment thought beyond the plan to find our land. Melissa sounded even more distant once I'd made that pronouncement, so I didn't pursue the conversation.

I said, "Just meet me in Anchorage. I'll make a reservation and call you back, maybe tomorrow, or a few days at the most, as soon as I get down to Anchorage. Are you all right?"

"I *miss* you," she said.

"Kill 'im!" someone screamed.

"I miss you, too," I said.

"*Outta* here! You're *gone*, Jack!"

I hung up the phone. I put both hands to my face, thumbs beneath my cheekbones, fingers touching in the center of my forehead. I remained like that until something stroked my neck and I jumped.

A very lovely woman stared right at me. She had curled dark hair and wet red lips. The skin revealed by her open fur stole was smooth and white. She lowered her gaze, shyly. Then she looked at me again and smiled. "I swallow," she said.

"I'm gone, Jack," I said.

I walked halfway down the block before I remembered to return for my snowshoes.

The first ride I got heading back south was from a middle-aged Eskimo. It was a year to the day since I had come to Alaska and I had never yet spoken with an Eskimo. I said that to him after he told me—in answer to my standard "Where are you from?"—that he lived on the Arctic coast.

"Guess you're glad I talk English, huh?" he replied.

His name was Murray Amukpuk. "But you can call me Murray." The lilt of his accent was unlike any speech I'd heard: amusement seemed to be its dominant characteristic.

He had been to the three-thousand-person metropolis of Barrow a few times, and to Fairbanks only once before ("To party"), but otherwise had lived his life in and around his village. He was delivering the car to his Anchorage cousin as a favor to his Fairbanks uncle. He had never before been to Anchorage. Nor had he ever driven a car. He drove in the middle of the road, wandering casually from shoulder to shoulder. "This road's a lot wider than a snowmachine trail," he said confidently. When another vehicle came toward us he pulled over to the side and stopped to let it pass.

I told him that I was going back to my land in the middle of the forest to build a home.

"What kind of game you got?" he asked, both hands on the steering wheel, dipping rhythmically across the yellow median line.

"Moose and salmon mostly," I said. "I've never thought about it much."

He nodded. "Hard to live without meat," he said.

"I don't even have a house built yet," I said.

"I guess you can live without a house," he said. "Might be hard to live without meat."

"We get most of our protein from beans," I said. Then I added, as much for myself as for him, "I've never actually hunted before."

He nodded again, a graceful gesture similar to the pro forma nod of psychiatrists when a client announces plans for suicide.

"Guess it's gonna be fun, huh?" he said, pulling over to the shoulder to let a truck pass—the *left* shoulder.

The semi laid on its horn as it roared by in a spray of snow, its trailer jackknifing behind.

"I think I'll get out here," I said as we idled, waiting for the snow spume to settle. "Will you be okay?"

"I don't know," he said. "I feel okay. It's kind of exciting. So I guess I'll be okay."

I spent the next two days and nights, after reaching the end of the Petersville Road, exploring the land I'd filed a claim on. I found my ridge by starting on the trail I'd made with Russ and then cutting off, instinctively, home. I marked every other tree I passed with a Boy Scout hatchet I'd picked up in a Fairbanks pawnshop. My trail was blazed for the summer hike.

I sat in my sleeping bag with all my clothes on thinking of wild game and construction and competence. It boggled me to consider any of it, so I ended up just listening to the breeze in the trees. I listened for moose and eagles. Then even that became a strain, so I just sat. For a long time, in the long night, I just sat.

I'd gone down to the creek bottom, where I thought I'd be warm out of the wind. I didn't yet understand that the cold settles to the bottoms of creeks, that ridgelines remain twenty degrees warmer in winter.

I shivered. But I felt okay. It was very exciting.

I couldn't wait to show Melissa and Janus.

I arrived in Anchorage resolved. I wasn't sure how fully Melissa would appreciate a wild ridgetop above a salmon creek amidst a hundred square miles of uninhabited ridgetops and salmon creeks, but I knew that she'd love a home. To get her a home required first getting cabin spikes and double-pane windows and fiberglass insulation and rolls of roofing paper and a big fancy cookstove in addition to other construction necessities that I kept adding to a growing supply list. To get enough of those necessities to begin building a home required working in Anchorage.

Anchorage was a boom town, still, five years after the Trans-Alaska Pipeline had been completed and the thousands of jobs it created had ended. Anchorage was still a boom town *because* of the pipeline. Two or three *thousand million* dollars each year in oil tax revenues fueled the state's economy. Anchorage, an urban hub of 250,000—half Alaska's population—was the repository of most of that money.

I hadn't much worry about earning bucks in Anchorage. I did, however, have hesitations about living there.

The first time I had seen Anchorage was when I came north on my summer vacation from New York. I had been given a ride by a wonderfully generous couple from rural Michigan who mined gold seasonally in Alaska. On the way toward the mine we stopped in Anchorage to visit mining camp friends of theirs. In a musty apartment building hallway we stood outside the friends' locked door, our happily shouted greetings answered only by perplexing whispers. Finally I was sent back out to the car. Fifteen minutes later I was joined by my traveling companions. They looked shaken. Inside the apartment was a woman who had been raped three days ago while her six-year-old son stood mute nearby. Her husband had gone early to the mining camp. The apartment door had been broken off its hinges by a man with a gun. He had pistol-whipped her into submission. She didn't want to visit with anyone after that, certainly not an unfamiliar man.

Anchorage, I subsequently learned, had, per capita, the highest rate of violent crime, alcoholism, wife abuse, child abuse, and rape in America. From the very first, I viewed Anchorage as an urban frontier, like Tombstone City or the South Bronx. But Anchorage was unique in that its statistically youthful population, a quarter of whom had arrived within five years, had migrated north not to pioneer or to find some kind of employment, but to become rich. Blazer-*and*-a-Bronco-*and*-a-satellite-TV-dish rich. Lizard-skin, hand-tooled, gold-toed-cowboy-boot rich. And if it took longer than expected to score that big-time Slope job, there was always McDonald's. Anchorage had the largest-grossing McDonald's in the world.

The city's rawness was exaggerated by the beauty of its setting. To the east, Anchorage ended abruptly at the glaciated Chugach Mountains, where bears roamed and Dall sheep scored the cliffsides. To the west, the city limits fell to the Pacific Ocean's Cook

Inlet, with tremendous tides second in amplitude only to Nova
Scotia's Bay of Fundy. Visible across the inlet were smoking volcanic
snow peaks. To the north, beyond a bridgeless arm of the curving
inlet, was the dark forest of the Susitna River Valley, at the top of
which I wanted to live.

Anchorage was isolated from Alaska by geography. A single road
headed north from town. But it was even more profoundly isolated
by population. Anchorage was pimps and police and Dallas oil
company executives who tried to avoid the fray high in the mirrored
glass offices of oil company skyscrapers. The rest of Alaska was Mel
Anderson in a beaver hat and Murray Amukpuk at ease.

I hoped that we could survive for a month or two while I hunted
and gathered basic building supplies. We really had no choice. It was
Anchorage or bust.

The day before Melissa and Janus arrived I rented an apartment.
It was the cheapest rent I could find, not counting the places in the
black ghetto, where I looked first until one prospective landlord—
Argentinian—tried to sell me some coke.

The morning before their early-afternoon flight I applied for a
proofreader's job at one of Anchorage's two type shops. The interview ran long because the owner was fixing the sole typesetting
machine and made me wait an hour and a half. I ended up rushing in
a cab to the airport.

The driver was Rudi Swartz, a twenty-five-year Anchorage resident, a German immigrant who wore a black bombardier's jacket
and black motorcycle boots. He was friendly.

"There any money in cabbing?" I asked.

"Vhy? You vant to be a driver?"

"I need to make some money," I said.

"I make two hundred dollars cash in my pocket on a veekend
night," he answered.

"Uh-huh," I said.

"You calling me a liar?" he said, slowing down.

I was thrown. "No! Hey! I don't know if you're serious."

He hit the accelerator again. "You asked. I'm telling you."

"Two hundred dollars a *day*?"

"On veekends. Maybe a hundred, hundred tventy in the veek. But on nights. I drive days this month 'cause I get tired of the drunks."

I was silent while I calculated. I ran out of fingers.

"Do you work five-day weeks?" I asked.

"Five. Seven. Two. Vhatever you vant."

We passed a Pizza Hut flanked by bars, a vacant lot filled with gray snow, a fifties whitewashed art deco gas station, another pizza joint, another bar, a bowling alley.

"How do I get a license?" I asked.

"Are you honest?" he replied at once.

"Honest?" I repeated.

"Cheaters steal fares. They make more, but I'm a road boss, and if I catch you I break your head."

"I'm honest," I said.

"Go to Ninth and L, fourth floor, take a test, pay fifty bucks, and that's it. Do you know the town?"

"I just got here," I said.

"You're honest," he said. "I could tell. That's vhy I'm telling you straight. Ve got a lot of Koreans and Albanians and Mexicans. They're cheaters."

"Al*ban*ians?" I said.

He shrugged. "I can't figure it out either. Used to be ve had only regular immigrants, like from Frisco and Seattle and Germany." He grinned. "But vhat the hell. Ve're on the last frontier."

I liked him for the innocent way he said "last frontier." In a Yellow Cab threading through lunch-hour traffic, with a Safeway mall on one side of the street and a Dairy Queen on the other, he wasn't mocking. He *believed* it.

I tipped him a five for a ten-dollar fare.

Melissa came down the boarding ramp looking wan but happy. We didn't speak for one of those long minutes that onlookers watch grinning—newlyweds in love! airport reunion!—while we embraced. Janus nestled between us.

Then she said, "You have *no idea* what it's like caring for an infant. I haven't slept in three weeks."

We took a cab back to our apartment. When I turned my attention to our cabdriver, Kim Hwan, he told me, in answer to my question about hacking, "Bad. No money. You do better something else." I stiffed him.

With the trunk full of kitchen utensils that had been in New York storage, we sat atop and among other necessary supplies: matching dinner plates and cups, fabric for curtains, pink and black place mats, a set of green glass jars to hold dried herbs. I told Melissa it would all come in handy since our Anchorage apartment was furnished with a bed, a table, a lamp, and little else.

I lay close to Melissa and Janus for the next fourteen hours. We all seemed to wake from short periodic dozes at once, marvelously. While Janus suckled, I tried to tell Melissa everything. She bravely listened to my flood of words until her eyelids lowered ("I'm listening!") and she drifted away.

At eight the next morning I walked to Ninth and L. I passed the test ("7: At which intersection is the Hotel Captain Cook?") by cheating off another applicant. Yellow Cab hired me two hours later for the night shift, 5:30 P.M. to 5:30 A.M. Then I ran to the typeshop and was told to report for work the next morning. I didn't sleep more than four hours at a stretch for the next fifty-nine days.

From the end of rush hour until bar closing—5:00 A.M.—I ferried drunks and whores and addicts and young white frustrated men who hadn't found what they'd come north seeking. I also chauffeured dislocated Natives—Athabaskans and Eskimos—whose pathos was particularly evident.

The drunks I took from bar to bar. There were ironworker bars and ICLU laborer bars, country-western bars and rock 'n' roll bars, VFW bars and even a couple of absurdly provincial gay bars where middle-aged men wore tar black hairpieces and called each other "Mary." But mainly there was Fourth Avenue.

The heart of downtown, and of the city itself, was a six-block stretch that at 5:00 A.M. was overrun with hundreds upon hundreds of people laughing and shrieking and singing and fighting and trying to find a cab. It was Times Square on New Year's Eve, every night. It was Dodge City during the height of the cattle drives. Every drunk in every bar in all the city seemed to end up on Fourth Avenue.

Ole was one of my regulars. I picked him up at the Pioneer Bar at 10:00 P.M. sharp and took him six blocks, for an expansive ten, to the Denali Bar, which had an interior swinging door that led directly into the Malemute Lounge, where people pissed on the floor and then got shot into the street at the hands of a seven-foot bouncer. Ole had homesteaded forty years before in the swamp forest behind Fireweed Lane, which was now a thoroughfare between the Seward Highway and Spenard Road's development. His original 160 acres had become a shopping mall and an oil-money-built high rise. He seemed as happy as a man could be who'd sold out for millions, living the dusk-to-dawn nightlife. But he always wanted to tell me tales of what it used to be like when he could take his yearly moose by aiming out of his bedroom window. We'd idle at curbside in front of the Denali ("I'll pay you triple, yah, you bet") so he could relive for me, an eager audience, the joy of Territory life in a rough-but-easy town where no one locked his door. I once made the mistake of asking him if he'd trade his yellow limo for his old trails, and he burst into tears.

The whores came in and out of the twenty-eight legal houses where I'd get thirty bucks a john for my recommendation. ("So where can I, you know, uh, like, I mean . . .") They got $150 an hour in-house and $200 for an out call. They called me "Slick Rick" because I always took my pay in bills and not favors. But most of them were ladies, and I got out to open the rear door for them. I knew them by name. Their *real* names. Not "Kahluha" or "Velvet," but Sally and Peggy.

The addicts circled the downtown blocks for an hour or two at a time—at $18 per—until they found their dealer back up against his neon-lit window front. Franny had been busted twice, so I helped her keep an eye out for the one or two beat cops who mostly broke up fights or shoveled the passed-out into the Community Service vans that waited at curbside, along with the cabs, to take *their* fares to the Salvation Army drunk tank out near the airport.

The young white frustrated men took out their frustrations on me.

"I'm maaad. I mean, I'm really maaaaaad. This place is a hole. They *lied* to me. Do you understand? They *lied*! I came here from (Detroit/Los Angeles/El Paso/America) and there ain't *nothin'*! Bull-*shit* on their promises. I'm the best pipe fitter in the goddamned country and I'm working in a fucking 7-Eleven. I can't even get laid! Will you take a check?"

The Natives were as out of place as Plains Indians on desert reservations. The Alaska Native Claims Settlement Act of 1972 that "granted" them first choice of Alaska's lands also gave them billions of dollars, which the hastily erected "Native corporations" promptly lost in a maze of financial dealings only Wall Street lawyers could properly understand. A lot of the new "shareholders" had been subsistence hunters until their first dividend checks altered their lives. They dumped their dog teams for snowmachines and abandoned the village potlatch for the nonstop party of Anchorage. Many of the resident urban Natives lived in squalid public plywood housing behind the downtown cemetery. Their small apartments disgorged first cousins and second cousins and in-laws visiting from the distant villages. They wanted to go "downtown" to drink beer and meet their relations in from the bush.

They were scorned by the cabbies because they didn't grasp the concept of a tip and were treated by most whites as "Nates" who couldn't even talk good. They only achieved equality at 5:00 A.M., when everyone spilled whooping and hollering into the street.

But for all the tragedy and violence of Anchorage, I went whooping and hollering through my days, too, because the city was as wild a place as could be found in any Louis L'Amour novel. There were no millions droning off to work, as in New York or Chicago, amidst a mingling of aberrant people to make things interesting. Anchorage was *all* aberrant people. The ones who had come to call it home were, by their definition, "Alaskans." And they lived inside an electric compound amidst recorded pollution that rivaled Mexico City's.

During the day, in the typeshop, I corrected the spelling of advertisements for Anchorage's booming ad agencies. "SoHio makes the Great Land great." "Tesoro Alaska fuels your dreams." "Fred's Landscaping for your home and business."

In between jobs I occasionally took naps in the back of a burned-out cab in the lot behind Joe's Cab Garage.

Melissa spent her days in the unassailable joy of new motherhood. She carried the baby in her arms wherever she went, not yet trusting a baby carrier or stroller to separate her from the touch that makes heavyweight champions and self-made millionaires confide to their biographers that they owe it all to Mom.

She went to the local library. She walked the downtown Park Strip with the other young mothers in a town where the median age was twenty-six. She drank peppermint tea and casually breast-fed Janus in the Bread Factory Natural Foods Restaurant. She made friends wherever she went.

Russ's wife, Gloria, became her best friend. They were both young mothers. They drove around Anchorage together, acquiring sale-priced roofing insulation and stovepipe and a cut-crystal vase, all of which was stored in Russ and Gloria's garage. "Gloria thinks I have 'charisma,'" Melissa said. "Isn't that sweet?"

People stopped her on the street to announce, usually shyly, sometimes with bold grins, that she positively *glowed*. These weren't, by her recounting, come-ons. They were spontaneous expressions of gratitude for an unexpected spot of sun in the gray winter.

Melissa accepted our separation for the nonstop schedule I worked because I was working, plainly, for us.

For small gifts of love to me she taped, at a new girlfriend's apartment, cassettes of Mozart and B. B. King. I brought her cut flowers and wads of bills. "A twenty tip from a crab fisherman who just made eight grand in twelve days." "A hundred and ten from a drunk I took to the House of Paradise, where three girls at once turned him into a bill-tossing spastic."

Janus just smiled at me. I just smiled at him. I was conscious at many points during every day that I was away from him, but it was worth it. It was a small price to pay for the years I dreamed about when we'd travel the mountains and explore the forests and catch fish, together, out in the wilderness, undistracted, home.

On my fourteenth night cruising the streets the full moon rose into a cleft between two serrated Chugach peaks. I was headed east toward the mountains in an alley behind Northern Lights Boulevard. I stopped. The western horizon was still colored in sunset. I stepped out of my cab. I stared. The moonlight sent blue shadows down the mountainsides, even with the rest of the sky radiant. I thought, "Why am I in this alley?"

My cab radio, which had been crackling with late rush-hour fares from oil buildings downtown, suddenly announced, "Got one going to Eagle River from Northern Lights and C."

I jumped back in the car and grabbed the mike. "I'm around the corner," I said, spinning wheels.

Eagle River was a twenty-five-dollar fare from town. It was a bedroom community of means on the other side of the first range of the Chugach, just under the moon. The river for which the community was named rose quickly to a glacier.

I dropped my fare at a big hillside home, pocketed thirty dollars, and drove a little way farther into the valley by the lingering daylight, my headlights off to better see the moon. I parked on a gravel road and without hesitation climbed up a hillside to the nearest peak, just to take a look.

A thousand feet and twenty minutes later I paused panting at the crest. Below were scattered yellow lights of houses. Farther to the west was the twilight sheen of the ocean. To the north was Denali and its flanking snow peaks against a cobalt blue sky. Between me and Denali were a hundred miles of dark forest, shadowless even under bright moonlight.

Anchorage was invisible behind the front range of the Chugach. Headlights from the cars traveling out the only road north looked like the afterburners of spaceships entering the void.

For an hour or two I stomped around atop alpine tundra and scree. My dominant thought was, "How long can I sacrifice my responsibility to leap up hillsides?"

I was an *adult*, for Christ's sake, with a family, and still I didn't think twice about scrambling up a mountain slope knowing at each step that I was losing income and possibly my very job.

But more than the necessary building supplies, more than educational toys to nurture an infant toward the fast track, more, even, than the ease of being ensconced in a wilderness homestead, I wanted the moment at the crest of a mountain in the full moonlight, because that's what I wanted my son to want. I was trying to earn something just as vital as cash dollars, just as requisite as food for a child: a legacy of freedom, the faith in beauty's power.

I didn't start down, stumbling in the moonlight, until I admitted that what we were working for, as a family, was the *need* to be drawn up mountains, into the unknown, to stand, alone, if only for a while, alive.

When I got back to my cab the radio squelched and then announced, amidst static, "Police are on their way to Eagle River. Anyone headed that way keep alert. Missing cab should not be touched until the police arrive."

"Wait!" I shouted. "Here I am! I . . . had a flat. I got lost! I'm okay!"

I got fired the next day.

To make matters even more fitting, I had my proofreading hours cut by half because the typesetting machine continued to malfunction.

I spent my suddenly free afternoon at Checker Cab, where I got hired for the night shift. "You look clean. You'll do," was the explanation.

I decided to get another job, just in case. I responded to an ad in the *Anchorage Daily News* for an advertising copywriter. I didn't quite know what a copywriter was supposed to do, but I figured it meant writing the ads I proofread at the typeshop.

On my interview the president took me into his carpeted office. He wore a pastel, obviously expensive suit and patent leather shoes. He was blond and coiffed. He owned the third-largest ad agency in Alaska. He was about my age.

"I was chief copywriter for the E. David Kach Agency in New York," I lied. "You've heard of JBL speakers? That's because of me."

Dave Kach was a high school buddy who wrote poems, not ads. I tossed the president a JBL ad I had ripped from a *New York Times* that a friend of Melissa's had mailed her as a joke. "Now I'm building a homestead in the forest," I continued, "so I won't be able to accept a salaried position. But I'll help you out for a consultant's fee."

Melissa had encouraged me to be confident. She knew the business world. "Start out strong," she had counseled, Janus in her arms. "If you *act* like you know what you're doing, they'll think you *do* know what you're doing. And you'll learn."

The president, behind his mahogany desk, was hesitant. I sat with one leg crossed over the other, a New York advertising star, a complete huckster, appropriately. Then he reached into his top desk drawer and took out a photograph. It was a ten-by-twelve black-and-white glossy of him with a ponytail and an American flag T-shirt. "I used to be interesting myself," he said, tossing the photo across his desk.

I wrote television and radio commercials for ARCO Petroleum and Bob's Bull's-Eye Hardware and Supply, among others.

I listened to my radio spots at night, in my cab, carting drunks from the Western Bar to the Montana Club. I was making *fifteen dollars an hour* at the ad agency. Big time!

The president's blond wife, a former model, who accepted me as an Ivy League advertising consultant, confided, "We know you're a genius because you look like you've slept in your clothes." I wanted so bad to tell her that I *did*, in the back of a rusting cab behind a garage with a pocket alarm clock near my head, set to ring in a couple of hours. But I only chuckled urbanely, like a Harvard man.

Since I could write my copy in a few hours at the agency, where I had my own fern-decorated office, I got yet another job. It was for the nights when I needed a break from the streets, or when my cab was down for repairs. I waitered in the Great Alaska Bush Company, the most popular of Anchorage's six nightlife establishments. There was also Kitty's, the Crazy Horse Paris I and II, the Wild Cherry, and Moby Dick's. All of them were topless-bottomless clubs, packed to the walls from opening to closing.

I brought overpriced drinks to men who tossed bills at stunning young women strutting on an electric runway a hand's reach away from the best tables. I knew most of the girls from cabbing. They made two hundred a night in small bills for "flashing pink."

"That's pink!" the deejay would shout over the booming sound system. "That's bush! Let's hear y'all say, *'Bush!'* "

"Bush!" the crowd would bellow as the girl on stage lay on her back kicking her legs toward the ceiling. *"Buuuuuuuush!"*

After my first night, when I tripped over my own feet trying to move between tables while staring at the show, I surprised myself by casually ignoring the naked women in order to sidle up to the tables where the glasses were empty, to suggest, "More champagne?" I got a cut of the hundred-dollar bottles of André pink champagne.

In the few hours that I was at "home" with my family, I'd slip next to Melissa on the bed and kiss our son repeatedly, too, until I dropped to sleep. When I woke, I'd reach for my rubber-band wad of bills to show Melissa.

"I got a double-pane window last night," I'd say. Or, "I got the insulation for the bedroom." Then I'd get up, still buzzing from lack of sleep and the intoxication of being on the loose in the largest nonstop party on earth, and race to my next job.

No wonder the Natives gravitated to Anchorage from villages one generation removed from the Stone Age. Ten thousand years of sensory deprivation and cyclical starvation had made the city Studio 54 for common folk. Open to all. An electric circus. And fun, fun, fun—with enough drugs.

My drug was cash money in my pocket. I had my own private car (Checker #151). I had the loveliest lover, who glowed. I had a penthouse apartment, even if it was only the top floor of a duplex. My New York desires had been fulfilled. My urban fantasies had become reality. I didn't even sleep much for fear of missing some of the action. And once I'd acknowledged that I could never ask for more from any city, I noticed the snow on the surrounding Chugach Mountains fading to brown hillside.

I noticed it while standing on the top deck of a downtown parking garage. The lot overlooked the inlet, which was, after almost two months, free of ice floes. The ocean cliffs were bronzed by that particularly intense sun that burns below heavy storm clouds in the gap between purple stratus and the gilded horizon. The city skyscrapers (sixteen stories tall!) reflected blazing light. The log cabins and clapboard storefronts on either side of them acquired the earth tones of South Pacific coastal villages. The dusty brown hills reminded me of Guadalajara, a booming Third World city where Indians wander in from the rural areas to mingle with shining development and squalor.

And I fit right in. I stood, fixed in amber like a fossilized insect at the height of its life, with a needle and thread poised over the crotch of my pants. I'd ripped them crawling groggily out through the busted window of my favorite cab shell behind Joe's Garage after a nap. I'd finessed a sewing kit from a maid's cart in the Hilton across the street. My Alaskan shopping bag was at my feet—a sleeping bag stuff sack—filled with my shopping bag belongings: toothbrush and toothpaste, nail clippers, comb, two pens, sunglasses, extra sweater, writing tablet, half a loaf of French bread, and bus schedule.

I brushed my teeth in public washrooms. I patched my crotch on rooftop garages. My father's worst fears had come true: I was an immigrant bum. I shunned—and was shunned by—respectable society. I walked the sidewalkless thoroughfares with my bag over my shoulder. And I was as happy as could be, because it was time to go home.

Winter fading! Ground thawing! That home could now be built.

I brought Melissa a glass of water from the bathroom after work. The bedroom was shadowed in moonlight.

"He's fussing," she said. "He won't go to sleep."

I handed her the glass. "It's my turn now," I said. "I just quit my jobs. I think we're ready."

"*I'm* ready," she said.

I lifted Janus and wrapped him in a baby blanket. I carried him like a thief to the vacant lot down the block next to the Lucky Seven

Trailer Park. At the edge of the city, stars touched the tops of the silhouetted mountains.

I pulled the blanket from around his face. "Moon," I said, pointing up. "Mooooon."

He grinned. He cooed.

Father and son stood together in a black gap amidst the electric gridwork, baying at the moon.

6.

WELL, THE FIRST DAYS
ARE THE HARDEST DAYS

The Petersville Road in summer was just as wide as the blade of a D-9 Cat and rutted by holes deep enough to drown a dog.

That's what Pecos said as we drove carefully down the road at ten or fifteen miles per hour. Pecos lived in a cabin a mile beyond Rosser, and kept an old three-quarter-ton Ford truck in the downtown Talkeetna railroad parking lot. Pecos had twice before hauled a truckload of supplies for us from Anchorage to a side-of-the-mining-road clearing where the construction materials were cached under plastic sheeting.

We had made those freight runs, however, in April, the last month of cold weather, when the part of the road that was occasionally snowplowed became like concrete from the alternating bright noon sun and freezing nights. In the summer, the road was best suited for prospectors with donkeys, or for Cats—the Caterpillar tractor company's various-sized bulldozers.

Pecos had a very long beard and even longer hair. He wore wire-rimmed glasses and heavy wool pants with suspenders. He looked the part of the proprietor and sole employee of Pecos's Dog Freighting. Though by winter he filled the caches of the last miners at the few still-active claims, he had been unable to dogsled any of our supplies to the ridgeline before the snows went.

There had been no trail. The snow had been too deep. The homesite was distant.

We wove between potholes, brushing greened branches that leaned into the road, until we reached a wide turnaround beyond which the road narrowed to an even less navigable track. This was the point where Pecos and I had twice stockpiled homestead provisions.

I didn't recognize it.

Where there had been ten-foot-tall snow berms there were now weeds trying to overrun the road amidst the gravel. The forest floor was a tangle of vegetation. Even after I spotted the plastic glint of the supply pile among the waist-high grasses I remained disoriented by the density of summer growth.

When I got out of the truck mosquitoes surrounded me. Pecos sprayed himself from boots to felt fedora with bug repellent, then tossed me the canister. After spraying myself twice over, I went to check beneath the tarp.

Everything was there: four-by-eight sheets of flooring plywood, rolls of fiberglass insulation, boxed triple-pane windows, tarred roofing paper, chain saw gas, cabin spikes, cement for the foundation footings, creosote, and a little sheet-metal wood stove. Pecos had helped me choose the proper materials. So had the library's *Building the Wilderness Cabin*.

I went back to the truck and helped Pecos wrestle a huge hawser-corded net to the cache. We had three nets, one for each load that a Jet Ranger helicopter would lift by cable sling the next afternoon and ferry into the forest.

Melissa was to be in charge of the road operation. She would come out from Talkeetna, where she'd been happily reacquainting herself with the Alaska she had first known, where our return from

Anchorage had been like a high school reunion: "What have you been *doing*?" How have you *been*?"

While she clipped the loaded slings to the dangling cable, I would be clearing a spot on the ridgeline, waiting for the drop. More than twenty-four hours for me to hike through the forest seemed plenty of time to reach the homesite, establish an area for the summer's building, and maybe even explore a little for signs of game.

Pecos and I finished unpacking the truck. We added cases of dried dates and spaghetti, bags of beans and rice, plus log-building tools: an axe, an adze, a peavey for rolling logs, a mattock for clearing sod, a five-pound mallet, and a beveled blade with handles a foot apart for peeling bark from the trees that would become the house.

Before I started into the woods Pecos said, "Now don't worry about the bears. If you do, you'll never make it. Every little sound will seem like death, and you'll spook."

I carried a machete for the brush, as Pecos had suggested. It was useless for bears. I left a 12-gauge shotgun in with the rest of the supplies because I *wasn't* worried about bears. I wasn't worried about anything. I was going home.

My only hesitation was that I didn't know where to go.

The open avenues between trees that in winter revealed the route were now filled with twelve-foot-tall alders sprung back up from beneath the snowpack, intertwining willows and dense shrubbery, ferns and vines and grasses. When I stepped away from the supply cache I couldn't see my feet beneath the vegetation. Each step was as if through a trapdoor, feeling blindly for something solid.

I located the first tree I'd blazed last winter. It was a birch. My hatchet mark oozed a pink sap. It looked like blood. It *was* blood, the festering wound of a mutilated trunk. Nobody had told me that trees bleed when they're blazed. The prospect of following a trail of blood home was disheartening until I acknowledged that without the markings the hike would take much longer. Navigating by compass and map would ignore the natural winter corridors as well, making the trail useless for a dogsled come the snows.

The bright pink birch cuts and the rivulets of orange sap on spruce stood out like neon against the forest green. The spruce boughs were olive green, darker in shadow. The broad-leafed alders were one shade of yellow lighter, mingling with brighter spring green birch leaves where birch branches draped low. The grasses were dull; the ferns and willows were vibrant. Patches of sphagnum moss were emerald where the ground was too moist for flowering plants.

I pushed through the brush for fifty yards. I carried a pack stuffed with a sleeping bag and tent and food and a canteen of water. The pack caught on alders.

I had seen this forest from Stanley's place. I had followed summer trails through it—to Marvin and Anna's, to Denny's and the Professor's. It had never occurred to me that those paths existed only as the result of hard work and years of use. The boreal forest had no natural summer corridors.

I began whacking at alder trunks with my machete. The three-inch trunks were like the bars of a cage.

Three blows! Four! I slashed the tree in two. I shoved the trunk into the foliage. Its weight snapped the stems of budding plants.

My God! Was I going to decimate a strip of this world just to be able to *walk* through it? I decided not to cut any more. I tried to slip through it like an Indian.

I was sweating. The sweat drew bugs. The bugs whined around my head. The sound was of desperation. Suck blood or die! Risk death for life! I killed the mosquitoes that landed on me. I killed them without guilt.

On Dead Dog Ridge, breezes from the Susitna had pushed the bugs back into the forest and I'd brushed them on their way when they harried me. I believed then, as Tibetans believe even now, that any killing is wrong.

But Tibetans live on a desolate plateau fifteen thousand feet above the Indus jungles. Life there is so scarce that any expression of it—any bug, any plant—deserves to be nurtured. Here in the upper Susitna Valley, seven hundred feet above sea level, I was beset by such a wild excess of life that I felt overwhelmed by it.

This was more intense than any tropical land I'd seen in Samoa or Java or East Africa. In Alaska! Clouds of bugs, clinging vegetation.

What had happened to the wide river plain with glacial mountains blue on the horizon? Where were the breezes?

I thought of bringing Melissa into this world and began slashing again with the machete.

I came to a thicket of devil's club, a chest-high plant with two-foot-broad leaves. The stalk was studded and the leaves edged with wicked thorns like porcupine quills. I had simply avoided it around Stanley's. Now, when I chopped at the leaves, the remaining stalk whipped up against my arm. I wore a cotton shirt and blue jeans. And I intended to hike through *miles* of this stuff?

I decided to turn back. No wonder so few people lived out in the boreal forest! Of course the Athabaskans would have settled on the banks of major rivers. No Indian in his right mind would march deep *into* the forest to live.

I headed back the way I'd come. But because I had been hesitant to clear a path, the green wall was as thick behind as ahead.

I paused, panting. Mosquitoes whined in my ears and bounced around my eyes. My legs were slimy with sweat and dew.

"I'll just ride in with the chopper," I thought.

But what then? How could I identify from the air an unmarked ridge in thousands of square miles of forest? And who would be on the ground to release the dangling net of supplies?

I lay down atop huge serrated ferns. Beneath them were delicate horsetail grasses. The canopy of birch leaves above was so thick the *sky* was a silhouette.

I crushed mosquitoes and black biting midges and anything else that dipped low—spiderwebs, benign mayflies, budding flowers.

I wiped the dead bugs on my shirt and took deep breaths. The air was dense, moist, oppressive. Groundwater began to soak through my back.

With my attention focused on the bugs I got good at nailing them. Reach. Clap! Wipe. I realized that this world was like any other: practice and attention allow ease. Clap! Wipe.

I got up and continued north, navigating by tree gash. I used the machete like a scythe, swinging rhythmically from side to side. When the alders rose thick I played samurai: one blow—*ha!*—to cleave the trunk.

Kill or die! I *would* massacre the floral life to make a path. I was no different from the Great Plains pioneers who annihilated the prairie grasses to make farms. I was no different from the Eskimos who gutted sentient mammals for meat. I was just as much a part of the tragedy of life as bears who slaughter moose calves and loggers who clear-cut redwoods.

It was too much to consider, so I just kept marching. One day I would sit with this reality. But not now. Now I had to hack my way between maimed trees to reach my pastoral dream.

I didn't stop again until I heard the creek. It sounded at first like wind in the trees, and the hope of a breeze made me straighten up. Then I remembered that in winter Russ and I had passed over a snow-buried creek—the far bank difficult to climb with skis and snowshoes.

I listened to the rush of the water. It sounded high, roily, but much more melodic than the thin wail of mosquitoes.

Then it hit me. The creek was *open*, flooded, without bridge.

At this time of year, mid-June, the Susitna River was near its highest, the result of snowmelt in the mountains and spring rains. From Stanley's cabin I had watched it running heavy with mud from collapsed banks, carrying whole trees.

For an instant I thought of building a raft. I'd fell saplings with the machete and lash them together with vines. But even if I could construct a raft that wouldn't be immediately torn apart, the brown water would carry me far downstream.

I gave up again. Before I turned back I pushed the last ten yards toward the creekbank just so I could report how deadly the crossing looked without a bridge.

Through ferns I saw that the water *was* swift and brown and high. It stretched at least thirty feet across. Branches bobbed in the current.

I clambered atop a massive fallen tree trunk—a cottonwood, a prehistoric tree with a trunk four feet thick, with branches that didn't begin to spread until fifty feet from the tree bottom.

The cottonwood trunk spanned the creek. Behind me, the roots torn from the earth were red and yellow and caked in mud. Across the water the branches were splayed around a birch that had a pink blaze mark on it. The water lapped at, but mostly coursed beneath, the fallen tree.

It hadn't straddled the creek when Russ and I had passed. I was sure of that because its branches, tangled in willows and grasses, were in full green leaf.

I walked across the cottonwood as casually as across a street.

Then I plunged back into the forest. All I thought was, "Well, that was easy." I didn't linger. I still had most of the way to go.

It wasn't until I stopped to sleep for the "night," hours later but with the subarctic sun still high, that I fully grasped that a perfect bridge spanned the creek *right on the trail.*

The almost constant summer sunlight of the far northern latitudes made the vegetation grow so thick I couldn't set up my tent, so I just burrowed in my bag. I lay awake breathing my own effluvia inside the sealed bag, thinking, "Holy shit." It was all holy and it was all shit. I couldn't think coherently. I needed to sleep. I couldn't sleep.

What if a bear found me? What if that cottonwood was a fever delusion and I had really *swum* the creek? I patted my clothes. They were soaked.

I tried to breathe. I was suffocating. I ripped open the bag and was immediately covered in bugs. I looked up at intricate layers of the forest.

I pulled the bag over me the way I used to pull the blankets over my head when clothes hanging in the bedroom closet had begun to stare back.

Where was I? How could anyone find my corpse when the brush closed? And the bears!

I fell into a horrible sleep, clutching my machete.

I awoke wetter than when I had lain down. The grasses seemed to have grown taller. I leaped up flailing at the bugs and crammed the sodden bag into the pack.

I had no idea how much farther I had to go. My map had no red arrow saying, "You Are Here." Every once in a while I imagined that I could hear a helicopter whirring into the uncleared forest, carrying the unbuilt house.

I didn't bother to slash at brush except when devil's club barred the way. By remaining in constant frantic motion I kept most of the bugs away. I crossed the wake of what could only have been a bear: flattened brush bowing up like the ribs of a canoe, a parting of the green sea. I wasn't spooked. I was annoyed that I had none of that power.

Suddenly I pushed out onto a long, narrow tundra meadow. I recognized it at once. At the top of the bronzed and russet fairway, through a short band of forest, was our ridge, a few miles from where I stood.

I had never actually walked on this tundra before. I had stood atop it supported by six feet of snow. I had flown over it on the flight to Denali. Now I stepped out onto a carpet of miniature plants—matted grasses and mosses and tiny flowering shrubs, a mosaic of flora rising no higher than my shins. Each step was like being on a trampoline. The ground was moist but not sodden. And the sky was revealed.

As I went farther, a steady breeze blew the bugs back into the forest. A long-legged bird swooped overhead with piercing cries. I ran, droplets flicking from my heels onto my legs.

It was like entering an amphitheater contained by tiers of trees: stunted black swamp spruce rising to billowed birch rising to the points of towering spruce. The trees echoed the cries of the circling birds. The sunlight lifted in heat ripples. There was a hallucinatory quality to it all. After the constricting forest, the expanse of tundra seemed fantastic. I felt like the first Masai tribesman to enter the huge verdant floor of the Rift Valley's Ngorongoro Crater, like a rookie taking center field in Yankee Stadium on opening day.

I jogged into the breeze, stopping only when I came to the edge of a large lake that extended from one flanking forest wall to the other. The lake, in winter, had been indistinguishable from the rest of the flatness.

The spongy tundra simply dropped off at the water, no sand bank, no gentle slope. I knelt and drank.

When I rose I saw a four-foot-tall mound of mud and sticks on the shore not far away. It looked like some ancient burial site. Had people been here before?

Then a beaver in the middle of the lake slapped its tail with a reverberating *thwack* and surfaced at once to glide in front of an iridescent wake, staring at me.

I walked to the crest of what I now realized was a beaver lodge. I stopped in ease for the first time since leaving the road. I didn't have to swat at bugs. The forest floor wasn't clutching at me. And I knew where I was.

I was in the tundra meadow where we'd play, where we'd swim, where we'd be the only people ever to enter this airy arena since the glaciers receded.

I curved around the shore of the lake, following a trail, a narrow dark indentation in the carpet of the tundra. The trail meandered a bit but headed north. I knew that moose and bear had made it, perhaps fox and wolves, too.

Less than a mile ahead the trees that bordered either side of the meadow arced to meet. Above those trees were the mountains. Wispy valley clouds shrouded the mountains from the rolling crests of their brown foothills to the midpoint of their blue ice buttresses— a band of mist that made the summits seem disconnected from the earth. It looked like the picture Alexander had given me of the Himalayas as seen from his monastery. It looked like a silvery-smooth Dali rendition of some floating Shangri-La.

I didn't hurry from the view. I shouted to hear my own voice return in successive distinct echoes. Dragonflies darted around me. I had seen vistas like this in glossy Sierra Club calendars in which photographers had captured some close-cropped quadrant of a Vanishing Paradise. All that vanished where I stood were my anxieties.

The sun had not reached its zenith. The helicopter was still hours away.

When I reentered the forest I followed my blaze marks for a few hundred yards to the crest of the ridgeline. I imagined I recognized the trees I'd stood among while Russ had skied off exploring. Then I *knew* that I recognized the spot where I had stood in winter, even now with the jungle burying that lone eagle feather.

I dropped my pack. I sliced ferns for a place to sit. For a long time I sat against a spruce trunk doing nothing except squeezing devil's club thorns from my arms. A breeze blew the bugs back from the ridge.

Surveying the area, it didn't take long to discover that there was only one possible place for a loaded net to be lowered through the canopy of leaves.

In that spot I gathered dried spruce twigs and birch bark to make a fire. Atop my kindling I laid green grass to create smoke, to mark our land for the helicopter pilot.

Then I covered myself with my bag and fell at once to sleep.

I awoke to the whop-whop-whop of rotors. I leaped up and struck a match to my kindling. It flared, then burst into flame, fanned by the draft of the chopper that I groggily realized was hovering directly above me.

The net of supplies was already drifting toward me. The pilot must have been a pro with maps to spot me sleeping in the clearing. I crashed through the brush to meet the sling. My fire roared.

I thought, "Oh, no! A forest fire!"

I ran back to the fire to kick it apart. It was too hot to touch.

The heavily laden net thudded into a trunk. I stumbled to the net and released the cable clip. When I unhooked it, I fell back as the helicopter lifted away.

I struggled to the fire on my hands and knees. It was just a smoldering pile of brush, as benign as a campfire in a drizzle.

I felt dumb. This was not California desert chaparral. I was in a rain forest. A forest fire here in full summer would require first the siphoning off of billions of gallons of water stored in the towering greenery.

Forty-five minutes later the helicopter returned with the second sling load. The pilot was remarkable to have made the turnaround so quickly. Melissa must have been strong to grab the heavy steel clip dangling beneath the prop wash and secure it to the net load. At $190 per hour I was grateful for their competence.

I had dragged the plywood and roofing paper and containers of gas from the first load. When the second came swinging down, I clipped the empty net in its place.

When the final drop arrived, the chopper unexpectedly began to settle lower. With its blades just a few yards from the wildly whipping branches surrounding them, a door slid open and Denny leaped out, paratrooper style, five feet above the ground. He rolled through the grasses and ran zigzag beneath the wash.

"You'll need support!" he yelled as he grabbed supplies from the remaining net. When it was empty we clipped it and its twin to the cable that was once again waving overhead. The chopper banked away and in an ear-ringing minute there was silence.

"He was in Nam, too!" Denny said, pointing overhead to the departed pilot. "Medevac! A hero!" He grinned.

"What are you doing here?" I said.

"First Airborne," he said, saluting. "I couldn't leave you out here alone. I came over with Melissa. Besides, I love this stuff!"

I was still stunned by the noise and activity. "How is she?" I said.

"She's the best little trooper you could want," he replied. "Just before I clipped the final sling to the Ranger and climbed aboard, she gave me this big hug and cried, 'Oh, Denny, don't let anything happen to him!'" He chuckled.

Then, because I was silent, he added, "So I told her that we'd be so far out of touch with the rest of the world that if anything *did* happen we'd be crawling with maggots before anyone found us."

I started to tell him that he should never say things like that to Melissa, but he broke in, "Just kidding! Just kidding! But it's true."

Then he lowered his head and sighed.

I was still trying to integrate his presence and the roar of the helicopter into my isolation.

He glanced up, lowered his gaze, and sighed again, loudly.

"*What?*" I said.

"Oh. It's nothing," he said quickly. "Just the inevitable loss that comes with any great gain." He looked around. "Boy you found a great spot!"

"What loss?" I said.

"All your dogs were stolen," he said. "You had them chained across the tracks from the Fairview. They must have looked good, even though they were Marvin's schizy little racing dogs, because now they're gone. Melissa was upset, but I convinced her that you can come up with a *much* better team."

I was dumbfounded. Who would steal dogs? "But . . . why?" I asked.

"In five or ten years you'll see dogsled racing on 'ABC's Wide World of Sports,' " he predicted. "It'll be big business. Do you know that *car* racing is the most popular sport in America?"

I was thinking about our dogs. Once I saw that Denny was serious, that they were gone, I was relieved. We would have spent close to five hundred dollars just to keep them fed and cared for in Talkeetna until the snows came. Then I was saddened that any of our meager assets could be gone. Finally I accepted Denny's dictum that gain necessitates a loss, that there is no such thing as the miracle of the cottonwood across the creek without *something* happening to balance the luck. And Melissa was fine. And here we were.

"So how about right over there?" Denny said impatiently.

I looked where he pointed. "For the house?"

"Sure! Right among those birch. It's perfect! Real secluded. Like a little nest."

I shook my head. "Too enclosed. We'd have to cut all those trees out."

Denny sighed again, theatrically. "For a split-level duplex with skylights?"

"Well. Something like that. I've sketched some plans."

Denny grinned. "I *knew* I had to come! You've got it all wrong! You can't build your home *first*. You need a little place to live so you can take your time building and do it *right*."

"Don't most people start out living in a tent?" I asked. "I've got a pretty good one. It lasted me on Denali."

He laughed. "You think *Melissa* will live in a *tent* for six months?"

"Where else would we live?"

"I'll show you," he said.

He started sifting through the scattered supplies. "Did you bring an adze and a mattock?" he asked with a tone that suggested I probably hadn't and was, therefore, a dummy.

"And a peavey and a big peeler," I said.

He looked up at me, genuinely pleased. "I underestimated you," he said. "Now we can really do it."

What we did was spend six days building a ten-foot by twelve-foot cabin from twenty-five or thirty young spruce, each about five inches thick. We dug away the top layer of sod with the mattock to lay the floor. We felled the trees with the chain saw, limbed them with a single-bladed axe. We flattened two sides of the wall logs with the adze. We rolled the roof logs into position with the peavey. The log peeler we didn't need to use.

"Watch this!" said Denny, taking a thick cabin spike and slicing through the bark down a length of log. He pulled the bark away with his hands as if he were slipping the skin off a snake.

"You can only do this for a month or two after the sap starts to run," he explained. "Otherwise you have to scrape with the peeler. Doesn't it smell sweet?"

It smelled like pine syrup, like thick mapled evergreen.

We worked fourteen hours a day. Denny had an aviator's watch, with a stopwatch feature. "Twelve hours twenty-six minutes and still going strong!"

And the trees we took would live forever, I hoped, in their bower.

After work we sat around a campfire cooking beans and rice. There was a brilliant sunset—at 1:00 A.M.—when the sky was clear, and a silvered twilight when there were clouds. The songbirds didn't differentiate. They began adding their dimension to the forest each evening about the time when our energies began to flag.

Denny was overjoyed to discover that I had brought in a small battery-powered radio/cassette player. He listened to the news on Anchorage's 50,000-watt AM station. He had been following the 1982 Israeli invasion of Lebanon. He didn't want to miss any of the action.

I wanted to listen to the birds. When they sang at dusk it was like the music of whales in a silent green ocean. There was one song that thrilled me.

"Thrilled?" Denny asked, chagrined.

"Listen!" I answered.

The song was a trill that spiraled up until ending in notes so faint that they blended with their own echo. I could never tell where the bird was perched. It was ventriloquism. It was magic.

Denny tried to familiarize me with the play-by-play of international war. It was so distant to me, the nightly news was so baroque, that he might as well have been introducing me to UFO sketches in the *National Enquirer* with an ingenuous "Isn't it amazing?"

"But this is *real*!" Denny insisted, fiddling with the radio dial to get Radio Moscow from Siberia.

"Uh-huh," I said, trying to locate the echo bird.

During the day I concentrated on building. *I* was chagrined that I had assumed I'd learn its subtleties on my own, without any practical instruction. I had read books in Anchorage. But I discovered that it was like trying to learn boxing from a manual, sculpting by going to a museum. Log building was an art. It took practice.

I knew from my studies that green spruce logs shrink one inch, when dried, for every foot of diameter. But I had no idea how to pin them appropriately so they would settle tight. I learned how to frame a window opening so the glass wouldn't be crushed by the settling, and how to roll roofing logs across a slope that slanted steeply.

Denny was an eager teacher. "If I had learned all this *before* building my place—well, I probably never would have done it," he said.

On the seventh day we rested. The doorframe lacked a door, but Denny convinced me that it would be easy to build. I believed him, not from faith but from experience.

We lolled around the clearing admiring our work, eating the last of twenty-five pounds of dried dates. Then we started out for the road.

We both assumed that the walk out would be a greater effort than hoisting—five times a day—a three-hundred-pound spruce log to our shoulders to stagger together up a ridge. I assumed it from having done it. Denny was merely hopeful. "No trail! Real wilderness!"

We got lost only twice, because the blaze marks were on the *other* side of the trees. We marched along in a straight line, turned to spot the last axe mark, saw nothing, and said, in chorus, "This way!" pointing in opposite directions.

But it seemed impossible to imagine that anything tragic could happen after we had negotiated the dangers of chain saws and axes and the skitter of sap-greased logs on a steeply sloping roof.

It was foolish to be so confident so far from help. But it made the trip swift. We didn't once mention maggots.

Melissa was in the kitchen of the Teepee Bar/Restaurant/Motel when I found her the following day. She wore an apron, her hair in a bun. She was stirring a large pot. When she saw me she ran into my arms, kissed me, then ran back to the stove.

"This can't burn," she explained.

She was catering a wedding. The bartendress of the Teepee was getting married in the morning. Melissa was going to lay a spread for the reception in the Fairview such as Talkeetna had never seen. This was her debut as a chef in town. She wanted everything to be perfect.

"We built a place to live," I said, as if announcing the discovery of the mother lode.

"Stir this," she said.

I stirred. "The logs of our little cabin are all peeled and the roof will never collapse," I said.

She acted as if she *expected* me to have done things right. I liked that. I put down my spatula and went to the corner where Janus was asleep in a car seat. I nuzzled him. I started to lift him into my arms.

"Don't let that burn!" Melissa cried as she carried a huge metal-handled pot to a table.

I was baffled. I wanted to wake my boy and hug him and say,

"Your daddy's back!" while he laughed in my embrace. But Melissa was serious. She seemed more serious about her pot than about my need to hold my son. But no, she wasn't aware that I was so serious about him. She was trying to keep three balls—or pots—in the air at once, and couldn't focus on much of anything else.

But I had just built our first home! Why couldn't she focus on *that*?

"This job," I thought, "must be as important to her in this world as the cabin was to me in the remote forest." I let Janus sleep. I surprised myself by returning to my post instead of balking and saying, "Hey! Are you listening to me?"

I saw the intricacies of human interaction as plainly as I had seen the layers of summer flora. My isolation for just a week, compromised though it was ("Okay, I'll *prove* to you that Israel could have taken Hanoi in a month!"), left me hesitant to judge circumstances that otherwise would have made me snap. Who knew what lay beneath the surface?

"Where is the ginger?" Melissa cried. "Where did I leave the ginger?"

I thought, "This is much stranger than when I returned from Denali. Why am I just standing over this stove so placidly? Why don't I feel betrayed, adrift, discouraged by these separate worlds we're living in?" I licked my spatula. Almond frosting!

After a week of beans and rice and dried dates, the frosting was like Proust's madeleine—if his cake had reminded him of *nothing* familiar. It was an unexpected treat, like blue ice above gold tundra, like a fern mattress in the ridgeline's breezes.

For the next half hour I tried to describe for Melissa what I had seen. I told her about the incomprehensible vegetation and the ease of the tundra's freedom. I told her how solidly our little cabin had been built, how much I'd learned about carving notches with a chain saw and about how to fell trees so they'd drop where I wanted.

Her responses were cursory. Shrimp paella demanded her attention.

When Janus woke I got my chance to hold him. As I expected, he laughed in my arms. Then he looked around and announced his hunger with a six-month-old's decisiveness.

Melissa turned off the last burners and suckled him. I waited for her to relax and ask more about the land.

Instead she brushed a strand of hair from her face, fussed with the baby, and said, "So when are *we* going to get married?"

"Ah," I said before I could stop myself.

"Is that an answer?" she said, looking at me.

"We *are* married," I said.

"We are *not* married," she said.

"What do you want?" I asked.

"A *real* wedding," she replied, still staring at me. "A big reception and a cake and bridesmaids."

I started laughing. I laughed because I had imagined human interaction to be as bewildering and complex as the summer jungle. I was relieved to think that occasionally there were simple explanations.

"I can't believe that you are *laughing* at *me*," said Melissa with a death-ray tone.

"I'm *not* laughing at you!" I said.

She opened her eyes wider. I took a step back.

"I just . . . I mean . . . Jesus! It was just so *different* out there that it's taking me a while to get back in step. I—"

"You are still talking about what's *out there*," she interrupted.

"No! I'm right here. I'm sorry. I just . . . oh boy. I just can't fit *that* into *this*."

She didn't bother to respond to something so lame.

"We *are* married," I said, to say something.

"Because we made it from the Professor's to Stanley's? Because we have a baby? While you continue to play explorer and I have to deal with things alone?"

"Melissa," I tried to reason. "I am as committed to you as can possibly be. We've chosen a life—together!—that can only bring us closer. The ritual with a cake is coming. So is the reception in our own home, with the French doors open to the greenhouse."

It wasn't what she wanted to hear. I was surprised. Janus released the nipple and howled. Melissa tried to pacify him. He didn't want to be pacified.

"*Now* look what you've done," she said, quivering.

I didn't believe that a preacher walking into the kitchen to reiterate our vows, followed by a bridal party strewing corsages, would satisfy all her concerns. More seemed to be preoccupying her than weddings.

"You're wearing Grandma's ring," I suddenly remembered.

My grandmother had given her own diamond wedding ring to Melissa. It had been waiting, unexpectedly, in our general-delivery mail when we went into Talkeetna a few days after finding our way back to Stanley's from the Professor's.

"Our dreams are coming true," I said.

"Living in the woods is *your* dream," she said.

The next day was easier. Every resident of the town who came to the reception told Melissa that they had never seen such food as she had prepared. When the bride hugged her and said, "And the cake was perfect!" Melissa said, "Rick's the one who did the frosting."

We slept on the floor of a friend's house. It was like a honeymoon. Melissa was yielding and loving.

I didn't question her happiness. When she whispered, "It's scary to think about, but I can't wait to see what it's like out there," I was glad that she was able, now, to consider the land.

The next morning I caught a ride to Anchorage. I needed to make more money to replace the supplies Denny and I had used up. Talkeetna was a helpful buffer between the homestead and the city.

After two days and nights, I returned by train with more boxed windows and spikes and roofing paper and enough food to last us through summer. The attendants in the baggage car recognized me. We jested about my need for more supplies. When I told them that this new stuff was for a homestead near the foothills of the Alaska Range, the senior attendant clapped me on the back and rushed to the bar car to bring me a beer. "You just won me a fifty," he said when he returned. "These other jokers bet that you'd be back in town before summer. We've seen a couple others like you, but they didn't last long."

I didn't know whether to be heartened by my tenacity or humiliated by the impression I had given. By the time we reached Talkeetna, I was only perplexed that the odds were against anyone trying to move into the bush.

Melissa and I dragged our supplies to the airstrip and loaded them into a net. I was excited to think how amazed she would be by the ridgeline. It was romantic and adventurous, and we weren't just tourists.

She would fly out with the helicopter. She would see only the beauty, without the struggle. The road into Talkeetna had been paved just eight years before. Until then there was no land access to Talkeetna except by train or heavy-tired jeep. The highway to Fairbanks hadn't even been pushed as far as the Petersville Road until about that same time.

I was glad to discover that access to the start of our trail had once been by hard work: prospectors plodding behind donkeys.

Still, our trail remained a difficult route. The grasses were now taller than my head. The bugs were awful. I was unable to concentrate on anything but step and clap.

At the creek, the water was red. I hurried across the cottonwood bridge, then doubled back. The red was from salmon—more than I could count—hovering in the current a few inches below the surface. The fish were two feet long, three, *four*. I could have walked across the water on their backs. When I took a step into the stream they vanished with wakes like torpedoes.

I stared at the water. It was blue with white riffles. The brown runoff had subsided. "Damnit, I *saw* you!" I shouted at the invisible salmon, shaking my fist.

I hadn't been back in the forest for an hour, and already I was overwhelmed by the extent of its life.

When I broke out onto the tundra at dusk it looked just as it had. A richer color. More dots of flower. Just as it should be, was, will be.

The bugs receded. The water flicked at my heels as I ran. A pair of loons rocketed overhead like artillery shells, their wings beating so fast the sky shone through.

I followed the game trail up toward the vista of mountains, but stopped. A pile of scat filled the trail. It was like a lava dome, studded with pieces of . . . what? I knelt down. I pushed the pile apart with my machete. Clods of hair, pieces of yellowed root or twig, strands of grasses.

Quickly I tried to pat the mound back into shape. "Oh boy oh boy oh boy," I said aloud.

This was the *bear's* trail. It was *his* scat. Maybe he wanted it there, just as it was, undisturbed.

I had been looking forward to pausing under the mountains. Now I only wanted to get off the tundra. "My" vista from "my" amphitheater was not mine to admire at the moment.

I talked loudly as I hurried into the forest and up to the ridge. What I said was unintelligible. The message was, "Here I come! Because I have no choice! Please don't eat me!"

When I saw the little cabin I started to race into its sanctuary but then paused. In the first place, there was no door to keep bears out. But I also admitted that I didn't want to duck inside away from this world so fast.

Then something happened that would recur at some point almost every day from then on. As I stared at the amber logs in their green bower I thought, "This is enough." Even if a bear came crashing through the alders and gnawed my skull there would be a legacy. Even if the birch that touched the roof fell through the ridgepoles the shell would remain, overgrown in time with lichens and vines, but evident. Even if nothing more was added to what had already been done, it was proof that great dreams could be reached. Maybe not held. But reached.

Who knew what the next moment would bring? I had just gone from the streets of Anchorage to familial hope in Talkeetna then to adrenal fear on the trail and finally to this refuge. What next?

Next was a step to examine the cabin. Then another step. Then—surprise!—no sign of bears.

I spent most of the "night" splitting logs with a chain saw to build a door. Denny was right. It was simple. The door fit as snugly into the frame as if it had been machined.

The next afternoon the last of our supplies were lowered to the ground. I unclipped the sling, then waited, standing atop the net, to extend a hand to Melissa. With the other hand I shielded my face against the rotor-whipped ashes from the campfire.

Melissa tried to make the step through the open door and hesitated. The helicopter rose up as if upon a wave. On a downswing she handed me Janus. I tucked him under my arm like a football. Then she jumped. I caught her. The three of us pirouetted clumsily, but we didn't fall. The chopper roared up to treetop.

"All right!" I shouted.

"All *right!*" she shouted.

I passed off Janus and cleared the net. When it was secured and the helicopter on its way back to town, we kissed.

"Have you ever *seen* what it looks like from up there?" Melissa cried. "It's all green. Everywhere! I can't tell you how beautiful it is!"

I was glad that she had ridden from Talkeetna to our clearing so easily. I wanted her to feel connected to the points of human habitation in this enormous valley. I wanted her to feel safe.

"Look!" I said, pointing to our little cabin.

I took her hand. "Oh," she said. "Oh, it's perfect!"

Then I turned to point at the jungle. "And over there is where we'll build our *real* house."

She stared at the devil's club and alder and ferns. She blinked. A mosquito landed on her forehead. She slapped.

"But this is *done!*" she said, returning to the sight of our little cabin.

I spent the next few days building a table and shelves and a bed platform. I built from split logs. The result was "rustic," we decided. But as crude as my furniture was, it worked.

Melissa cooked on a Coleman double-burner gas stove atop the new table, next to the grain grinder. She baked in a metal Dutch oven that fit over one burner. We slept on a foam mattress that covered most of a four-by-eight sheet of plywood supported by stumps. With our pile of dried food in one corner and the wood stove mounted in another and the bed filling more than half the floor area, we had little room to move.

But we agreed that our first home was "cozy."

I hung a mosquito net around the bed. Over the door Melissa tacked a tablecloth that had been her mother's. We let the sun shine unimpeded through the windows.

During the day it was seventy degrees. Through the long luminous twilight the temperature dipped into the fifties, but the cabin logs retained enough heat to keep us comfortable. We needed no wood stove fire.

Melissa had brought potatoes and carrots and cabbage from Talkeetna—fresh vegetables that wouldn't quickly rot. We kept cheese and tofu and dried salmon under ferns in the shade of the cabin's north wall.

The six-month-old baby claimed the wide bed as his domain. He crawled around it, laughing, from the low windows in one wall to the drop-off on the other side.

"He likes it here," said Melissa. "He's more alive than I've seen him in a long time."

I was goofy with pleasure that she could see it, too.

From around nine in the evening until the midnight sunset, when the sun slid *sideways* against the 17,400-foot peak flanking Denali, the light was a color that could be touched, like brass. Molten columns of pollen and dust hung in the air. Each of the countless gnats and midges and moths and mayflies that darted in front of the sun trailed a streak of light. Each leaf had a nimbus, our hair held a halo. Melissa and I sat at the window and watched. Even the baby slowed down, as if suspended in liquid gold.

" 'Liquid gold' doesn't even come close," said Melissa.

"Copper Caribbean seawater?" I asked.

"Worse," she said.

"Your turn," I said.

She laughed. "I wouldn't even try to describe it."

Once we'd fixed up our temporary home, I began spending almost all my waking hours outside. I dropped a dozen trees directly along the crest of the ridge above the spring. The trees didn't crash down. They settled slowly, eased to the ground by the branches of their neighbors.

I accepted responsibility for each of their deaths. It was preposterous to imagine that they were "only" trees. Just as matter-of-factly as Eskimos believe that whales give themselves to men who would otherwise starve, I assumed that my carnage retained some element of grace, if not because of the prayer that I offered before each cutting, then because I left the healthiest trees standing. It was hard to tell at first glance that spruce had been culled from the densely forested ridge. Still, it was difficult to come to terms with the destruction I created just because I wanted to be here.

Melissa remained mainly in the little cabin, cooking and caring for the baby and writing letters to distant places like New York and Talkeetna. I didn't blame her for wanting to remain connected to the familiar.

The only dark cloud that settled over those radiant first days came when I tried to get our CB radio to work. It was our emergency link with the rest of the world. It was also dead. The result of the thumping air drop? Fate?

"Great!" I announced after admitting that it was useless. "Now we *have* to be aware of every step. I mean, we *have* to."

Melissa wasn't as enthusiastic. "What if something happens?"

"It won't. It can't. That's all there is to it."

"And what if Janus gets sick?"

"Nobody that happy gets sick."

"Or if he falls off the bed and breaks an arm?"

"Janus," I said, "doesn't fall."

"He's a *baby*!"

"But if you believe it, then he'll believe it. That's how children work. If you *know* that they're beautiful, then they'll *be* beautiful, in amazing ways. If you know that—"

"You're not listening!" she said.

"*You're* not listening!" I replied.

Janus woke suddenly from a nap and said, "Whaa?" It wasn't a cry. It was more a surprised question: "What's going on?"

Melissa and I stopped.

Just that momentary pause broke our rhythm. Instead of Melissa's saying, "*You* think that it's a great *adventure* to make us all suffer because you didn't have it together to do things *right*," she said nothing.

Instead of my replying, "Well, if you had any faith that what we're doing is blessed you wouldn't be so goddamned full of fear," I said nothing.

Janus looked out the window and grinned. A gray jay sat on the sill, pecking at wheat berries we'd scattered.

"Isn't this a lesson," I said quietly.

"There's no way to escape each other here, is there?" said Melissa as she sat on the bed beside the child.

"That's exactly what I was thinking," I said.

"I know," she said.

I sat beside her. "I'll bet that being so far out in this world *does* increase psychic ability," I said.

"Increases stress, too," said Melissa.

"But—think about it—now we're more connected to the sky than we are to anything else. We're not trying to be successful or clever or cool or friendly or fashionable or *anything* that society values. And if you abandon the connection to what 'they' think is important, then what's left is the other ninety percent of our brains. Like reading thoughts. Or sensing the migration of birds. Or knowing that it's only a rabbit and not a bear rustling behind the alders. Do you know what I'm trying to say?"

Melissa smiled. "Remember when you waited for me at Fiorello's across from Lincoln Center? And I was late because I had to do inventory for the next week? And you kept sitting in the café drinking wine until they closed, so that when I finally got there you were standing on Broadway looking across the street with your hands behind your back? You didn't even *glance* at me. You said, 'Can you understand the passion and exaltation that has marked every atom of that marble?' Or something like that. Do you remember? That's the way you sound now."

I didn't remember. But I got the message.

"New York *is* intense," I said. "It's a *human* intensity. But this world is just as intense. And it has nothing to do with people."

She lifted her blouse and drew Janus to her breast.

"We've just traded one overwhelming world for another," I said. "But here there's just light and wind and ice on the horizons."

"And bugs," she said.

"And bugs."

In a week the bugs subsided. We still slept under the mosquito net, but it wasn't speckled in the morning with mosquitoes.

When the bugs faded the rain came. At first it was tropical: huge thunderheads drifting overhead to pelt the ground with large drops before dissipating to a cool breeze. But then it became monsoon: a silver-gray drizzle that rose to torrent that fell to drizzle. For weeks.

Instead of ringing sunlight there was soft mist. No tangerine radiance at 2:00 A.M. No mountains.

On rainy days in New York I would occasionally turn to the Muzak station and sit at the window, humming old songs but otherwise doing nothing. In the summer forest I still hummed, but I didn't stop moving.

I dug pilings for the house. I dug twenty different holes a foot wide and four feet deep to plant the dried spruce logs that I had coated with creosote to retard rot. The horizontal house logs would rest atop the pilings, a foot above the mildewed ground.

The first six inches that I dug were sod and topsoil. Russ was right: the next foot was clay, and then rocks. There were pebbles and stones and boulders that I tried to cleave with an axe-head chisel struck with a five-pound mallet. There was granite and quartz and shale. But no gold.

I looked for gold.

When the pilings were set in their square—four to a side, with the remaining ones in the middle of the square to support the floor joists—I broke out the come-along.

The come-along is a winch with two hundred feet of half-inch manila rope. I knotted one end of the rope around a fallen spruce out in the forest and ran the free end through the winch, which was fastened by a heavy chain to a standing tree. Then I began to crank, tugging on the handle.

Click-click-click. Three turns of the ratchet slid a log an inch. One inch. If the log didn't get stuck against the brush it plowed up I could slide it smoothly out of the forest.

Usually it got stuck. I could pluck a note on the taut rope when I went out to free the burrowed tip of the log.

After three or four hours of this kind of labor I had the first log pulled up to its pilings. I used the peavey to turn the log horizontal to its pilings. Then I built a ramp from the tailings I'd dug from the foundation holes.

I levered one end of the thirty-foot log up the ramp to rest on the creosoted stump. I lashed it down with rope. Then I built another ramp at the other end to do the same thing.

After a few abortive tries at keeping the first end lashed to its stump so it didn't slide off, I had the log steady on its foundation. I pounded it flush with a twelve-inch cabin spike after drilling a six-inch hole with the hand bit, and then using another spike to counter-sink my first one.

It took two days from the time I first rigged the come-along until I could call Melissa over from the little cabin a hundred feet through the jungle to announce, "Look!"

She stood in the rain without a slicker. "I knew you could do it!" she said.

"I was hoping you'd say that," I said.

She smiled. She kissed me on the cheek. "I know," she said.

One log up. A hundred left to go.

Log building on this scale wasn't as easy as I'd thought.

. . .

Two weeks later the rains stopped. I had finished the four sill logs on which the rest of the house would rise. Each fourteen-inch-thick log weighed a half ton. I hadn't even come close to rolling one onto my leg.

Melissa hadn't even come close to burning down the little cabin when the gasoline pressure stove flared, yellow flame spreading toward the ceiling. She shut it down efficiently.

Out in the forest, maggots starved to death because we didn't screw up. I felt no guilt.

It was deep summer, July by the calendar, but the days of the month were meaningless. Our radio/tape player had introduced Mozart's *Magic Flute* to the songbirds until the six D cells died. When the birds stopped singing in order to feed their newborn young, the sound of the forest was just wind in the trees, except for the buzz of the chain saw and the sudden announcements of a passing raven.

The path down to the spring required maintenance every other day. I chopped at grasses and ferns to keep the way wide enough for me and the five-gallon plastic bucket that I used to haul water. The bucket had held sixty pounds of honey, now decanted into smaller containers. Our water was sweet. It remained sweet long after the honey scent was gone. Even when spruce grouse crapped in the pool the water remained sweet. If we could have bottled it, we could have afforded coolies.

I thought of coolies as I cut and peeled and hoisted and notched logs. I thought of the legions of workers who carried the stone to build the Great Wall of China. I thought of a painting in a grade-school history book: an army of loinclothed men tugging the blocks of the Pyramids into place from a distant horizon. I kept kicking aside rocks hoping to find gold with which to enlist help.

In thinking of the history-book Egyptians, I remembered that they had used logs as skids to ease the passage of their load. That proved to be a tremendous help in getting the trees out of the forest. I placed one round pole under the front of a peeled tree, lifted the tree atop the pole with the peavey, and then added more skids as I winched. Easy street.

Other idle thoughts produced other useful help. I remembered that Mr. Oster, our handyman next-door neighbor when I was a kid, had used a string stretched tight to indicate horizontal when he was building his patio. I remembered it because I was thinking of the games we used to play in that patio as it was being constructed, especially Cars and Trucks, into which we pumped "gas" from the cement mixer. Our play building equipment then went, "Vrooom, brumm-brumm-brumm." I even made the appropriate sounds of childhood as I leveled logs.

And so the day would pass, one vivid distant memory after another.

Melissa continued to keep to the little cabin. The single room of the cabin always smelled like fresh bread. When I tried to get her to walk with me farther into the forest she laughed. "You can't *get* any farther than here," she said. "We are *in* the wilderness. Up to our necks. Besides, Janus is content right here."

I carried Janus into the twilight each evening. He grabbed at leaves and examined the flowers I held him near until he tried to eat them. When sounds of wind or bird altered the silence, he stood up in my arms and cocked his head like any forest animal.

My secret pride was my bedtime walks with him. Melissa was grateful for the reprieve from mothering. I was glad for the break from building.

When two rounds were up—eight logs, two per side—I rested in the center of the rectangle daydreaming of the roof. A snowshoe hare, brown in its summer clothing, hopped up to the logs, paused, slipped under the sill log, leaped *over* the logs on the other side after almost brushing my leg, and disappeared.

"Well," I thought.

Immediately a marten appeared. It darted from side to side following the hare's trail. It passed in front of me as casually as had the hare. When it came to the far wall it paused and looked back at me.

"It went thataway," I said, pointing.

The predator sniffed around some more, found the trail, and slipped into the brush.

As I stood marveling at how easily I was accepted into the forest's life, the hare returned, moving a little more quickly but still almost playfully. It hopped in a veering line past the building. Then the predator came sniffing and stopping and hurrying.

It was like a Keystone Kops routine.

I wanted to go back and tell Melissa. But before I could clamber over the house logs, the hare came racing past at a full run. It moved so quickly I was startled. I sat back on the logs.

I waited for the hunter, and he came, hesitantly, trying to discern one trail from another. He looked baffled. If I had had a bone, I would have tossed it to him.

I sat for a while trying to decide if it was possible to have fun with the imminence of death. Then I looked to my uncrushed legs, my uninfected scrapes, and didn't know whether to laugh or to shudder.

That night the bear came.

Melissa elbowed me awake. She had lain listening to Something until she was convinced that it wasn't wind or mice. I got up with the spasmodic movements of exhaustion and stumbled to the north window.

There was a bear chewing cheese directly below me. It looked up. Its head, when raised, was level with mine. Flecks of white goat cheddar on its muzzle were like spots of slaver.

The bear was enormous. It was as massive as a rhinoceros, as ominous as a killer whale.

I was petrified. Then, as it continued to look calmly at me, chewing a wad of cheese, it began to shrink to the size of an average black bear, a 250-pound Saint Bernard with two-inch teeth.

"Melissa!" I hissed. "Quick!"

The bear bent back to its feast. Melissa jumped up. When she saw the bear she said, "It's a *bear*!" She didn't whisper.

The bear stepped back.

"He's eating all our food!" Melissa cried.

The bear began to lope away.

I rushed to the door. "Aaawrrr, git outta here!" I yelled.

The bear had vanished.

I ran inside and grabbed the shotgun. Its only use, after all, was bear protection. Bolting outside, I pumped a shell into the chamber and fired into the sky. The force knocked me backward. Shredded leaves drifted down like confetti.

The first sound I heard after the ringing ceased was Janus crying.

"It was a bear!" I said, ducking back inside. "A bear!"

"Did you see how his muscles rippled when he ran?" said Melissa. "Have you ever seen anything like that?"

"I wasn't scared," I said. "It was too sudden. I didn't know *what* to feel."

"I knew there was something there," said Melissa. "I couldn't tell at first if I was just imagining it, but then I *knew*!"

"He stared right at us," I said. "Just *that* far away!"

Melissa started to add more about our encounter when we both realized that Janus was indeed howling on the bed. We reached to pick him up at once. His face was contorted with the purple grimace of babies who aren't used to crying without a parent immediately lifting to soothe.

Melissa stuck a nipple in his mouth. "A bear!" she said.

Janus fussed and then sucked.

I began to laugh. "Can you imagine how we'd feel if it had been a grizzly? Griz are three times the size. Four! It could have knocked the window out by *breathing*!"

Melissa lost some of her initial excitement. She swallowed her next breath, then quickly nuzzled Janus to hide her expression. When she looked up she said, "You're just kidding, right?"

"I'm just kidding," I agreed.

"You're not kidding," decided Melissa. Her face was panicked.

Denny had repeatedly counseled me to go slow, not to push hard. And here I was gleefully describing the power of bears. I had blown it.

"Aw, come on," I said. "Didn't you see how scared Bob was?"

Melissa arched her eyebrows. "Bob?"

"Sure! Bob the bear. Our circus clown. One word from you and he bolted. He did a *somersault* trying to get away!"

"I didn't see that," said Melissa.

"Bob was more terrified than we ever were," I announced. "He's probably still running!"

Bears in the forest triggered a fear that extended back fifty thousand years to the time we competed with them for caves. But a bear named Bob was from a children's book. He might eat our food, but he'd perform tumbling tricks in return.

Melissa wasn't convinced. I wasn't either. It took us a long time to get back to sleep. Janus was the most animated. He bubbled and rolled and stared out the window.

"See?" I said. "He wants Bob to come back."

Melissa said nothing. She reached for my hand. I gladly interwove our fingers.

In the morning I went outside to see what Bob had eaten. He had eaten everything.

"I guess it's time to make my way into Anchorage to bring back more supplies," I said.

"But not today," Melissa said.

We had awakened late. I spent the rest of the day—my first abbreviated shift—pushing through the forest to find the next round of spruce for our walls. I found ten with straight trunks that seemed ready to lay down their lives for the crypt of our house. At each step I listened for bears.

That night we had a serious discussion.

"You're a breast-feeding mother who needs protein," I argued. "I don't think beans are enough."

"I agree," said Melissa. "But maybe there are salmon in the creek."

In the morning I went down to the creek. I saw nothing. We lived five miles from the ground seep that was the source of our creek. Salmon that reached this point were ready to spawn, after thousands of miles of ocean currents and glacial silt and beaver dams.

"Maybe you can shoot a bird or something," Melissa said.

I hoisted the shotgun and stomped through the forest. I had shot a gun only once before in my life. It had returned confetti. Murray Amukpuk had been right. We needed meat. But I hadn't the faintest idea how to track game.

We lay in bed discussing what should be added to the town list. I wrote 12-gauge shells and chain saw gas and a wood chisel. Melissa suggested soap to wash diapers and a book on herbs and cans of tuna.

"I won't be gone long. Just listen to Janus," I counseled. "He's aware of what's going on."

She narrowed her eyes. "Go fast," she said.

I went fast. I jogged down the tundra. I played Bear on a Rampage through the forest.

When I reached Anchorage I got a cab to drive for the night. I was ruthless. I wrestled drunks from the taxi, demanding not just the fare but a tip. I exceeded the speed limit by as much as the transmission would allow. I burst into the ad agency at 6:00 A.M. with my executive key and wrote three commercials in an hour. Then I ran from supermarket to hardware store to gun shop before taking a bus to the Eagle River exit, on the outskirts of Anchorage.

From there I hitchhiked. I didn't wait with my thumb stuck out. I stepped into the traffic lane waving my arms. The first car that came north had no choice but to stop.

"My wife's ready to give birth any minute and I've got to get home!" I shouted.

I blustered my way up to the Petersville Road. Even if my angels, whom I throttled by the neck, didn't believe my story, they believed my intensity.

When I got out at the head of a gravel mining road I hoped that Mel Anderson would come by. He didn't. I rode the final miles inside a Winnebago with Florida license plates. "Are you sure this road'll take us up to Mount McKinley?" asked the innocent older couple in front.

"You'll never get any closer," I said as we jolted from rut to rut.

When we got to the end of the road they thanked me profusely

("If not for you we never would have gone this way!") and then took pictures as I shouldered my eighty-pound pack, a gallon gas can in each hand.

"Good luck!" they cried as I waded into the forest.

Each step was a joke. I felt like Atlas standing up to his chest in the Mediterranean. I didn't laugh. When I tripped and fell to my knees I *begged* for a bear to come clear the way.

The tundra was not a relief. I sank up to my shins in buoyant vegetation. At the edge of the lake I tried to step across a narrow slough the beavers had dug from their lodge to the trees in order to reach food. It was less than two feet wide. It was a short step across. I missed.

I dropped in over my head. I could feel no bottom.

Without releasing my metal gas cans I clawed at the bank—metal against mush—until my head was free. I gasped. I hurled both cans and grabbed at the tundra.

My pack was wedged in the channel. I wrestled it free and clambered out. Without pausing I picked up the gas and kept moving. The sky was translucent.

A cumulus cloud, a small glow of purple, radiated the last color of the departed sun.

I stopped. Heavy slog, sudden sorrow, unexpected light. I said it aloud: "Heavy slog, sudden sorrow, unexpected light."

I was on the home stretch.

The door to the little cabin was open, just as I had left it, shrouded by a wafting tablecloth.

I shouted. "I'm home!"

There was no response.

I dropped my pack and stepped inside.

Melissa was sitting bolt upright in bed. Her eyes were wide and unblinking. She was dressed all in white. Janus was at her breast.

We stared at each other.

"I was so afraid," she whispered without moving, "I was paralyzed."

I collapsed on the bed.

. . .

Sixteen hours later I woke. Melissa had cooked a huge breakfast: scalloped potatoes and onions and tofu with cheese.

I could smell it. But I couldn't move. I felt drugged. The cabin was warm from the sun. The warmth was narcotic. I drifted in and out of consciousness, but I remained unwilling to drift into memory.

"I started a garden," said Melissa.

A garden! We were supposed to have a garden. It was impossible to keep journeying in and out of Anchorage. But Denny had no garden. Marvin and Anna had no garden. They didn't need it to survive. They lived a few hours from a store, down the railroad tracks.

We hadn't started a garden because we had arrived on the ridgeline in mid-June. The growing season in the Susitna Valley lasts until the end of August. Plants need to be started indoors in April. *Guinness Book of World Records* vegetables come from theSusitna Valley because of the constant summer light, but only if the seeds are germinated when snow still covers the ground.

"A garden," I said dreamily.

"I went out into the forest this morning," said Melissa. "I chopped away the brush. Then I used the shovel to turn over some ground."

"That's great!" I said, sitting up, falling back.

"It'll probably be for next year," said Melissa.

I tried to imagine next year. I couldn't imagine the next minute.

"I took Janus with me," she said. "I put him in the baby pack and put a head net over him so he wouldn't get bit. He didn't complain once."

"You worked outside with Janus?" I asked. I tried to picture it, and drew a blank.

"We got lots of work done," she said.

I heard only her tone. It was strong and confident.

I sat up. "Smells good," I said.

She carried an iron skillet to me. "How do you feel?" she asked.

"I feel . . . blasted. How do you feel?"

"Great. I'm taking charge."

Melissa handed me a mug of water. "I went down to the spring, too," she said. "I got five gallons."

I focused on her and remembered, in a rush, the sorrow of seeing her pinned to the bed with Janus clutching at her breast. I drank the water in a gulp. It tasted sweet. It was like orange juice to an electroshock patient.

"Thanks," I said. "Thank you."

"We missed you," she said.

"I fell into a beaver slough. I went in over my head. I almost drowned. But I never for a moment believed that I wouldn't get back here. Boy that smells good."

She sat on the edge of the bed. "Do you want to hold your son?"

I held my son. He pissed out the side of his diaper. The stream dribbled down my shirt.

I wouldn't have cared if he had saturated my breakfast.

The complications I had seen upon my midnight arrival were gone in the afternoon of my awakening. I could only think that Melissa needed a home where she would feel secure, a *real* home.

"I've got to get to work," I said.

"You've got to eat," she said.

I ate. Janus sped around the bed, showing off. "You are a rock," I said.

He crawled to the edge of the bed, rocked, and then did a somersault to the floor.

"He's all right!" Melissa and I both said at the same time. Four arms hugged him up at once.

He looked startled, but didn't cry. I laughed.

"Don't laugh!" Melissa commanded. "He'll just do it again."

I bit my cheeks. She was right. Janus struggled between the parent sandwich. He lifted his arms free and held them over his head like a victorious prizefighter.

When Melissa and I went outside—together—she carried the baby. I carried the Johnny-Jump-Up.

The Johnny-Jump-Up was a gift from Russ and Gloria. It was a canvas seat attached to a long spring with a clamp hook at the top. We had left it buried under supplies in the little cabin.

Now we attached it to a thick spruce bough near the building site. When Janus sat in it, his feet touched the ground on a downward bounce so he could spring back up. He boinged up and down, up and down, giggling and cooing. I draped our mosquito net like a pyramid around his perch.

"I can peel logs now!" said Melissa.

I was proud that we all were, finally, working together.

When Janus tired of bouncing he slowly oscillated to a feet-hovering sleep, his head nodded against his shoulder. His little legs dangled. When a woodpecker riveted or loon cried he snapped awake (boing, boing), twisting in his seat to locate the sound.

His ease allowed Melissa to become the Come-Along Queen of Alaska. As I cranked, she levered massive logs up onto their skids and kept the logs moving. She peeled the logs before winching, tugging off the bark out in the forest, while I notched those trees we had already brought in.

When we returned to the little cabin at the end of the day we were as solid a pioneer family as history had known. For the moment. I began to believe that we could, in fact, get the roof on before summer's end.

In two weeks we winched, hoisted, and notched two more rounds. The framework looked like a fortress. The amount of work two people could accomplish was three or four times what one could do. But it was hard work.

The obvious joy Janus took in being outside helped keep us going. Melissa was stoic. I pushed. The result of pushing is birth.

Then Melissa woke me in the night and said, "Listen!"

Without any thought I went to the window. I saw nothing. I went outside. There was only wind in the trees.

I lay back beside Melissa and said, "No bear."

I closed my eyes. I couldn't sleep.

Melissa whispered, "Are you awake?"

I nodded.

"How long do you think this is going to go on?" she said.

I realized that we were both too tired to sleep. "Go slow or you'll lose her," I could hear Denny say.

"We're doing great," I said.

"Do you think we'll ever take a break?" she said.

She spoke so gently that my heart broke. "Coolies don't get vacations," I said.

She smiled. I knew she was smiling though I couldn't see her face. I knew that she knew that I knew she was smiling.

"Good thing we aren't coolies," I added.

Her need to have contact with other people seemed less compelling than her need simply to get *out of the woods*. But then I realized that for her, they were probably the same thing. I had enough contact with other people just where we were. I had my family. I didn't particularly need the perspective of social lunches and late-night bars and current movies and high school reunions. I liked them. But the perspective of the wilderness seemed, to me, more alluring.

In the morning we took a vacation.

For the first time Melissa walked the trail to the road. She had been on the ridgeline for six weeks.

She was stunned when we entered the tundra. She had never known there was such freedom so close to our small clearing.

But after an hour slashing through the forest at the bottom of the meadow she said, "I never knew how far away we were."

I carried Janus in the baby backpack. I tucked the supply pack under one arm. With my free hand I hacked at brush. It hadn't stopped growing. But I was familiar with the way, and there was evidence of a trail most of the route.

Melissa sang songs to inform the bears of our passage. She punctuated "You Can't Always Get What You Want" with "Are we almost there?"

An hour before we reached the road, clouds settled and dumped a heavy rain on us. "We're almost there," I said.

We hitched into Talkeetna. We stayed for two days at Pecos's town pied-à-terre—a little plywood shack near the Teepee—sleeping on the floor. Melissa was excited to see everyone she knew. I wasn't at all excited to watch the rain continue to pour out of the sky, torrentially. Marvin wasn't in the Fairview, nor was Rosser, nor Denny, nor Pecos. Maybe they knew that a flood was coming.

But I did find a dog, a white husky, a year-old pup whose owner wanted to get rid of him. He would be our lookout for bears. Melissa named him Leonard, for no identifiable reason.

On the morning of the third day I was unable to stay any longer. "The rain is only going to get worse," I argued. "If we don't get home now, we won't be able to cross the creek."

Melissa was surprised. "You mean we'll be trapped *out*?" she said.

It seemed odd to me, too, to think of being barred from a place that, in flood, we'd be trapped *in*. But I was worried about the little cabin's roof leaking. I was worried about the trees I'd felled near the creek. Would they be washed away? I had no idea.

"Should we just try?" I asked.

Melissa nodded, bravely. "Janus doesn't like being bounced on my lap anymore," she said. "He's been whining a lot."

That made me sure. We asked a friend to drive us north, and reached our trail head in an uninterrupted downpour.

I lifted a heavy pack of food to my back. Melissa hoisted Janus, wrapped in rain gear. We hiked to the creek. The dog tried to escape, whimpering, but he had nowhere to go. The cottonwood bridge was buried beneath brown water.

I tried to steer us to a different crossing. I wanted there to be *some* bridge across the creek. Water came up to our knees wherever we walked.

"Forget it!" said Melissa.

"This way," I said.

We returned to the road, beaten. We were sodden. My shoulders ached. The dog cowered.

I left Melissa under the umbrella of a huge birch and began walking up the road. I walked for miles. A miner in a six-wheel truck came sloppily along and I flagged him down. When I reached a phone I called the helicopter from Talkeetna.

As I splashed back down the road a pickup came from behind

me. In it were two young men from Michigan in trucker's caps. They were on vacation because "There sure ain't no jobs up here like we sort of hoped." They were four-wheeling the back roads because they'd drunk too much beer to deal with the slow-moving Winnebagos on the Anchorage-Fairbanks highway. They pressed a beer on me.

We rocketed down the muddy road and then we all nearly died.

"Jesus H. Christ!" shouted the driver when the truck's veering skid stopped and the bumper hung rocking above brown churning water.

A steel-girdered bridge that I had crossed a few hours before was gone. It was *gone*. Fifty feet of flood separated sections of road.

We all got out in the rain. We all stared at the creek. No one spoke. The water splashed up around our feet.

Then a helicopter flew low overhead, following the road. It banked in the distance and returned. Without cutting speed it came in for a landing behind the truck.

I ran under the spray of the rotors. I jerked open the door and clambered in. Before I could even reach a seat we lifted off.

Those two guys from Michigan are probably still trying to figure it out, over beers, in a bar with Tigers and Lions pennants on the wall.

In a minute we landed again. I hadn't been able to move from where I clung. Melissa ran out from beneath her shelter and handed me Janus. I helped her aboard and then ran back to grab the dog by the neck. I shoved him into the chopper.

Then we were airborne. I tried to follow our route. It was useless. Everything out the rain-streaked window was green and brown and the same.

I wanted to say something to the pilot, but he didn't glance back. I thought, "Emergency medevac in Nam," and left him alone.

Melissa and I conversed in long gazes. Melissa's eyes said, "Nobody told me that I'd have to stand under a dripping tree for a chilly afternoon trying to nurse a baby beneath a poncho."

My glance said, "But isn't this exciting? What an adventure! For only a hundred ninety-two bucks an hour!"

Melissa's steely stare said, "That CB we took into town to get fixed better work now, because if it doesn't we're dead."

"But isn't this exciting? What an adventure!"

She looked away.

When we reached the homestead I dropped our life's savings into the copilot's seat. We were now officially, once again, broke. Then I jumped out and rolled.

Melissa handed me Janus, pushed the dog out the door, and then leaped to the ground.

For the next day, while I fussed with the CB, the dog dug holes under the cabin.

When I got the CB rigged, when I got the little red light to glow—power on!—I flipped through channels asking for response.

There was nothing on any of the twenty-one channels except static. I went outside and played with the antenna. "Hello! Hello! Does anybody copy?"

Nobody copied. We were too far away. The range of the radio was too short, or else there were no other people in the upper Susitna Valley with CB radios.

"Testing! Testing! Do I have any contact?"

Melissa hung over my shoulder. It wasn't a test to her. It was survival. She had made the walk out and seen how remote we were. She had seen the flood on the way in and been stunned by its power.

I felt the way I used to when I would telephone a hesitant lover at the appointed hour and listen to the phone ring thirty-three times: first chagrined, then annoyed, and finally relieved: *free!*

The rain continued to fall. The dog continued to hide.

I went outside to wrestle with slick logs. Melissa stayed in the little cabin. Leonard whimpered during the day and barked furiously when we went to bed. Bears! Shadows! Paranoia!

None of it heartened Melissa.

I did my best to cheer her, but with the first massive low-pressure system of the summer weighted upon us, with the watchdog crying, "Watch out! Watch out!" for most of the "night," with the inescapable admission of our utter isolation, my cheer was like that of a drunk at a funeral.

Then Leonard died.

He disappeared from his customary hole under the cabin. I called for him for an hour before giving up and getting to work. At that point I was encouraged by his absence. It was a sign of his strength, of his security, to wander the forest.

At the end of a desultory day trying to imagine the roof, of exploring the forest for new wall logs, I went down to the creek. I wanted to see what it looked like. I had seen it a rippling brook no higher than my boot tops. I had seen it eight feet deep carving out chunks of bank. And still the rain had continued. I wouldn't have been surprised to find a Spanish galleon bobbing past.

I was shocked to find Leonard beside the lapping current, legs stretched straight out, spittle on his muzzle.

He was so stiff I couldn't even bend his head up. I suddenly didn't have the strength to drag him back to higher ground.

I sat beside the creek for a long while. I listened to the dark water. Drops from overhanging trees plopped around me.

I couldn't go back up and tell Melissa because I was scared. Even in my eager confidence that nothing could happen to us if we paid attention, something had happened.

Spores on breezes have devastated civilizations. Inexplicable plagues have annihilated vibrant cities. And we were alone. With a diseased dog. Who dug holes beneath the floor under our bed.

A raven flew past, slowly, with only the faint whoosh of its wings. Ravens had been, until that moment, elegant black eagles that I had seen circling the upper slopes of Denali, incredible creatures who could live, I had heard, for a hundred years. Now I could only think of Poe. Bad sign. Bad sign.

When I felt thoroughly chilled I walked back up the ridge.

"Where have you been?" said Melissa anxiously.

"Leonard must have picked up a bug in town," I said. "I think he's dead."

"You *think* he's dead?"

"He's dead," I said.

Melissa got up from the bed and spooned me a plate of food. She didn't say anything.

I rested the plate on my lap.

"I was afraid something had happened," she said.

Neither of us spoke until I had stripped off my clothes and climbed beside her in bed.

When we had squirmed around to position Janus between us, I said, "I really love you, you know."

Melissa didn't answer. She lay with her hands on Janus's head. I held his little feet.

We were both confronted with the proximity of death. We couldn't speak. Death was a presence so immediate we couldn't talk it away.

We slept like that—the child between us, each of us protecting him—until we woke blinking. The cabin was flooded with light.

"The sun's back," I said.

"I can see," she said.

Janus lifted himself free of our constricting embrace and began the day. He crawled to the end of the bed, looked around, and strained forward like a small truck in gear with its emergency brake on.

"He doesn't know what's going on," Melissa said.

"He knows," I said.

"Don't you fall!" Melissa told him.

He giggled. He began to roll off the edge. I grabbed him up. He squealed in delight.

"I don't think I can handle this," Melissa said with the tone of a new lottery winner whose home had just burned to the ground.

I tossed Janus up like a balloon until my arms were tired. Then I handed him to his mother. She immediately wrapped him in her arms.

"I'm not sure I can handle this either," I confided. "It's too much. I can't believe the rains have just *stopped*."

Melissa sat upright. "Say that again," she said.

"Say what?"

"Just tell me that you're over your head, too."

I hesitated. I looked around. "Sunlight!" I cried. "Clear skies!"

Melissa narrowed her eyes. She wanted confirmation for the sorrow of the night, for the tragedy implicit in our world. I didn't give it to her.

I didn't simply sit next to her in affirmation that our lives hung by a thread and we couldn't see what the thread was connected to.

"I can see clearly now," I began singing. "The rains have gone."

Melissa was silent.

"I can see all obstacles in our way."

I was aware that I was that drunk at a funeral shouting, "Oh, here come the pearly gates! Golden harps! Why be sad?" but I was unable to meet her gaze.

I was afraid for our tenuous security. I was more afraid than she was. I felt helpless to keep us safe. If I acknowledged it, she might worry more. So I avoided it all.

This incapacity jeopardized our life together more than did my inability to hunt food or to build swiftly. Melissa was asking only for validation that she wasn't crazy to believe our survival was precarious. And I made her feel alone, and isolated.

I buried Leonard under sphagnum moss. I recoiled when I had to touch the dog to pull him into his grave. I dropped atop him the gloves I had used.

But as soon as I had patted the dirt mound with the back of the shovel blade I became aware of the flowers. Beside the grave was a bed of purple flowers interspersed with red wild roses. As I started up the ridge I stepped between scatterings of tiny yellow flowers pinned to the ground beneath tall grasses. Blue bell-shaped clusters hung from long bent stalks. Even the two-foot-tall pyramid-shaped remains of a rotted tree stump held mosses with minute red tips on their green hairs.

With the abrupt swing of mood with which I was beginning to become familiar, I bent to examine the richness of life. Lemon yellow mushrooms pushed up through shards of rust-colored bark.

Where had all this sudden color come from? The rains? Or was I just now able to see it?

Instead of living in a constricting rain forest I felt as though we'd entered a botanical garden. A beetle with an iridescent carapace crawled up a blade of grass. Its wing covers were mostly gold and green, but the colors shifted through the rainbow as it moved.

Then it crawled right into a spider's web I hadn't noticed. It twitched as the spider ventured out to kill it. In the layer between the ground blooms and the hanging blossoms were more spiderwebs than I wanted to count, because I must have destroyed hundreds walking down the ridge and I'd do the same going up. And among them exquisite insects died.

I hurried up to the building site. Surrounded by the rock-solid rectangle of logs I felt relief. The work was rote, but it was balm. I spent an hour notching logs until the last of the clouds blew off from the mountains.

The peaks, in their mantle of new snow that had fallen at the higher elevations, were so bright I went back to the little cabin for sunglasses.

Melissa was asleep curled around Janus.

Once again my mood swung. How could we even *think* of living here when death was invisible and everywhere?

I abandoned the sunglasses and went back to the building site. I squinted at the Range. It was so close and yet so far beyond my wavering world that I began to recognize grace. Grace is an acceptance of things as they are. Things as they are is God.

I dropped to my knees in benediction.

I noticed, out of the corner of my eye, a gap between one piling and the sill log that should have been supported by it.

I thought, "All right! The log's already shrinking and drying." I wedged a piece of chain saw debris into the opening.

Then I tried to return to God. But I was curious to see if there were any other gaps around the foundation. On my knees, I circled the house.

There were no other gaps.

Melissa came outside and put Janus in the Johnny-Jump-Up. I didn't know whether to interpret her expression as resigned or withdrawn or simply as an indication of being tired. But when Janus first left her hands and lifted himself into the air, a wind came up that bent the tops of the trees. It was warm and scented and revealed the underside of birch leaves to be silver. It cleared the air in arcing gusts. Janus laughed aloud, repeatedly.

Melissa and I looked at each other. Nothing unsettled had been resolved. The future was still unimaginable. But something vital had been renewed. It might have been as simple as a deep breath, compelled by beauty. It might have been as complicated as love or commitment.

We spent the rest of the short Alaskan summer practicing grace by practicing log construction. Melissa spent days at a time, usually during rains, in the little cabin. But she still peeled logs.

"It's not *security* I miss now so much as my friends," she said at one point. "Our life is so solitary."

I said that I understood, but I was, at the same time, baffled that living so intimately with "nature," as Goethe called the source of his sustenance, didn't heal us of our secret trepidations.

By the middle of August, less than three weeks after the flood, I abandoned the come-along. On my shoulders I carried six-foot sections of eight-inch-thick trees out of the forest to then spike upright atop the horizontal logs. *Stockading* was the technical term: 150-pound vertically fixed pieces of the walls instead of the click-click-click of the come-along dragging much larger logs a few hundred yards. No notching, either. But lots of spikes. It made the house rise faster.

The walls *had* to be finished before raising the ridgepoles. Without the ridgepoles there could be no roof. The roof was requisite before the snows.

I began to work sixteen-hour days. There were days of slog when I was plagued by twitching muscles. There were days of sorrow, especially when a pulley rig broke loose and sent a thirty-foot ridgepole careening through three wall logs like a battering ram. When the sun angled into the room, there was such radiance as made me imagine we lived so far out at the edge that we could look *down* into stars.

One morning the winds shifted. They blew not out of the south, from the Pacific, but from the north, from glaciers, from the arctic ice pack. The birch leaves, in the space of a few days, turned yellow and then gold. I had never seen autumn arrive so quickly. There were no maple reds. There was only a blizzard of yellow and gold.

And then there was snow.

We woke with our arms around each other. We could see our breaths. Janus rocketed up to crawl to the window and then ricocheted back.

The world was white!

I went outside. The sun in the east through skeletal branches gave no immediate warmth. Whoa!

Winter! In September!

I stood outside until my feet grew cold in the rubber boots I wore for rain. I stomped around making tracks, then ducked back inside.

I built a fire. I was exhilarated. All my senses had been rearranged. This was my ascetic's reward after months of being immured in jungle.

But the roof wasn't on.

Only an inch of snow had fallen during the night. But I was impressed by the speed with which seasons changed.

"I'm going to get the ridgepoles up today!" I announced while Melissa watched me hop around the cabin.

I didn't eat breakfast or lunch. I climbed a birch, hung a pulley from a thick branch above the house frame, and tried to hoist a huge log up. It slid higher, like a whale breaching, then slid back.

I kept working until it began to grow dark. I could see the moon on the horizon. It was the first time since late April that the moon was visible against a dark sky. Melissa came out wrapped in a parka. I sat astride a log fifteen feet off the ground.

"Are you going to sleep?" she asked.

I nearly shouted, "No!" but glanced down. She looked lonely. She looked sad.

"Won't you feel better knowing that our home will keep us safe all winter?" I said.

She just stared up at me. I banged a last spike flush. She went back to the little cabin.

I slid to the ground. I put away the chain saw and the axe and the pulley and the rest of the tools in case it snowed again. When I went inside to stoke the stove she was asleep.

"We're almost there," I whispered as I snuggled beside her. She didn't respond. Janus rolled over into my arms.

The next day another front came through, dropping another inch of snow. The logs were too slick to handle. When I slipped and fell heavily on one arm, I jumped up and cried, "Yeah!" Nothing could throw me.

Melissa threw me.

"I want to go into Talkeetna," she said.

I pretended she was joking.

"This is *winter*," she said. "We're not prepared."

"But I'm almost ready to get the rafters up!"

"You aren't listening to me," she said. "I don't like this. I haven't been out in seven weeks. I don't want to stay here. You are pushing too hard and something is going to happen."

"The roof!" I said. "That's what'll happen. It'll keep the snows out, and I can finish it in a month."

"Rick," she said. "This has gone too far."

I refused to admit that I had seriously miscalculated, that I had assumed we would be lacquering the kitchen table by now, yet the ceiling was still open to the sky. If we left now, we'd live at Stanley's until the spring while snow buried the shell of the house. I'd have nothing to do except brood. Janus would crawl around somebody else's house and think of it as home. I wanted him to know the security of his own home. I wanted him to grow up with the variations of the wilderness. I wanted Melissa to hang tough. I wanted more miracles. More!

7.

FOR EVERY ACTION
THERE'S AN EQUAL AND
OPPOSITE NEGLIGENCE

We went to Talkeetna.

I didn't go without a struggle. I didn't give up in order to save my family, nor from an easy faith that the dream of completing the house would be reached in time. I gave up because I couldn't make Melissa stay.

We went back to Stanley's. It was like returning to subsidized university housing after a field trip to Borneo. Melissa felt safe. I pointed out that a year and a half ago she had been in tears because Dead Dog Ridge seemed like the asteroid belt to her, and now it was suburbia.

She shrugged. She was happy. She didn't want to quibble.

I was grateful. I had seen that isolation beneath snow peaks was too intense for either of us to handle. Neither of us was able to stand exposed to the world and say, "Yes." No matter what came, inevitably, naturally, furiously, "Yes."

We had a long way to go.

164

Janus couldn't have cared less about where we were, physically or philosophically. He explored knot holes in the floor. He crawled around the front yard giggling. He was in tune with his world. Melissa and I were still trying to create ours.

I spent the first few days back at Stanley's in unexpected pleasure. We had food and wood, and there was nothing to build. So I played with the ten-month-old baby all day. From the time he rolled onto my chest in the morning and announced, "Beh!" to the time he nodded out at night, I wasn't more than two feet from him. He was fun. He was magic. He was alert to everything going on in the world—colors and textures and the moods of his parents.

"Well duh," Melissa said. "What else would you think? He's your son."

"Yeah, but look at the way he examines little pieces of wood in the kindling box. He's *studying* them. He's going to be a naturalist."

Melissa rolled her eyes, but smiled.

"And look at how he prowls near the door testing the difference in temperature between the stove and the doorjamb. He's conducting an experiment."

I began to understand how Melissa could have been content to remain in the little cabin when the mountains and the forest gave me such wonder. I actually felt cheated that I had spent so much time at work when the child was so involving, too.

Then he began to whine. He didn't want to be nursed. He didn't want to be bounced up and down in my arms while I sang the *William Tell* Overture: "Buh-da-*bum*, buh-da bum-de-dum."

"He's had too much stimulation," said Melissa.

In exasperation I pulled a parka over us and kicked open the door to get a breath of air.

He rose up in my arms and cooed. The moon was full in his face, creased by dark branches. While I fussed with the parka to keep him covered he continued to stare, without complaint.

"Moon," I whispered.

He didn't need me to tell him. I felt like an intruder, like a taxi driver who's brought a pilgrim to Lourdes and then hangs around offering a travelogue.

I rocked him back and forth. His eyes remained fixed on the moon until he fell asleep.

When we went back inside Melissa said, "What did you *do?*"

"Nothing," I said. "Really."

Marvin and Anna were in Georgia spending a long vacation with family, showing off their own firstborn. Their child and ours had been born six days apart. Lara had been delivered, by accident, in the Rossers' cabin while Rosser, manfully and hysterically, had hooked up his team to race blindly into the night for help. A neighbor had tied the cord with a shoelace sanitized in the cookstove oven. I was sorry Marvin and Anna weren't around. I hadn't seen them since our children were born.

Denny took up our social slack. With characteristic suddenness he popped into the cabin.

"I knew you couldn't cut a winter out there!" he announced. "But it's all right! You're all still together!"

"We're just taking a break," said Melissa.

I was amazed to hear *her* say it. So was Denny. He began to hop around like a punch-drunk fighter.

"Hard-core!" he said. "That's hard-core! Ooh, I can't believe it! I'm jealous! Do you have a sister? If she's like you I've *got* to meet her!"

Melissa was pleased but tried not to show it. "As soon as we get more winter supplies we'll probably go back out," she said, the first I'd heard of our plans.

Denny was in hyperbolic ecstasy. "That's great! You don't know how great that makes me feel! When I heard you were back I was worried. But now I have an offer."

He sat down and busied himself with unbuttoning the layers of his wool shirts.

"I *missed* you!" Melissa said suddenly. She went over to give him a hug. Denny looked as if he wanted to hide, but then he rose to the occasion, grinning and embarrassed but mostly grinning.

It was like a family reunion.

"Boy, that's even better than your cooking," Denny said.

Melissa went to the stove to heat something up.

"Hey!" said Denny. "How'd you like my five excellent giant dogs and a fourteen-foot wood Yukon freighting sled for the winter? I just passed my ATP. I got my Airline Transport Pilot rating. I'm qualified to fly a 747! Aren't you proud of me?"

"A 747?" I said. I looked at Melissa. She said, with her hand raised to her mouth, holding an imaginary mike, "This is Captain Denny speaking. The flight deck is now open to visitors. Ladies first! One at a time. No rush. We've got a long flight."

Denny laughed. "I've got two bush companies bidding for my services. I'm going to be a professional! I'll just be flying little 185s and 207s, but a 207 holds six passengers! You have to be really good to take a 207 up from some remote village in a snowstorm and fly a hundred and fifty miles by instruments to land at some other remote village. I'll be the main man for Bush Air in Bethel or Air North in Fort Yukon."

"I'm impressed," I said, without exaggeration.

Denny knew that his skills were exceptional. But like a prodigal son, he was glad to know that we knew it, too. "I'm going to be gone for a while, though," he said. "But now that I know you're serious, I'll let you use my team if you promise to take really good care of them."

"They'll probably be glad to get off their chains," I said.

Denny hung his head guiltily. "I know, I know. I've been going in and out of Anchorage for my rating so much this past year, I practically haven't run them at all. They've just stayed in town, getting lazy. But they're really good dogs. Big! No one runs big freighting dogs." He sighed. "But I suppose you grew to like those little goofy racing dogs of Marvin's. Zoom zoom, yap yap yap."

"I'd rather be able to haul a cookstove home," I said.

"Right!" Denny agreed. "Six-hundred-pound loads! Drive right through storms and up the frozen creeks."

"This is a real blessing," said Melissa.

"For me, too," said Denny. "If you promise to take good care of them."

"I promise," said Melissa.

"It's a deal!" Denny said. "Just don't be intimidated by Jake. He's my leader. He's killed a few dogs in his time, but if you let him know *you're* the Alpha wolf in the pack, he won't try to rip your throat out."

Melissa blanched and then said, "But he's really very sweet, right?"

"A complete sweetheart," Denny agreed.

Jake was mean and snarling.

We met him in town a few days later, where we went to do laundry. In a washing machine. With quarters. Instead of squeezing diapers by hand over an aluminum pan and then using spruce boughs for a clothesline. Diapers had been a tedious job for most of the summer. I was impressed by how easy it had become.

Melissa and I, carrying Janus in his baby pack, towing our wash in a plastic sled, had walked to town. The tracks had been clear of snow. Heat from the still-unfrozen Susitna River had warmed things up. Voluminous clouds hung over the Alaska Range, out toward our ridgeline—snow in the hinterlands.

Denny, from Anchorage, had sent us a "Bush Pipeline" message by commercial AM radio telling us to meet him. Three different Anchorage stations, at advertised times, broadcast personal messages to bush residents who had no phones: "To Jane: I can't live without you. From Butch"; "To the gang on the beaver pond: I found a carb for the snowmachine. I'll try to be home by noon. From Blackjack"; "To my real good buddies at Stanley's: Meet me in town tomorrow at one so I can show you the dogs. From Captain Denny."

Denny met us outside the Fairview. Melissa was standing on Main Street involved in conversation with a new friend—an immediate friend, after just five minutes' conversation: a young single woman studying to be a helicopter mechanic who had been struck by Melissa's femininity and style in woolly Talkeetna. I stood idly to the side, drinking a beer, appreciating, for the first time in a year, that Melissa *was* a West Side New Yorker in rural Alaska.

The day was bright autumn, though the trees were bare and ankle-deep snow crusted the ground. Janus was content on my back, playing with my hair.

Denny drove up in a pickup with dog boxes in the bed. He jumped out. "Communications technology brings us together *on time*!" he said. "And who are *you*?" he added at once, addressing Melissa's friend.

"This is Tanya," said Melissa. "She's—"

"I've been *waiting* to meet you!" said Denny. "I've seen you around town a few times, but I use dogs instead of choppers so I haven't had the chance."

Tanya was very attractive.

The dog box farthest to the back of the truck quaked and then roared. "Oops! Jake knows we're here," Denny said. "I picked up the team at the dog-sitter's." He went to the row of plywood boxes and opened a door. Jake, a bear-sized wolf, leaped out.

Denny grabbed an axe handle from the truck bed, casually, and commanded, "Down!" Jake got down.

Denny opened Jake's jaws with one hand and stuck his wrist in Jake's mouth. Jake didn't bite. "See?" said Denny. "Gentle as a lamb."

Denny ruffled the dog's fur and began cuffing its head playfully.

Jake and Denny danced around like sumo wrestlers.

"Want to see the rest of them?" Denny asked.

"Not quite yet," said Melissa.

"Are you the new pilot in town?" Tanya asked.

Denny wrestled his dog to a sitting position and puffed up. Then, at once, he deflated. "But I'm on my way to Bethel in the morning," he said, as if unwilling to accept his fate. "That's closer to Siberia than to Talkeetna," he added, sinking lower.

Jake suddenly licked his face.

Denny, the archetypal woodsman, turned from the pretty girl and nuzzled his lead dog. The axe handle dropped to the ground.

"But I'll be back!" he said, rallying.

"When?" I asked, stepping forward.

Melissa and Tanya withdrew to their conversation. Denny and I did, too. We talked about feeding schedules and freight loads and dominance patterns among the dogs. I could no longer eavesdrop on Melissa, but I could see how animated she was.

I was aware of how easily she had adapted to this odd Alaskan world of all-night bars and lumberjack-shirted dog mushers, with girlfriends who fixed helicopters and carved moose. She hadn't compromised her femininity or her vivacity. But I was also aware of dark storm clouds out near the Alaska Range.

"It *always* snows more out where you are," Denny explained. "You're higher in elevation, weeks more advanced in the seasons. And you'd be a fool to lose someone like Melissa."

I assured him that I'd try to make her happy and I'd always carry the axe handle when I ran his dogs.

A week later I ran his dogs to the homesite. It hadn't snowed much in Talkeetna since we'd walked out from the homestead. But when we got to the other side of the Susitna River, fifty road miles farther into the valley, there was fresh snow at the start of our trail, ten new inches.

Melissa had helped me unload Denny's five dogs from his truck, standing behind me with the axe handle as I lifted them to the ground. Jake was docile.

The plan was for me to mush home, set a trail, and then, in time, come back out for Melissa and Janus.

Melissa was in no rush. She was content to be near town, either at Stanley's, where adventurous friends came to visit, or within a five-block radius of the Fairview and the B&K General Store, near the majority of the population.

I was in a rush to get home. Even though the recent snow partially obscured the trail, Jake knew exactly where to go. By scent? Because it was once again full winter and the route between trees was revealed, ferns fallen, grasses buried?

It was so easy I wanted to turn the team around to tell Melissa. But in the forest, the trees were too closely spaced to turn such a large sled. It was like driving a Mack truck after a sports car—a Rosserghini.

When we came to the large tundra lake, it was frozen. I stopped to examine the thickness of the ice. When I'd brushed away the snow I could see silvered bubbles suspended deep in the black ice. When I stomped, no cracks appeared.

We sailed across.

The next day I used the dogs to haul logs from the forest. I dropped three or four stockades into the sled and brought the load easily up to the building site. No more thigh-trembling slogs with just one hundred-and-fifty-pound log ground into my shoulder. Two people, I'd seen, could accomplish four times as much as just one. But one man with a good dog team was as effective. The house would be done in a month!

Then it snowed.

It snowed a ton. It snowed enough to bury any indication of the trail. It snowed enough to bury the trees I'd felled in the forest. It snowed a foot during the night and another foot the following day.

The snow was wet, heavy, sticky. It came so thickly I couldn't see the trees across the creek except as gray two-dimensional apparitions. Another flood. But without sound. Without turbulence. And just as disturbing.

I spent a day first shoveling off the exposed logs of the house, then shoveling out the dogs' houses, then again the logs.

On the morning of the third day I harnessed the team to reach the road. Jake plunged responsibly into a drift, plowed out the other side like a dolphin, dove into the next drift, and balked. I went up to him with the axe handle. He snarled. I retreated. We all retreated.

It took two hours to get the sled and the dogs turned around. The snow was like tidal water. The dogs didn't want to wade through it. Lines tangled. When Jake jumped the next biggest dog, I beat them apart with the axe handle. If I had tried to separate them with just shouts and a boot toe they would have killed each other, and then, perhaps, me.

After I'd chained them again to their trees, I fell into the little cabin exhausted. Wet flakes continued to drop.

I made a huge pot of survival stew—rice with canned tomatoes and tuna—and then lay numb on the bed, bloated and resigned.

When I woke—after ten hours? fourteen?—I saw trees bending beneath a huge wind. I checked the thermometer. Thirty-seven degrees above zero Fahrenheit.

It was a chinook wind: a tropical current from the Pacific turning the already wet snow to glue. Snow plopped from branches like cow patties.

"I'm trapped," I admitted. "The sled just sinks in this stuff. Sinks and sticks. What would a real arctic adventurer do?"

I didn't know.

I fed the dogs. I shoved thigh-deep through the snow until I was soaked. Then I stoked the stove and read Jack London by kerosene lantern until, finding no helpful advice, I fell asleep.

I woke chilled. The sky had cleared. The temperature had dropped. The thermometer read ten above. Wind was gusting, but now from the north.

When I went outside I sank less into the snow. New snow falls moist when it falls in quantity, but then it settles. Of *course* I knew this, but from where? Jack London? Archetypal memory?

I put on snowshoes. I couldn't imagine why I had felt trapped, burdened, alone.

I walked fifty yards beyond the point I had reached with the dogs. The snow, beneath its upper layer of cold crystal, was still sodden. It stuck to the shoes. It was like walking with lead weights on each leg.

That's how I could have been worried. I was panting and sweating. Even if I reached the road and, ultimately, Talkeetna, there was little hope that I could bring Melissa and Janus into a winter where she would be confronted, again, with the anxieties of flood.

I put my faith in the trail. If I could make it firm, visibly linking the homestead with the rest of the world, it might help her to feel connected.

I returned to the little cabin, fed the dogs, dug out the shell of the larger house, and then put up two more stockades so that I could point to progress.

By late afternoon I started out. The dogs swam through the billowed snow, but they didn't balk. I walked ahead with the snowshoes, Jake following gratefully on my heels. I carried my ice axe, which I used to whack the snow from the shoes with each step. I lifted a heavy foot—whack!—and put down a light one.

Between the bottom of the tundra and the road we were all ready to stop, exhausted. By starlight I snapped spruce boughs from nearby trees and spread my bag atop their insulation. The dogs collapsed where they stood.

I slept like a hero. No dog chewed its harness.

The next day I chained them near the road and hitched to Talkeetna. I still wasn't sure what we'd do, but I knew what I had done. I sang a Jimmy Cliff song, walking to the highway to catch a ride, an up-tempo reggae song about faith and trust and the need for tribulations to make us remember gratitude.

Melissa seemed unnaturally happy when I tracked her down at a friend's house in town. I hadn't assumed that she'd be snowbound at Stanley's up the tracks.

"Praise God!" she cried as she hugged me.

I made light of what I'd been through. "It was a bit of a struggle," I said, "but nothing I couldn't handle."

Melissa didn't notice that I wanted her to say, "But how could you have made it through such a storm?" Talkeetna was deep in snow, too.

Instead she said, "I prayed that you'd be all right! I knew the Lord would protect you!"

I tossed Janus up and down—whee! whee!—while he laughed. "I made a trail that should last all winter," I said.

Melissa remained with a very bright smile. When I returned to sit beside her, smiling my own fatuous grin, she said, "I have something important to tell you."

Immediately I thought, "Pregnant!" My grin vanished. I was not ready. I was definitely not ready.

I stared at her, expecting the worst, hoping for reprieve.

"I've accepted Jesus," she said.

"Are you pregnant?" I replied.

She looked confused. "No!" she said. "Listen! I've accepted the Lord."

I burst out laughing. "Me too!" I said. "Every day in every way. Do we have a choice?"

"The choice is Satan," she said darkly.

I feigned shock. "You mean . . . *de debbil*?"

"This is serious," she said seriously.

I felt the little plywood room in the middle of town begin to close in. "Haven't you *always* tried to follow God's way?" I asked.

"Well, of course."

"So what's different now?"

She was taken aback. "Nothing, if you put it like that."

"Then why is it so important?"

"Because I'm verbalizing it now," she said.

"What does *that* mean?"

"That means I'm saying it aloud."

The room began to lean on me.

"That means it's more *real*," she added. "It's like a *vow*."

"But what *difference* does it make?" I repeated.

Melissa hesitated. She plainly hadn't expected a devil's advocate. "I just thought you should know," she said.

I looked at her closely. Even with her eager enthusiasm muted I could still see her happiness. I didn't understand it, but I didn't want to take *any* pleasure away from her. I had just come from desolation and its unexpected reprieve. God only knew what trial might await us next.

"So tell me more," I said, rocking my boy. "This must have been a good time for you in town."

Melissa started by describing the loneliness she had felt when she returned to Talkeetna after dropping me off at the end of the road. She had felt adrift, disconnected from everything except our child. That sense of being on her own, isolated from family, from her mother who had died of cancer, from her father who didn't care, from any home, was her personal cross to bear. She had begun chatting with a stranger, making a new friend, as was her gift. Charlene had responded by sharing the story of her own turbulent life, which culminated in accepting Jesus and finding peace. Charlene introduced Melissa to other members of the Talkeetna Charismatic Church, all of them young, many of them ex-druggies or adventurers who were now raising families. They had opened their homes to Melissa. They had, until that week, dismissed Melissa as just another of the "up-the-tracks" people who frequented the Fairview instead of church.

Melissa, from up the tracks, had bridged the gap between the polarized factions of the gold-mining town. She had taken a water baptism the day before I returned and had been greeted by shouts of "Hallelujah!" She had friends everywhere.

I didn't know how to respond. I had met a few of the local Christians, and those few struck me as being as insular as small-town religious zealots anywhere. But Melissa seemed as happy as I had seen her since she first rode into town on a dogsled. The embrace of most of Talkeetna's diverse population made her feel whole.

"So will you come with me to church on Sunday?" she concluded.

"I left Denny's dogs at the road," I said. "I have to get back to feed them."

"It would bring us so much closer if you would accept Jesus," she said.

"Melissa, I am racing to finish our home so we can accept each other."

"After you've been baptized," she replied.

I had decided on the slog out that there was no way I'd risk frostbite to a baby. But now *I* felt lonely. I wanted support.

"What do you think about flying out with a bush plane?" I asked.

Melissa was surprised. "During a cold snap? With Janus?"

We had never known a winter on our own land. "If it breaks?" I suggested.

I could see her struggling with the anticipation of isolation after the warmth of her communion in town. Who would want to leave loving support for the unknown?

"Sure," she said.

"Praise Jah," I said.

"Jesus," she corrected.

"Same thing," I said.

"It is *not* the same thing!" she bristled. "And there is no way that I can marry you until you accept the Lord as your personal Savior."

The next day I returned home. I felt burdened. I had been unable to get a ride until almost dark. By the time I got the dogs hitched I couldn't discern a blue harness from black.

"For many of us today, intimate relationships have become the new wilderness, bringing us face to face with all our gods and demons," Alexander had recently written me.

The dogs took off so heavily that I had to push behind the sled. After a hundred paces we stopped.

The stars through the trees were silver dots of a pointtillist painting viewed from too close up to reveal any pattern.

We slogged another hundred paces. We stopped.

When I lifted my head from the push behind the sled I could see the horizon beyond the naked boughs. I could see the trail far ahead. The night wasn't dark.

The dogs picked up the pace. I rode the runners until the dogs slowed, but I kept them moving by pedaling as if on a scooter. I ducked the branches silhouetted against the glowing snowpack.

After we crossed the creek I saw the green arc of the aurora lift from the north. The forest was lit with green glow and blue snow-light, mocking the tales of the dark Alaskan winter.

The beauty and light were unexpected. I had anticipated great frustration, long struggle. The luminous landscape lifted my spirits. How could Melissa not appreciate such a world?

When we finally broke out onto the tundra the dogs began to run. I could see the border of trees a mile ahead as plainly as in early morning light. The clarity of air in the cold was breath-taking.

Jake led north. Jake, or his peers, would lead us into the farthest reaches of this bright valley. Into the mountains. Up glaciers.

When we reentered the forest at the top of the tundra the sky suddenly exploded. I grabbed at the handlebars of the sled. The dogs, all at once, sat down.

Reds and yellows and blues lit the treetops. "Nuclear attack!" I thought, a child of the Cold War.

I cowered against the coming roar. There was silence. The sky whirled.

"Hut-hut!" I cried, hoping to reach the sanctuary of the ridgeline. The dogs remained seated and stared.

An incredible aurora waved and curled. The dogs didn't move. The tops of the trees didn't bend. No sound surrounded.

I leaned against the handlebars and saw my gloved hands flicker as if in firelight.

This was the most obvious sign I'd been given in my life. It was a sign of . . . what? Unexpected radiance? Celestial power?

Snow that had been kicked into the sled burned red and then yellow. I looked up, as motionless as the dogs.

And the display vanished. White impressions were fixed against the sky like negative images in photographs. The fireworks burst had trailed to silver cloud.

The dogs stood and shook themselves as if coming out of a river.

Jake tugged. The sled moved. Was this a common occurrence that the dogs accepted as easily as their duty?

When we reached the ridgeline, Jake licked my hands as I led him to his chain. None of the other dogs balked. We had all seen . . . something—God or grace or unspeakable wonder. We had all stopped in recognition of it.

I hurried to give them food, in gratitude for their strength, so that I could be done with chores and get some sleep. I was, in fact, over my head. But in light. In light.

I awoke to silence. There was no rhythmic breath at my side from mother or son, no bug or bear or the pulse of my own fear. I lay in my bag, its cowl pulled around my head, appreciating stillness. It seemed like peace.

When I got up to start a fire I checked the thermometer. I didn't doubt that it was ten below zero Fahrenheit. But I wasn't sure what that meant. Silence, certainly. But what for Melissa and Janus? Could I imagine them out in such a deepening cold snap?

No way. Without actually addressing it, I knew that twenty and thirty below were not just possible, but inevitable. My only association was to the energy-sapping inertia I'd experienced in Fairbanks.

But here in the forest, though the sun from the south through bare branches died at my feet after the longest journey it would know to reach this planet, there were prisms where it burrowed beneath snow crystals.

The arctic weather stayed. I slapped my hands against my legs often to keep the blood flowing. But the only real complication of those first deep winter days of building came when I whanged on a twelve-inch spike and saw the hammer rocket back toward my skull. I was too surprised to duck. I took the full blow in the forehead. Frozen logs! Red auroras at noon! I rocked at the top of my home-made ladder—a triangle of split spruce logs crossed by poles—and laughed.

Of course I'd be stunned. Everything about such weather was stunning.

I learned to swing the mallet sidearm and anticipate the bounce.

Three days later the weather broke. Clouds returned. The temperature rose thirty degrees.

I snowshoed out to the tundra and stomped a landing strip that I marked with small cut swamp spruce laid in a twenty-foot-long arrow.

That afternoon the Super Cub landed on skis. I was waiting with the dogs. Melissa had brought fresh food. She was exhilarated from the flight and wary about what might come next.

I loaded family and supplies in the sled and headed home. Janus was fascinated by the dogs. He kept popping up from his mother's embrace to see what was happening. He seemed wary, too, as the sled rolled and dipped through the forest like a sailboat in high seas, but he whined only when we stopped.

Icicles hung from the eaves of the little cabin. The vegetation that Melissa had come to know as familiar—even if dusted with the first snow that had compelled our departure—was gone. I could see, through Melissa's eyes, how different our world had become.

I could feel her shiver, even in the relative warmth of twenty above, even after we had stepped into the little cabin where the stove was lit.

"Well," she said, sitting on the bed in her parka. "At least I can appreciate now what you've been through."

"Isn't it lovely?" I asked, trying very hard not to insist.

"Nobody in town can believe we're out here in winter," she replied.

"But look at Janus," I said impulsively.

He was like a zoo animal let loose from his cage. He squirmed from her arms onto the bed and then raced in widening circles.

"That's why I came so quickly," Melissa said. "He was getting to be impossible."

I jumped outside and grabbed a fistful of spruce needles that I then crushed under his nose. He paused to sniff. "And the moon's coming, too," I told him.

Snows came instead. Then clearing winds. Then arctic cold.

Melissa kept the fire in the stove burning. In Talkeetna I had found a pair of used army-surplus Korean War forty-below vapor-barrier Bunny boots for me. But none for her. It was reason enough for her to stay inside. She read the Bible.

I spent hours introducing Janus to the *real* winter—to moose tracks near the larger house made before a dog team was near, to icicles and stars. He complained when I took him *in* from the cold. The dogs, like their wolf ancestors, just curled in a ball, their tails over their noses.

Melissa cleared a space inside the crowded cabin where I carried stockade logs to thaw. When she peeled them, the sap like liquid incense was ground into the floor.

It was not much fun for her. The work was without immediate reward. The bigger house was still just a frame of logs, without a roof. The roofing materials were buried beneath the snow.

I tried to make it fun for her. I tried to excite her about the clarity of the sky, but the clearest skies were, as always, also the coldest. I tried to lead her up the log ladder to the framework of the second floor, which would be our bedroom, above which was nothing, below which was ice. It was all like fixing a climbing novice to a bivouac against a sheer rock face and exclaiming, "But look how far up we are!"

A few days later Melissa and I woke to mewing. Outside, I found three new furred pups nuzzled against the only female dog's belly.

Melissa became animated. "We have babies!" she cried.

I was startled that I hadn't even known the bitch was pregnant.

"Now we have our *own* team!" said Melissa.

I refused to accept mongrels. Some stray dog in Talkeetna had entered the dog lot where Denny's dogs had been fed. The father could have been a cocker spaniel or toy collie.

Melissa blithely named the pups at once. Norton, she pronounced the largest, though whether for the Norton 750 Commando motorcycle I had ridden in New York or for Ralph Cramden's sidekick wasn't clear. Van Dyke for the largest female, after Alexander's Van Dyke Ltd. kaleidoscopes. Dick for a pup that was obviously a male. Dick's name was my contribution.

Melissa began feeding Hoonah, the mother, as much as she could eat. Melissa insisted that we keep the pups, while I argued for a "better" breeding.

"We owe this to Denny," she said adamantly. "I just know that they'll be great dogs."

I humored her. I couldn't imagine that they'd be anything but useless mutts.

Ten days later I made the mistake of saying, "Look how much light there still is at nine o'clock!"

Melissa picked up the windup clock she'd brought from Talkeetna. "It's four-thirty," she said.

I wanted to deny the time. I denigrated the clock's ability to keep time.

Melissa stared at me as if I were a jailer and then lay down on the bed to nurse Janus.

My back suddenly began to ache. My back was never without ache, but now it gripped into knots. I lay beside her.

Janus rose from his dinner, looked at me, grinned, and then furiously dove back to eating.

After a minute of relative silence—Melissa breathing in long waves, Janus slurping—I said, "Do you think you'd like to go back east and show Janus to everyone?"

More silence followed. I lifted myself painfully to see that Melissa was weeping. I rolled onto my stomach.

"It's only a week of cabbing," I said. "If I'm lucky."

My head was burrowed into my arms. Melissa touched my back, and the pain eased.

"You know what Jesus said," I continued. " 'Share your blessing with everyone, especially relatives and old friends.' Proverbs 6:19."

Melissa's hand remained on the small of my back like a heating pad.

"Besides," I added, "the whores are probably hurting for business since I stopped bringing them johns."

Melissa's touch stiffened, and then relaxed. She began massaging me with both hands. Janus rolled to my head and tried to suck on my nose. I made a face. He giggled.

We went out, with Melissa and Janus swaddled together in a sleeping bag nestled back in the sled. Across the tundra the dogs pulled us as if down an amusement park water slide. When we reentered the forest, the sled careened like a roller coaster. On the downswings, snow cascaded into the sled. Melissa laughed, and even though it came out more a gasp, it bolstered our confidence.

Twice I was unable to control the sled and it angled up on one runner and then dumped on its side into the snow. As I wrestled the sled upright, Melissa said, "I'm okay!" and Janus licked the melted snow running down his face.

This was how I expected us to live—massive jungle in the summer and roller coaster rides in the winter.

When we reached the road, we drove the team between the track that a snowmachine had grooved in the unplowed snow. When we reached the highway I chained the dogs back in the trees.

I divided ten pounds of dog food among them. Melissa paced back and forth with Janus, watching the road.

Finally a squad car came out of the night.

I flagged it down. When we got inside I explained what we were doing.

"I grew up on a homestead," Officer DeHart said to us. "Fifty miles down the highway from here, before there even *was* a highway."

He lifted the police radio mike from the flickering dash and said, "I've got a 10-86 into Talkeetna," while we huddled in back.

"Cold and desperate hitchhikers," I assumed the code meant.

I've never been so fond of police before or since.

"I heard there was new homestead land out here," said Officer DeHart. "But I didn't know anyone had tried to homestead."

"It's hard," said Melissa.

"Yeah, it wasn't always fun for me," said Officer DeHart, as the squad car's brights illuminated the highway's flanking wall of forest. "Us kids had chores from morning to night."

A moose appeared in the middle of the road. DeHart slowed, killed his lights, and when he turned them on again, without having hit the brakes, the moose was gone. A dozen people are seriously injured or killed each winter by hitting moose on Alaska's highways.

"I don't know that I'd want my own kids to live that kind of life," he said. "It's hard."

"It's hard," Melissa echoed.

"But I sure did like it," he said. "All told."

We slept on the floor of Tanya's cabin a few blocks from the Fairview. Melissa stayed up late, talking about her coming travels.

In the morning we borrowed a truck from someone I didn't know. "This is Fred!" explained Melissa. "Don't you know Fred-and-Judy?"

Most people we'd met at latitude 62 were known not by their surnames but by their affiliations: "Mike-and-Debbie." "Scott-and-Tricia." I still didn't know the man Melissa was introducing.

"Oh, sure! *Fred,*" I said, shaking hands.

"Fred knows that you might stay a few extra days in Anchorage to work," Melissa explained. "But he's not going anywhere soon."

Fred, a gentle, bearded man, nodded his assent. I made a mental note to give him half our winnings in the next Publisher's Clearing House Five-Million-Dollar Sweepstakes.

On the way to the Anchorage airport Melissa was bubbling. Traveling back to the life she had left after the life we were trying to create was as much an adventure as flying into winter wilderness.

I stopped at the ad agency to borrow enough money for the plane ticket. For collateral I offered not my services but the thousand-dollar Permanent Fund dividend check that every Alaskan resident would soon receive—the distributed interest from the billions of dollars in the state's oil-tax-bloated coffers. It was the first of what was projected to be annual payments.

Twenty minutes after her flight left, I was hunkered down in a cab. In front of the Montana Club, I wrestled my first fare from the backseat and demanded a five for a three-dollar ride. I got a ten. I crumpled it into a ball and stuffed it into my shirt pocket.

I accelerated toward a yellow light, got caught by the red, and sat fuming at the intersection until I glanced out the window. In a beige Mercedes in the next lane, the president of the ad agency and his wife sat staring at me. I tried to duck. They looked stricken.

The next morning, after I'd changed my Bunny boots for my thrift-store wing tips and a ratty sports coat, the president's wife came hesitantly into my office and blurted, "You mean you *don't* have an independent income?"

"I'm writing an article for *Commentary* about the last frontier town in America," I said smoothly. "Research takes me afield."

"Oh," she said. "Oh, thank goodness." She struck a pose. "And what do you plan to say?"

"That travesty and despair reside even in the blondest breast," I said.

"I see," she said, backing out my door, her hand at her throat.

A day later, at 5:00 A.M., after dropping off my cab, I drove Fred's truck back to Talkeetna, then hitched farther north.

I had left Denny's dogs for two days without food. But at least I had food for them now. I fed them bacon from a Safeway and cheese from a 7-Eleven.

No new snow had fallen. The Petersville Road had been plowed. We ran down the slick road and veered onto our trail so suddenly that I dumped myself in the snow. For a few yards I was dragged behind the sled. When the dogs stopped I got up laughing. Going home!

I spent the next four weeks trying to get the roof on. At first it was a joy. Within a few days it became as frustrating as trying to build a suspension bridge without an instruction manual.

I kept chain-sawing rafters to fit a flat plane. Roofs should be flat, sloping down. My roof bucked and twisted, sloping down. I had imagined three large dormers with windows overlooking the mountains. For some reason that design resulted in a roof that curved bizarrely.

I drove the dogs out to the road, killing a day.

I called Melissa at my parents' house. She cried. Something wasn't right, but she couldn't tell me what was wrong.

I called a master log builder in a distant part of the state, whose name I had gotten from books on log building. He laughed. "What you got, if I understand you right, is a hyperbolic parabola," he explained. When I said nothing, he added, "That means the roof is like a bird's wing in flight—flat at the peak and then curving along down to the feather tips. Must be pretty tricky, eh?"

The roof did not look like a bird's wing in flight. It looked like the skeleton of a petrified albatross that had died in an unnatural position.

But even at my most frustrated, as I sat astride a log fifteen feet off the ground trying to hammer a rafter so it wouldn't stick up like a cowlick, there was the land. Maybe Sisyphus has a panorama at his crest like my ridgeline's, which is why he doesn't just give up.

Regrets and revelations came and went. I raged against bent spikes and looked up at snow peaks to laugh. "Who struggles through snow?" asked Ho-san. "Is this me, or my thousand fears? They lead the way!"

. . .

When Melissa returned she brought surprising news. "Nobody can do what we're trying to do and still be happy," she said after I'd run with Janus from one end of the airport terminal to the other and back, after I'd squeezed us all in a family sandwich, after the reunion had quieted.

"Alexander gave me proof for you," she said.

"How *is* he?" I asked. I had spoken with her by phone twice when she was in Chicago, once at her aunt's home in Pennsylvania, and not at all in New York.

"Oh, he's pretty bright," she said. "I mean, he *shines*. He gave me this." She took a sheaf of stapled Xeroxed pages from her carry-on bag. "It's a Harvard study of isolation and the stress it produces. Isolation *always* produces stress. I suppose the saints can handle it, but saints don't have children."

"How are you?" I said. "How have you been?"

She brushed a strand of hair from her face. "I'm okay," she said. "It hasn't been easy, but at least I know now what we're up against."

"Stress," I prompted.

"You don't know!" she replied.

I tried to look at her papers, but couldn't. "How has Janus been? Was this a good time for him?"

He was like a different child. Almost five weeks of change! I wouldn't have been surprised if he had said, bass voiced, "And how have you been, Dad? Was this a good time for *you*?"

His eyes only said, "My dad! My dad!"

"He was a year-old baby!" said Melissa lightly.

I didn't understand what she meant. I remembered the times on the phone when Janus was crying as she spoke. I also knew that he could be such a joy that nothing else mattered.

Then I realized that I didn't care what she meant. I couldn't do a thing about what was past. We were all together, again, and the most I could ask for was to keep us together. We hadn't resolved religion or location or conflicting need. But it hadn't *kept* us apart.

"I've been building us a pretty unusual roof," I offered. "If I were a sculptor I'd never finish it. I'd just charge admission to see the framework."

"But what do you think of *this*?" said Melissa, indicating Alexander's study.

"I can't concentrate on it," I said. "Tell me what it says."

As we walked to the baggage claim Melissa told me. Isolation in sensory deprivation tanks creates hallucinations. It heightens fears and exaggerates exaltation. Isolation produces powerful change.

"And then when the people they studied got back to *other* people, they were disoriented," she concluded. "They weren't sure *what* was real."

"I'm glad to see you," I said.

"That's just because you've been alone for so long," she said.

I let it pass.

We loaded her bags in the back of the truck I'd borrowed from Marvin. For four hours we drove through the night up the snow-bound highway, Janus exhausted in Melissa's arms, Melissa as close beside me as the gearshift would allow. I wore the White Sox cap Janus had been given in Chicago. We were classic 1980s Alaskans: half-ton pickup, median-age couple with child, baseball cap.

We were also the classic white Alaskan bush family: struggling to stay together.

"I need other people," said Melissa. "I need to feel *connected*."

"I think I understand," I replied. "For the last month I've felt so connected to the trees and the sky that I've been a little sorry to go back inside."

"I mean to *people*," she explained.

"Like my parents in Chicago and your Aunt Rose and Lamonda?" I asked.

"Oh, God," she said, sighing. "They didn't understand me. They had no idea where I was at."

"You felt isolated," I said dutifully.

"I ended up hallucinating on Madison Avenue!" she said. "I used to *love* Madison Avenue. Godiva Chocolates is on Madison Avenue! But everyone who passed me was so weird! They rushed down the block thinking about their new chinaware or their stupid career or the time they were losing by bumping into me and Janus. And I used to *be* like them! I wanted to trip them up and shout, 'Don't you know how *nowhere* you are?' "

I took my hand from the stick shift and rested it in her lap.

"Do you know what Lamonda said? She said, 'You are absolutely out of your mind for wanting to go back.' I came unglued. I said, 'You don't have any idea! Your boyfriend is a coke freak and you take Valium to get to sleep and *you're* telling *me* that *I'm* crazy?' Oh, I wish you could see what Seventy-fifth Street looks like after having been in Alaska! I couldn't even sleep in my own apartment! That's when I went to Alexander's."

I slowed down to forty-five to keep the tires in the snow grooves. "Alexander," I said, thinking of the solitude of his loft.

Melissa laughed. She seemed to know what I was thinking. "At least it's quiet there. But talk about weird! After he pulled out the studio couch for us, I could hear the messages people left on his answering machine. 'I'm at Studio in the john because I can hear myself in here and I miss your touch.' 'It's three A.M. but I had to call because I'm not sure if it's worth it to go on living.' 'I'm only calling because nobody else understands me and even talking to your machine is better than talking to myself.' That's where everyone was at: nowhere! It was like being in the Twilight Zone!"

"I guess that's why Alexander and I are both trying to create a retreat," I said. "A place of beauty where we can get away from the random sorrow that pops up everywhere."

"But he's still in the thick of it!" Melissa said. "And you're so far out there's *nothing* keeping you grounded except me."

"And our home and the mountains."

She leaned back in her seat. "*I* need to be connected to *reality.*"

I noticed that I had gotten back up to sixty. I slowed.

"The Bible says that communion is necessary," Melissa said. "That's why Paul founded the church. That's why sane people come together on Sundays."

"There's never been a religious tradition on earth that didn't value the solitude of private union with God," I said. "The way to the top of the mount has always been alone."

"But Moses came down!" she said. "Jesus came out of the desert! Didn't Buddha spend the rest of his life among *people*?"

"So I guess you're waiting to get back to Talkeetna?"

"I'm waiting to get back *somewhere*," she said.

We slept the night in a twenty-five-dollar room in the Fairview, above the bar. Janus woke when I carried him upstairs. He reached for my face and smiled. I was so startled by his love that I grabbed a handrail to keep from falling back. With his hand still on my cheek he drifted back to sleep.

In the morning Melissa said, "I'm not ready to go back out."

I didn't argue. I spent the next few days baby-sitting while she visited with her friends. She said, "I feel like I'm home." I walked with the child on the frozen river plain. We studied sastrugi—the wind-sculpted mesas and canyons a few inches in height and depth carved into the snowpack. We studied frozen water baubles at the edges of open river leads.

Then I went back out, alone.

I spent the rest of the winter finishing the house. For three or four days I chain-sawed logs, nailed plywood to hyperbolic rafters, whanged on spikes, each night driving the dogs to the road to haul more plywood and more spikes and more building supplies from my cache. During the days intermediate to building I went into Talkeetna, to be with my family and to restock my supplies. And so a week passed, and then another.

Melissa came out occasionally to keep our connection immediate. When she rode rolling in the dogsled to the ridgeline she was wonderful. She exclaimed at the progress I'd made and whirled through the cleaning of the little cabin.

Wilderness is an ideal that sages and cave bears grasp, without associations, without intent. I was no cave bear and light-years from the sages. I just wanted continuity, a lasting home where my son could see what was real: death interwoven with life, inexplicable sorrow and sudden radiance. I wanted Huck Finn's idyll and Crazy Horse's bond to the natural world.

I was the son of an immigrant from southern Italy. I wanted family. I had fathered a son by a woman who was almost pure-blood Italian. Family! Lasting! Through planetary convolutions and the coming millennium.

When spring came—the last week of April—the house was finished. Roofing paper kept the rains out. The three-thousand-dollar cookstove, for which Alexander had loaned us the money, gleamed in its corner. Triple-pane windows overlooked glaciers.

We could finally celebrate. When we all came home on the last of the dwindling snow, I brought a bottle of Moët & Chandon champagne in the sled with Melissa and Janus. The tundra was becoming bare, though sled-packed snow remained on the trail like a glistening ribbon.

While I chained the dogs beneath their trees Melissa opened the split-log door to our new home.

I gathered an armful of dried spruce, knocked the snow from my boots, and went in to join her.

She stood in the middle of the room, the ceiling ten feet overhead, blue light illuminating the logs. She was silent. I lit the kindling. Wisps of white smoke curled from the firebox, rising to the billowed yellow fiberglass insulation that hid the complicated log work. The insulation, supported by clear plastic sheeting, looked like a gold thunderhead. The floor didn't sag.

Janus squirmed in Melissa's arms. She put him down. He lifted himself to his feet and tottered from wall to wall like a bumper car.

"Well," said Melissa.

"There's still a lot of work to do," I said, noting, with a surprise I tried to hide, that nothing impeded Janus's circuit: no furniture, no furnishings, not even a carpet. It had all been *done* last time I'd looked. Suddenly it looked barren.

Melissa nodded.

The smoke gave way to crackling. Heat waves shimmered above the shiny cast-iron cooking surface.

"Come look upstairs," I said quickly.

We climbed a makeshift log ladder. "I'll build regular stairs," I said when one of the cross-logs creaked under her weight.

There was a mattress upstairs, on the floor, covered with a quilt. I'd left the huge log ridgepoles exposed. Melissa hit her head on one. She hit hard. She stumbled to the bed and sat down.

I knelt beside her and rubbed the bruise. It was a moment for reconciliation. I ran my hands from her head to her neck. Janus, downstairs, laughed like a boy in a funhouse.

Melissa remained bent over. She didn't relax beneath my touch. "How do you feel about being here?" I asked bravely.

She looked up with tears in her eyes. "I don't know," she whispered. "It's so beautiful. But it's so far away. I *want* to be happy, but . . ." She lay back against my arms, hesitantly.

We listened to the slap of Janus's feet on the bare boards downstairs. The rising warmth of the stove thickened around us. I lifted one hand from her neck and touched the small of her back. She seemed to stiffen.

I bolted up and went downstairs. I stoked the stove. I rolled around with Janus until he made it plain that he'd rather explore the floor. Then I grabbed the champagne out of the pack. When I got to the top of the ladder I popped the cork. It bounced off an exposed ridgepole and rolled to her feet.

"To the whole wide world!" I called, taking a swig.

I went to the bed and handed her the bottle. She rested it in her lap, smiling, her eyelashes still damp. "And to us," she said, handing me the bottle.

She hadn't drunk. She saw my perplexity. "One of my vows is to abstain from alcohol," she said.

I sat beside her. I took another sip. The champagne bubbled over. I stuck the bottle's neck in my mouth. The froth went up my nose. "What vows?" I managed to ask.

"Last Sunday I went before the congregation and asked for direction from God. Everyone prayed for me. It was so powerful! People cried! Then I heard the voice of the Lord tell me to follow in His steps. I heard Him as plainly as I hear Janus. You can't imagine how peaceful it was. I have my calling! I know why I've come here!"

I gripped the bottle by the neck. "Is it for our sake?" I asked.

"Of course!" she said. She sank back against my chest. "And for everyone who's been through so much pain and confusion."

I held her in my arms. From downstairs came a *thump*, silence, and then a giggle.

"I've spent most of the last month in *tears*," she said.

"You didn't tell me."

"I couldn't. I was afraid you wouldn't think I was strong enough or brave enough. My ministry is *people*. People *respond* to me. I *hear* their pains. I *feel* for them. I come here to the end of the earth and then back again. They look to me to know what's real in the world."

"*This* is real!" I said, a little too loudly. "You can't *get* any closer to the world. There is no way to insulate yourself from the stars unless you keep your eyes shut tight. That doesn't take strength or bravery. It takes clarity, eyes open."

Melissa took a deep breath and then began to sob. Janus called, "Whaa?" I took a long gulp of champagne.

I went downstairs and brought Janus up. He seemed amazed to find that there was more of the world than he had just explored. He fidgeted out of my arms and tottered to the edge of the floor to stare seven feet down. He drew back, peered over the edge, and squealed in excitement.

"Don't let him fall!" cried Melissa.

I grabbed Janus up. "I need to build a wall up here," I said.

Janus refused to be held. Both Melissa and I crawled around after him. It might have been comic—a conga line following a disco dancer—if it hadn't been so sad. We didn't trust anything.

We allowed him his circuit of the upstairs loft. Then I held him close to his mother, so she could suckle him. He grinned at me, winked at her, and dropped off to a peaceful sleep.

Melissa and I resumed our conversation. I tried to make a case for the wonder of being safe in a landscape that for millennia had been a terrible struggle. We had a metal wood stove and triple-pane glass windows and a cache of dried foods. We had a stash of split kindling and a fiberglass-insulated roof. No dark caves. No need to hunt through deep snows for food. And yet we could see what our distant ancestors had seen beyond the ring of their campfire: the blue radiance of glaciers, the presence of God. We lived the life fifty thousand years of travail imagined. Here! Secured!

Melissa answered by begging me to accept the necessity of human interaction. Everywhere on earth there always has been connection to the community. What right did we have to ignore that truth?

I said that we *did* have a connection to *many* people, good friends near and far, but our home was where we nurtured the connection to each other. I just wanted us to be happy.

Melissa just wanted us to be happy.

I ended up drinking the whole bottle of celebratory champagne alone, standing in a moonlit window. I fell asleep downstairs, beneath yellow clouds. When I stumbled back upstairs, shivering, Melissa was asleep.

We went back to Talkeetna the next day. So much snow had melted in the space of one warm late-April day that the tundra looked flooded.

Some of our friends had been hired to clear a forty-foot swath of forest for a power line that would extend from Fairbanks to Anchorage. Others of our friends were incensed that the land near their homes could be scarred for a power plant that had yet to be built, for an electrical need that Alaska would require only if the population density rose to that of Connecticut's.

I signed on. I made twenty-five dollars an hour to chain-saw old forest growth to stubble. I rose at dawn to walk to the helicopter pad near the airstrip, there to be ferried into the forest with the rest of the crew. Melissa and Janus and I lived in a tent on the banks of the Susitna River. Melissa never once complained that there was no place to rent in town.

We were part of a tent city sprung up from the needs of workers brought from distant parts of the state. Alaska's economy has always cycled through periods of boom and bust, and this was the greatest boom Talkeetna had known for fifty years.

I earned enough that summer to repay Alexander's loan, to buy our own car, to allow Melissa a semblance of financial security for the first time since we had moved north.

Not until September did I go back home for the first time since I had stood with my champagne in the moonlight.

Bears had destroyed the outhouse. One window of the little cabin was busted out, but there was no sign of entry. Fifty pounds of cached organic brown rice had not enticed any forest animals. But the bags of red beans and of lentils were empty. I found their contents under the bed pillow, in my winter boots, filling the upright receptacle of the grain grinder.

I cleaned up the winter larder of mice and shrews. I swept it all into a great heap in the middle of the floor. The effort, after the hike in and the anxiety about what I might find, took the last of my energy. I couldn't even walk to the larger house, where the door was nailed shut.

In the morning the bean pile was gone. My boots were full. There were even beans under my pillow. I was upset that rodents had walked under my head while I slept. Then I laughed. We were nurturing the forest life! We were ministering to all the beasts of the field. If I caught any of them eating our food I'd whack them with a stick, but until then—what an abundance we had created!

I yanked the nails from the larger house's door. It swung open easily, a perfect fit. I felt as I had when I first entered the Cathedral of Notre Dame. The light reflected from snow peaks through the triple-pane windows was like light from blue stained glass. The glowing stockades were like a hundred Stations of the Cross—each log lifted from my shoulder into position.

And then I returned to common sight, checking my work for holes. The huge horizontal log supporting the second floor had begun to sag. I made a mental note to shore it up.

I went to the window. With the magic of coincidence a moose stepped from behind dying alders, browsed, and slowly ambled across the yard. I thought, suddenly, of grabbing the gun to get our winter's meat. It was hunting season. But any life here seemed now to be blessed. I watched as the moose disappeared between spruce.

. . .

I returned to Talkeetna for Melissa and Janus. I felt rich to reach the
road and simply start the V-8 engine of our "new" 1972 Chrysler
New Yorker with sixty-five thousand miles on its odometer.

When we all hiked home there were neither bugs nor constricting
grasses. Ice rimmed the shore of the tundra lake. The devil's club
leaves were gold. Rose hips along the trail had been frosted and
sweetened. We plucked them as we walked.

We moved immediately into our home. It took days of dragging
shelves and tables and clothes and food from the little cabin. Melissa
was sorry to leave the little cabin. "It was hard for me to move from
Pennsylvania to Manhattan," she said, "because I had to abandon a
familiar life. Then we moved to Alaska, which took . . . a lot. And
now just moving into here seems complicated, too, but I can't really
say why."

It was difficult for me, too. But I knew why. This was *it*. There
was nothing else we could anticipate to create our security. If we
didn't settle into a routine of ease and harmony and trust, there
would be only cold winds and deep snows coming.

Melissa and I both yawned our way to an early bedtime; we slept
fitfully, while Janus acted like a prince in his palace.

In the following days we avoided awkward discussions.

The winds came cold. They blew the last leaves from the birches
in showers of bronze. Then the snows descended.

The snows came in a storm. Flakes whipped against the north
windows to melt and run in rivulets that froze. Gusts of black night
wind drove the smoke from the stove back into the house in clouds so
dense we had to retreat to the little cabin. Once inside the now-gutted
house that had been the stage of so much hope we both broke down.

"How great to have this security," I said.

"Our house smells like a fire!" Melissa said.

"It'll clear."

"It'll always have that smoke stink!"

"Nonsense. We'll air it. But now we're safe."

"We're desperate!"

"Little things like this are inevitable," I said.

"What a terrible way to live," she replied. "One unexpected worry after another."

"That's life anywhere," I said.

"That's not life. That's *survival*."

I began to shout. Melissa began to shriek. Janus wailed as we ripped each other apart.

"I want to go home!" cried Melissa.

"You *are* home!" I yelled.

In the morning we patched things up. We aired the house. Melissa worked silently, like a victim in a war zone.

The next day the balcony wall I was trying to build on the second floor lost a log that could have hit Melissa with Janus in her arms. We fought again. When would come the black lacquer table? How long could we live on the edge, where logs fell?

We patched things up, again.

The twenty-one-month-old child, who had begun to show signs of talking—"Muhmuh, muhmuh"—returned to "Beh!"

With the horror of statistical inevitability, we proved that Alexander's university study was accurate.

We were isolated from each other. I demanded that she confirm that we were creating a life amidst uncommon beauty. Melissa wanted my admission that it was not without daily struggle. Our domestic strife could have been that of upper-middle-class Americans torn between the assumed ease of a spacious city condo and the actual demands of a twelve-hour workday that made career the primary priority.

"What are we living for?" I shouted.

"For Janus!" she answered, rising up in bed.

"Right!" I agreed. "A home where he can see the world. The ability to discover God by walking out the door."

"There are bears outside the door! And the winter!"

"That's what I mean!" I said, getting up to pace. "Maybe I'm too aggressive. I'm sorry for it. But I was born in America. I want what I want. That seems terrible to say. But I've seen such grace, too. I've seen too much to insist that *I* know what's right. Look! Look out the window! *That* is real. *There* is God."

Melissa was silent. When I returned from my mania I saw that she was sobbing.

I sagged. I crawled back to bed.

The next afternoon I nailed the door shut behind us. We were all dressed for a hike.

I hit the final nail so hard I startled myself. Melissa was watching me. I looked up to the mountains but caught her stare.

"So this is it?" she asked, Janus in her arms.

"This is just one more slog out," I said, trying to be light, sounding like death.

"I can't tell you how sad this is for me," Melissa said.

I didn't want to hear of any sorrow. I had closed the door hoping for her to say, "Wait!" I wanted her to reveal such commitment and wonder as would make us break out of our pattern to stand exposed before the sky and accept our bond to the forest and mountains and each other.

Janus was eager to move farther into the day. Melissa hoisted him into the baby pack I lifted to my back. I tucked the snowshoes under one arm. We started out.

"Well, I guess this *is* it," I said, stomping inches deep into the snow.

The bitterness in my tone made me hike faster.

As we broke out onto the tundra, scattered clouds blew north. The sun, ahead to the south, illuminated our feet where we trod. The sun was like a brass gong. It rang in the bare trees.

I felt like Whymper descending from the first successful climb of the Matterhorn: after his rope had broken and his companions had plum-meted to their deaths, a radiant cross had risen into the clearing sky.

Janus rose up in his pack on my back and reached his hands to the horizon. I saw his little fingers over my head.

I stopped. Melissa, behind me, stopped. Janus didn't move, arms extended.

I could hear Melissa weeping. I stared at the child's hands reaching for the light. They were my hands, the breadth of palm, the thickness of thumb, the crook in the little finger.

"Oh! If only you could see!" said Melissa.

I wanted to turn around, but we were on the trail out. I took a step and kicked up a plume of new snow. The golden fog around my feet was like a nebula, as marvelous as any isolation tank hallucination. I didn't know, suddenly, whether I was wildly happy or sad. All I could think was, "We're headed out. We're done. We are done. And I have no idea what such beauty means."

When we entered the forest again I started walking faster. "Rick! Slow down!" Melissa cried.

I concentrated on lifting each leg above the snow and moving at the limit of my ability. Janus, at such a pace, bounced. He giggled.

"Rick!" shouted Melissa. "Please!"

That's when I stopped. "Please *what*?" I shouted over my shoulder. "Please go back? That's not what you want. Please let me take us *slowly* away from our home? Please just *accept* it? I can't!" I whirled around to face her. "I can't!"

I still wanted her to walk up to me in embrace. She paused, five steps behind. I waited. The forest was silent. No dramatic bear leaped from behind a snowdrift. No rampaging moose burst across the trail.

We were alone. The sun shone around our feet.

Janus, startled by our cries, fidgeted. When he began to whine I kept walking, slower but steadily. No word was spoken until we finally reached the road.

"Just don't speed," Melissa said when we'd gotten into the car.

I drove so slowly an angel could have alighted on the roof. Miles passed. And then more miles.

I pulled into the railroad parking lot in Talkeetna. We sat for a minute. Janus rose from his sleep and bounced. "Can you hold him?" Melissa said softly. "I want to go see the pastor."

I held Janus. Melissa opened the door, stepped out, bowed her head, and left. Janus and I went into the Fairview.

"Yo!" called Rosser when we came into the bar.

"Give that man a Michelob!" called Marvin.

I went behind the beer taps and took a room key from the hook on the wall. Then I went upstairs with Janus. The silence behind us was the silence of a morgue.

Early in the morning I went to the pastor's house. I knocked on the door, hesitantly. No answer came. I heard the murmur of voices. I went inside, Janus in my arms.

Across the fluorescent-lit kitchen, in the living room, Melissa sat in an armchair flanked by all the young elders of her church. The pastor rose from a straight-backed chair and stood behind her. He rested his hands on her shoulders.

"I think Janus and I'll just go back out," I said.

Melissa nodded.

"We'll be fine," I said. "There's nothing to worry about." Janus began to play with my nose.

"She just needs to be alone now," the pastor said quietly.

I nodded.

Janus grabbed at my hair and squealed, "Beh!"

"Really, we'll be fine," I said.

Melissa made a motion to rise, but the pastor held her back. She tried to smile. "I know," she whispered.

"We love you," I said. "Please don't worry." Janus squirmed around in my arms.

I backed out the door. The last thing I saw was Melissa with her head in her hands while her circle of support closed around her.

Once outside the door I drew such a deep breath that I involuntarily lifted Janus into the air. He started to laugh at the motion that usually became a "Wheee!" But he stopped when he saw that I wasn't playing with him.

I saw his confusion. I tossed him up and said, "Wheee!" so loudly he was surprised. Then, hesitantly, he laughed.

I loaded our three new pups—now grown—in the back of the car along with the two new dogs our dog-sitters had given us for free.

On the roof of the car I lashed the lightweight, plastic-bottomed toboggan sled that Pecos had built for us during the summer, stored with the dogs in town.

As we drove out the spur road to the highway I was aware that Janus sat in the passenger seat alone, without his mom, without a breast or bottle. He knelt against the dash and said, "Ooh! Beh! Ah!"

We reached the end of the Petersville Road without complaint.

I harnessed Norton, ten months old, in lead. He had never before pulled a sled. Nor had any of the other dogs, who now barked in their traces behind Norton.

"It's just us now, buddy," I said as I burrowed Janus into a down sleeping bag at the back of the sled.

When I released the line tied taut around a tree the dogs took off more powerfully than I could have imagined. I had had no idea what to expect from them. Puppies whining in the snow? Greater difficulty than what we had known?

Norton tugged hard. The forest flew past. Pearls of snow kicked back into the sled.

I whoaed the team so I could lean over the handlebars and fix Janus's covers.

He reached both hands up to me, his head tilted back. He said, plainly, "My dod."

We stared at each other. I bent farther down to kiss him on the forehead. The dogs jerked and began racing on up the trail.

I stood back on the sled runners to keep us from tipping over.

Then I burst into tears.

8.

PERSPECTIVES

"It's rice cream and honey with raisins," I explained. Janus sat at the new black lacquer log table in his new spruce-stump chair, hesitantly examining his bowl.

"Uck?" he asked.

"No, it's great stuff. Watch." I shoveled a big spoonful into my mouth. "Mmmm. *Good!*"

He waited to see if I'd suddenly spit it on the floor gagging. I dug up another spoonful. "It's the *best!*"

He lifted his own helping, eagerly.

Atta boy!

Then he stuck it toward my face. I leaned back.

In that moment's pause his hand wavered and the food plopped onto the table.

He laughed. He sucked on the empty spoon.

"Mmmm!" he mocked. " 'Ood!"

"You realize, of course, that you are now weaned," I said.

He grinned.

"I mean, you have no alternative but to try everything at the breakfast table, because you haven't had any chi-chi for weeks."

"Chi-chi" was the term Melissa and I used for breast-feeding. The half-Mexican wife of my best friend in Chicago claimed that it was a common expression. It sounded better than "tit."

At this reminder of his mom Janus looked around, first over one shoulder, then over the other. This was the longest he had ever been away from her, but he hadn't complained.

"Your mom *wants* you to eat," I added.

He understood me. He was not quite two years old, but he understood everything I said as long as it was immediate, like "No" or "I love you" or "Time for breakfast!"

His own verbal communication was less clearly enunciated, but I understood everything he said, too. Happiness has a simple vocabulary.

I was aware that it wasn't my parenting that had allowed him to become weaned so casually. It wasn't my love or my cooking. It was our world.

We spent most of our days outside.

We went for morning walks after breakfast. I put on snowshoes, settled him into his baby pack on my back, and we made trails: down to the creek where burbles of water streamed out to freeze in long slick lanes along which I slid him like a curling stone; out to the tundra by different routes where spruce grouse occasionally burst from low branches to fly twenty yards before roosting again; deep into the forest where we discovered animal tracks or an eagle feather in the snow.

We went for evening walks after the "Bush Pipeline" broadcast. For the last few weeks we—or, rather, I—had waited for Melissa to send us a message on our D-cell-powered radio. When the announcer concluded, "And that's it for the 'Pipeline' tonight, brought to you by Susitna Air, dependable charters to the bush," I sagged, while Janus, unable to decipher the rapid radio-announcer speech, continued to make towers from his colored Lego blocks.

That's when I would hoist him up and we'd go back outside.

First we fed the dogs. On well-packed trails I lugged a plastic five-gallon bucket of hydrated kibble while the child followed. At each dog's house I ladled food into a metal dish while Janus petted the dog's head. He was as tall as their shoulders. They licked his face, lapped their food, licked his face, never growling. On clear nights we could see every dip and rise in the trail—even after terrestrial twilight had passed through nautical twilight and beyond astronomical twilight to stars. When clouds settled, though enough radiance still remained for us to see to the far corners of the homestead, I wore a miner's headlamp so that the child wouldn't stumble in the shadowless glow. The yellow beam gilded him so that he seemed to float ahead of me, my tottering cherub.

The dogs were our lifeline. They hauled our wood to heat the house. They waited ready to race to the road if an emergency required more medical care than my $12.95 first-aid kit could provide. They were our transport to mountains.

Only dimly did I question the ability of these eleven-month-old huskies to pull a sled. I assumed that their breeding as sled dogs made it difficult for them *not* to pull. Occasionally, however, I wondered whether their propensity to pull might be less like a chicken's instinct to peck and more a wild serendipity. I knew that Joe Redington, the founder of the thousand-mile Anchorage-to-Nome Iditarod sled dog race, had to breed a few hundred dogs to get ten good ones.

Ultimately, I believed that our dogs responded to love, that they knew what we needed through a deeper sentience than I could grasp and were eager to reciprocate our love.

They required some training, though, in the finer points of our needs. I insisted that the dogs whoa when I said so—and *stay* stopped—because traveling with a child demanded a team that could be easily controlled. I learned that the hierarchy of a wolf pack was duplicated in these almost-wolves. If I was lax in my discipline, they were lax in compliance. A dog as excitable as Van Dyke needed sharp cuffs periodically to remind her that I was the Alpha dog—the boss—and what I said was law.

A dog like Norton, on the other hand, got the message the first time, and remembered it. His job as leader was to keep the line tight, especially when I was hooking up the other dogs behind him. If he wandered around, everything would end up tangled. If he tugged, the others would follow, and I'd end up chasing. He kept the line extended by the strength of his will. When we took off, he remained a step ahead of the pursuing dogs, the line connecting all five never sagging to the ground.

After feeding the dogs, we stomped around the house atop snow the dogs had trampled when they were loosed from their chains to romp. We dug snow caves. We examined dried grasses and seeds insulated from the night air by the snow cover. We listened for the dogs to send up their inevitable nightly song: the haunting tenor chorus of wolves who have eaten well. Gray jays scolded us when we frightened them from the rim of the dog food bucket where they pecked at leftover food. If we held out kibble in our hands and remained still, they alighted, gripping our fingers with their small talons. The boy didn't flinch. We named the boldest jay Braver. When an owl hooted in the distance the jays vanished.

This much became routine. It seemed as if we had always explored the woods in the morning, played in the homestead clearing after the 7:00 P.M. "Bush Pipeline." I was aware that my perspective was a child's, where a week is a year and a moment's pleasure mitigates any lingering pain.

Our routine didn't vary. We had nothing to vary it. At first, when he napped in the afternoon, I peeled logs and spiked them in a grid to form the base of a table that I then covered in split poles and lacquered black. After that chore, I utilized my two free afternoon hours to peel huge logs for the foundation of the greenhouse that would attach to the south wall of the house. When Janus awoke, together we gathered kindling from the discarded branches of house logs. Each afternoon he proudly led the way down to the spring, where I filled our water buckets. When we hiked back up to the house he hummed.

Only at night, after he fell asleep beside me as I sang our version of Brahms Lullaby—"Lullaby, and good night, / Go to sleep, happy

Janus, / 'Cause your mama loves you so / And your daddy loves you, too . . ."—did I resume my private routine.

I worried.

I worried that he wouldn't remain content, that our excursions would pale or storms keep us housebound, that the need for his mom would become overpowering. And why *hadn't* Melissa sent us a message? She needed time to sort things out away from my judgments, away from our isolation. But I wanted to know what she was thinking!

Janus, breathing peacefully in the crook of my arm, knew without the slightest doubt that his mama loved him so and his daddy loved him, too.

In the morning, when the sky was clear and the Range hovered over the house, I said, pointing, "Mountain."

"Moun'n," he echoed.

His sudden capacity for speech seemed miraculous.

"Roger," I said.

He shook his head. "Jay-nut," he corrected, pronouncing his name.

Melissa had insisted on giving him "an identity," repeating his name to him from the week he was born. "Janus" this. "Janus" that. She had said, "I'm not sure who *I* am, but *he'll* know."

"My beautiful, wonderful little Janus," I said.

"*Big* Jay-nut," he replied.

I never called him "little" again.

And still I knew that I couldn't claim such unexpected health to be my doing at all.

"Look! The moon's back!"

"Moonee!"

When I was sixteen, during a period when all I read was science fiction, I read H. G. Wells's *The Island of Doctor Moreau*. As a newspaperman's son, unable to avoid the morning papers and the radio news at noon and Walter Cronkite at dinnertime, I was aware that much of the human world was comprised of bellicose posturing and privation and despair. I withdrew into tales of a better future. Doctor Moreau introduced the notion that better *people* could be created.

Years later, when I reread the book, I was disturbed to realize that the mad doctor's "better" life was surgically manufactured. The fact that my original memory was only of hope is evidence that I wanted *wholeness* pretty badly.

When I looked at Janus alone with the moon in the forest, I knew I had a laboratory in which to test Rousseau's theory of the "noble savage," which presumes a natural goodness inherent in us all. I certainly hadn't been trying to concoct any experiment. Mostly I'd been trying to build a roof that didn't leak. But here it was: a *tabula rasa* world—with sorrow, certainly, at the peripheries, but a world in which few cultural influences intruded.

Janus, however, showed me that *Homo sapiens*, especially at the age of two, was more eager to practice dominance than benevolence. He liked to *win*.

We played games—wrestling in bed in the morning, racing around the house (slap, slap, slap of bare baby feet on the varnished plywood floor), hide-and-seek—that at first befuddled and then annoyed the hell out of him when he didn't "beat."

After we discovered that the curious markings in the safflower margarine on the dinner table were from the pecks of chickadees who fluttered inside at dawn through the ill-fitting upstairs porch door's jamb (we woke one morning to chirps downstairs), Janus was excited to "keep" the birds where he could get at them.

At that point I did a quick backtrack on my hope that the wilderness child was benign. My ingenuous boy was instinctively in need of control. Adam and Eve seemed a pretty accurate myth.

But Janus also insisted upon love. He demanded that the birds be fed, that the dogs be allowed to romp free of their chains, that fallen pinecones not be touched in case they had "babies." He brought me gifts ten times a day: clusters of new pine needles, crayon drawings, scraps of birch bark that did look, as he pointed out, like mountains.

I saw a capacity for caring in my aggressive child that heartened me. He didn't have to be taught that the world is worthy of trust, nurturing, *whole*.

That's certainly what I *wanted* to see. But when he fussed and refused to take a nap, I calmed him to sleep, always, by taking him outside, where he cocked his head for bird song and lay back in my arms to stare up at the trees.

That was the extent of my "scientific" investigation: going outside. What's to study about happiness?

On the eighteenth day of our first days alone, Melissa sent a radio message. "To Rick and my precious Janus on the ridgeline: I love you and miss you. I am fine. I hope everything's fine there. From Mom."

"That was from your mom!" I cried.

Janus looked up from the Golden Book that he held upside down, turning pages from back to front, nodding to himself and murmuring, sagely, "Yep," in reply to what he "read."

"Chi-chi!" he shouted.

"Yeah, well forget about that for a while," I said as I lifted him up.

He nestled in my embrace and tried to lift my shirt. I didn't distract him. Among some tribes in Africa, men will pacify insistent adopted children by giving them a teat. I let him find my nipple.

He sucked for a full minute, staring at me. I stared at him. It could have been a powerful bond.

It wasn't.

"Time to feed the dogs?" I asked.

He released me and nodded eagerly.

"Then maybe we can go explore for the owl. I think it lives in the trees behind Norton. Would you like that?"

He ran for his snowsuit.

We didn't find the owl, but we found the tiny tracks of a vole in the snow. We dug carefully where the track disappeared beneath a tree and found some brown droppings atop the hoarfrost—a foot under the top layer of snow—at the opening between two exposed roots.

"That's where he lives," I announced. "Do you want to give the little mouse some food?"

He did. We left wheat berries at the hole.

"Now he'll be our friend, too," I said. "Like all the other animals."

Such was the real nature of our bond.

Melissa's radio message was repeated each night for the next three days, as was standard "Bush Pipeline" procedure. But I was still surprised to have such consistent communication from the distant human universe.

On the third night of "To Rick and my precious Janus . . ." we went out on our walk to stand beneath a great auroral display. Directly overhead, shafts of green fell from a pulsing oval. The mountains on the horizon seemed transluminated—glowing within from a light beyond. We quickly fed the dogs and then carried a ground pad and sleeping bag from the house to lay in the snow. We sat to take off our boots, then zipped the bag around us. It was twenty above, and calm.

While I lay on my back with Janus's back against my chest, his head up against my chin, we stared at the zenith from which the lights spread. I told him that God was drawing pictures in the sky. I told him that no other boy in all the world was lying in the snow with his dad watching the northern lights overhead. I told him that I loved him.

He was silent, but aware. When I realized, in time, that he was asleep, I rolled him beside me. Then, surprisingly, I slept too.

I woke to squirms. I lifted him to his knees and pulled down his pants. He peed into the snow. His head wobbled from side to side sleepily. I nestled him again beside me because it seemed easier than putting on my boots, raising him in my arms, and stumbling into the dark house. He sighed once, pursed and contracted his lips with a sucking motion, and nodded off. I looked up at stars, the aurora gone, the night blue.

With a sudden tremor I realized that we could camp together in the winter. We could sleep in the snow, casually. We could, I had no doubts, drive the dogs to the mountains and spend a day or two. He liked to explore. Neither of us thought twice about sleeping "out in the woods." For what seemed like hours I watched the stars revolve above the spruce, but when we both woke together in the morning I accepted that I had dropped back to sleep almost at once, watching only interior horizons.

We hopped back to the house and made a fire. Janus got his crayons from beneath the table and scribbled on drawing paper while I made rice cream with raisins. Not until the next day, when I jotted in my journal, did I realize that he had, at the time, been drawing God's pictures.

That was the day a moose wandered into the clearing.

The dogs leaped up to bark furiously. I ran to the window. A very large moose stood ten yards from the house idly pawing beneath the snow. It seemed oblivious to the clamor around it, even after I kicked open the door, Janus in my arms, to shout, "Look!"

Plainly, this moose refused to believe that so much wild activity had invaded its domain.

I ran a few steps toward the moose, eager for Janus to see its size. It suddenly ran a few yards toward us, snorting.

As if hitting a wall, I stopped and began to walk backward, my knees weak, my feet shuffling like a little windup toy. "Isn't he big?" I said, trying to sound composed.

There was no way to miss seeing that the moose was the size of a half-ton pickup, and annoyed.

I was angry with myself for introducing Janus to big game while frantic adrenaline coursed through me. Of course the boy would sense that fear was predominant, that moose were *scary*.

He cried, plainly, "No!"

The sound of his voice galvanized me. I turned to hurry toward safety.

He wrestled almost out of my arms. "No!" he repeated.

I stumbled. I lost my grip on him. As he slid to the ground I saw that he wasn't terrified at all. He wasn't even concerned. He was excited. He wanted to go *closer* to the moose.

I sat in the snow, gripping him around the waist while he twisted to break free and approach the moose.

I tried to stifle a laugh, but it burst out like a Bronx cheer.

The moose, completely baffled, began high-stepping down the ridge. The dogs screamed at the ends of their chains.

That night, as we lay together to sleep, after blowing out the kerosene lantern, I made up a bedtime story about a moose that carries a boy on its back and flies through the forest to the mountains. Janus's eyes were bright. In Alaska, more people are charged by moose in one year than have ever been attacked by bears. We, too, had discovered the power of moose, but we had also seen their wonder.

The next day we went into Talkeetna. "Bring my baby," the radio message had said, like a brass gong.

"Want to see your mom?" I asked the boy, who was putting on his snowsuit—backward, feet in sleeves, zipper mysteriously vanished—in anticipation of our nightly walk outside.

"You bet!" he said, looking up from his consternation.

My father's favorite expression, in times of validation, was always, "You bet." Was this a genetically determined response? How *do* we learn our speech?

"Okay. Tomorrow we'll take the dogs to the road," I said.

Then, with a furious burst of frustration (distressingly like his dad), he pointed out ("Yahghh!") that he was still caught in the Medusa's-head tangle of his snowsuit.

I helped him free. We explored for owls. We saw a raven. It was perched in the top of a spruce, obvious against the sky. It said, "*Kluwok!*"

"That means, 'I see you down there,'" I explained.

"Yep," said the boy, casually.

Ravens, who can and do circle the upper slopes of Denali, who fly at thirty below, have more than a score of different, distinct calls. Most birds have two. Both Janus and I seemed to have understood our raven as plainly as had Poe. We were acquiring all manner of language.

In the morning we lit no fire. We took off in the cold.

I carried all the dogs' chains wrapped around the back of the sled. I also carried food for them, for their daily feeding, just in case the world was full of grace and forgiveness and I spent the night in Talkeetna with all my family.

The world, however, was complicated. Melissa was angry at me for "keeping" Janus so long. I pointed out that I had been waiting only for some communication from her.

She pointed out that she *had* sent a message four days ago, that she herself had listened to it be repeated *three nights in a row*, that she hadn't understood why we hadn't then replied.

I said *I* hadn't understood what she wanted until getting the *clear* request.

She said I should have *known*.

Janus tried to bring us together, running from mother to father, arms spread to hug, while Mom and Dad remained at opposite ends of the room.

I was horrified that Janus would see that this tension was from antagonism. Love is ease, and ease is trust, and trust is mandatory for being at home in the wild world. Antagonism is Not Love. But I had no idea what to do about it.

Some language is best learned young.

Melissa was indignant that I hadn't even considered how difficult an "independent" life was for her. I had been oblivious enough to her need for respite from the woods and from my insistence that she *like* it, that to her it seemed in character for me not to have thought at all about how hard a separate life would be for her—financially, emotionally, familially. I didn't *want* to think those thoughts, of course. I didn't want her to be "independent." But here we were again, proving how chaotic the breakup of family can be, overwhelmed by pain, which we expressed as anger.

"I'm going to have to work in town cooking *hamburgers*!" she cried. "While you do just what you want!"

"I'll go to Anchorage and work for a week!" I shouted.

"You don't know how much you've hurt me!" she replied.

Janus stopped in the middle of his circuit and said, calmly, like a ninety-dollar-an-hour marriage counselor, "Now what?"

Melissa was startled by her baby's sudden capacity to be articulate. I almost laughed, but I was afraid she'd misinterpret. Janus's composure was droll. His parents, unfortunately, were not.

"I'll be back," I said.

"I helped build that house!" she said.

"Bye, Dod!" said Janus.

For four nights in Anchorage I slept in the back of the car—when I slept—parked in vacant lots. I took one half day off to bomb back up the slick winter highway to dump fifty pounds of food for the waiting dogs, then returned to work. While carrying the dog food through the forest from the end of the road, my pace slowed so radically that I thought of Zeno's paradox: if I went only halfway to the dogs with each incremental advance, would I ever get there? I hoped not. I hoped I would continue to walk through the northern woods, ever so slowly, arriving not quite at an ending forever. The dogs heard me and burst into barks. I hurried.

When I came back to Talkeetna, richer, older, sadder, Melissa was calm. "I just need more time," she said. "I just need more time to get used to . . . everything."

I gave her the money I'd earned. "We'll listen to the radio," I said.

"Give me another week or two," she said.

Boy and dad went home, dad vibrating, boy relaxed. He was as glad to see the dogs as they were to see us. Like all carnivores denied a kill for a day, they were accepting of what they couldn't control. They raced home.

We fed them well. We fed ourselves richly—honey and rice cakes before dinner! We stayed up late, playing, exploring, telling stories.

In the morning I gave the dogs water flavored with canned tuna, then loaded the sled. Atop sleeping bag and tent and insulating pads, against a pack of dried grains and cheese and clothes, in front of a six-gallon stainless-steel cooking pot of dog kibble tied inside a burlap bag, I sat Janus.

The mountains north were clear. Clouds overhead that still held the heat to the earth were blowing south to expose clear sky, like the lid of an eye opening.

"Ready?" I asked after I'd secured the house and harnessed the dogs.

Janus nodded emphatically.

"Let's go!" I shouted.

We streaked through the yard, plummeted down the ridge, and dropped onto the creek all in the space of a breath, or, more accurately, a hundred hyperventilating breaths.

The snow on the creek was compressed, its base melted by the slightly warmer water flowing beneath its sarcophagus of ice. The creek bed wove back and forth in lazy oxbows. We were headed north, but often ran east and west and occasionally even back south rather than toward the mountains.

The snows that were billowed on the banks were like marshmallows, but I, a child of Welch's grape jelly and Campbell's soup and Snickers, didn't try to explain my perspective to a kid who knew only organically grown rice and wild berries.

The creek soon rose to a level plain. Our pace slowed as the snow grew softer and deeper. The thermometer I'd lashed to the back of the sled read thirty degrees Fahrenheit—warm for a boy in a snowsuit bouncing around. A cycle of clear cold followed by humid breezes had settled the snowpack. Conditions were perfect for an expedition. Ahead of us was a steep draw between flanking ridges.

I stopped to study my maps. Janus ate a handful of snow, and then a bag full of unsweetened carob chips and raisins that I pulled from my pocket to drop in his lap.

The map indicated that the route led up a hundred feet to a long tundra plain that extended almost uninterrupted to the foothills.

We had traveled two air miles, and a lot more by wandering creek, in less than an hour. Eight more miles to go, and all now direct. I was so exhilarated to find that we were, in fact, easily proximate to the snow peaks, that I couldn't eat the treat that Janus handed up to me over his shoulder.

We began plodding up the draw. Norton didn't hesitate. He

knew where I wanted him to go. I didn't even try to understand his prescience. But his competence was a sign, which I took to mean that possibilities were endless. The other dogs followed as surely as greyhounds behind a rabbit.

"Nnn*nortee*!" Janus cried suddenly.

"Good dog!" I echoed.

I was traveling into the wilderness with so many intuitively wise companions that I didn't for a moment pause to consider my own capacity.

I pushed the sled up the draw, rested panting when the dogs stopped, then pushed some more. At the top of the draw was not the vista I had imagined, but a saddle dipping too gently to be delineated on a hundred-foot contour map.

We picked up speed angling downward and then jerked suddenly to the left, *up* the adjacent ridge instead of gradually forward into the dip, before rising onto the tundra.

"Whoa!" I shouted.

What the hell was my genius lead dog doing?

He was following a trail, a snowmachine trail.

In two years I had seen no indication whatsoever that there were other people out here. And now, suddenly, on our maiden voyage to the corners of the earth: a well-traveled route.

We had no choice but to follow. The dogs were eager for solid footing. I was darkly suspicious and curious to see where we'd end up. Would we find Cyclops or Circe or the Lotus-eaters?

We discovered Penelope and Rex.

But first we passed chain-sawed tree stumps on the side of the trail, sawdust still fresh in parallel lines a foot apart: signs of a trunk cut to firewood lengths. Then we passed, burrowed in the snow where the trail rose steeply, a metal sled piled with gas cans and a small generator: whoever had hauled it this far was not just idly passing through. Then we saw the house in its clearing silhouetted against the sky, white smoke rising from a stovepipe: a lovely little frame house with a sheet-metal roof built at the highest point of the long ridge we had followed for a quick mile or two.

The dogs began to bark as they pulled closer. A man and woman hurried together out the door to stare suspiciously, then to grin, then to wave.

Penelope was tall and lissome. Rex was compact and burly, vibrant with energy.

"You're our neighbors!" he boomed. "Welcome!"

I was relieved that we were welcome because the dogs kept tugging even against my command and the brake and my out-stretched boot planted in the snow. When Norton was just a few yards away from where they stood on their porch, I threw the sled to its side and sat atop it. The dogs stopped. Janus didn't. When he was able to right himself from where he had sprawled in the snow, he went up to the two unfamiliar adults, threw out his arms, and announced, "Ta-da!"

"That man needs some hot chocolate," said the man.

We all went inside and got acquainted.

They had just finished their house that week—after a month of hauling and three weeks of frame construction: plywood and two-by-fours and a *normal* roof easily sheathed. Their trail began at an earlier point along the road than ours, looped back across the road, followed open tundra stretches, and finally curved up the ridge that led to their land. They'd met in a distant Alaskan strip joint, where Penelope was, improbably, the bartendress and where Rex, astutely, had singled her out, a woman among girls. Their desire to build a wilderness homestead grew out of a shared desire to accomplish something of great import that they were hesitant to reveal.

Their hesitancy allowed me to explain myself with commensurate vagueness. But I didn't demur intentionally. I was flabbergasted to find that adult conversation, after undivided attention to a two-year-old, was so complicated that I was tongue-tied.

"Fun!" I wanted to say, by way of explanation.

I could see that they took me to be a little simpleminded, harmless, and friendly.

"Tank yooo!" Janus sang, sipping his hot chocolate, rescuing me from dialogue.

"Yeah," I agreed. "Tanks. I mean thanks."

They exchanged glances and smiled tolerantly.

"We knew you were out here," said Rex, "because it's my business to know what's going on. Know what I mean?" His manner was intense and to the point. He wore a short black beard and a tight black knit cap.

I just nodded.

"Where's your wife?" asked Penelope. Her gaze was no less focused, but her voice was soft, balancing his drive. She wore a pair of man's Carhartt work overalls, but they didn't compromise her femininity.

"Gone," I said, searching for more accurate words, realizing that I'd said enough.

"That's what happens," said Rex conclusively, "unless you're working together for the same dream."

His words were so resonant that I just stared.

"But it's cool," he continued, trying to help me out. "You've obviously got it together enough to drive a good-looking team into"—he waved a hand—"this great unknown." I could see that his disposition, in speech and actions, was to be grand.

"We crossed your trail accidentally," I said, to say something.

He didn't bother to say, "I know."

"But I'm impressed to find a stable couple established so securely in such little time," I added.

I noticed that I had suddenly advanced one small step up from grinning dolt. But it had been comfortable simply to sit nodding without having to be articulate or impressive or responsive. Personality, in isolation, is irrelevant. "Who is this beggar at my door?" asked Ho-san. "What you seem? Or Buddha? In fact! Come in!"

"I like you," I concluded. I liked everyone who liked kids.

Janus extended his empty cup from where he sat in my lap.

"With pleasure," said Penelope. She rose from the floor beside the stove and lifted him to her hip, then went around a plywood partition to the kitchen area.

Their house, perhaps twelve feet by sixteen feet, was tidy: wall-to-wall remnant carpeting, a couch, an armchair, a propane four-burner range—all of which had required a staggering amount of hauling. I knew about hauling. If they'd utilized a helicopter, I would have heard it, even three or four miles away beyond a ridge. But they were closer to the road and had invested in a large snow-machine.

One wall was decorated in Rural Alaskan: a .22, a 12-gauge pump, and a large-bored rifle with a scope. An adjoining wall was covered with a bookshelf, floor to ceiling: *Solarizing Your Home* and *Modern Carpentry, Survival in the Twenty-first Century* (illustrations by Peter Max) and *Soma: Divine Mushroom of Immortality*, Lowry's *Under the Volcano* and *Complete Needlepoint*.

"So just you and the kid, huh?" asked Rex.

"And the dogs and the hills," I said.

"Must be a struggle," he said, lighting a small ivory pipe.

"Not anymore. Now it's a joy."

"Good!" he said with a quick laugh. Smoke snorted out his nostrils. "That heartens me." He handed me the pipe.

He told me how he'd moved from place to place around Alaska investigating the possibilities, acquiring skills, and finally, with Penelope's support, had taken the plunge into the forest to create what he'd always wanted. He still made it plain that he hadn't decided to tell me what that encompassed.

"I'm just glad to be out here for Janus," I said. "He's glad, too."

Penelope sat back down and rested Janus on one of her long legs. "Obviously," she said.

"And you know what?" said Rex, knocking out the pipe into an ashtray and leaning forward. "That's just what he'll be. That's who he is. We'll never be other than what we seem."

"Thank God," I said.

Rex lifted his head and laughed. "Well hey, neighbor," he said. "Glad to finally meet you. It's you and us and that's it."

"We don't think there'll be anyone else," said Penelope. "We checked the roadside last spring and found no other trail except yours. After two years, anyone who was going to homestead would have at least tried."

"But there're fifty other stakings," added Rex. "Land grabbers without guts. Greedy urbanites who hired guides. Real estate is real estate. Owning a piece of the *moon* through ads in *Parade* magazine attracted lots of money. Remember that? And *this* land is something to value. Know what I mean?"

I knew what he meant.

We talked of the weather, of blizzards and floods—not an idle conversation at this latitude. We talked of the weight of snow loads on the roof. Rex convinced me that a foot of snow on my six-hundred-square-foot roof would weigh thousands of pounds. An average winter dropped six or eight feet of snow. We joked about coolies with shovels.

After an hour Janus and I resumed our journey.

Penelope gave Janus a packet of Carnation hot chocolate powder.

"Anytime," called Rex. "Anytime at all!"

We followed the snowmachine trail for a few hundred yards until it veered away from the wide expanse of tundra that headed north. There I had to lead Norton by the collar off the trail and onto the plain. The horizon ahead was a wall of peaks. The central point was Denali. Norton, suddenly, proudly, began leading straight toward it.

"More friends!" I said as we traveled along. "The dogs and the mice and the moose and now Penelope and Rex."

Janus nodded, but without enthusiasm. He was facing into the wind. His cheeks were red. I stopped to burrow him into his bag.

"You can take a nap if you want," I said.

He immediately dropped off to sleep.

I stood on the runners with eyes wide open while cold-wind tears froze on the tips of my lashes. I could see the wide indentation of a glacial canyon far ahead. A dark river of trees was drawn up into it. The round-crested foothills, piercingly white, that sloped down to the canyon seemed fortified by the sharp rock summits rising beyond. I reached out a mittened hand to touch it all, so close did it look. And, by God, I touched it, though subsequently I considered, grudgingly, that it might have been just the pressure of the wind.

The tundra rolled down into creek gullies, then up again to higher plain, then through increasingly straggled bands of trees. We crossed no other trails except those of moose, small predators, and hares.

When we stopped, near tree line, in a grove of stunted black spruce, Janus jumped up from the sled as the dogs collapsed in the snow.

"Time to make a bonfire," I said.

The temperature, as the sky cleared, had dropped steadily. The sled thermometer read eighteen above.

I let the dogs lie as I broke dead limbs from trees and piled them into a depression I'd stomped in the snow. Janus paraded around, moving from me to the dogs, whom he petted, to the campfire branches, which he knelt down to examine. I took the machete from its leather sheath, which I'd lashed to the back of the sled, and chopped down a skinny dead tree.

While I worked, Janus grew slower in his rounds and finally held his hands out to me. "Dod!" he said with alarm.

"I know your hands are cold," I said. "But I'll have the fire going in a minute."

"*Dod!*" he repeated, more emphatically, looking stricken.

I wedged the machete in the cut I was making in the fallen trunk and came to him. I unzipped my parka, drew up my shirt, took off his mittens, and put his bare hands on my belly.

He rolled his eyes and leaned against me. "Ahh," he sighed.

I hugged him tight.

The following day, or perhaps the following week, I realized that I couldn't remember how I'd known so surely the best method to warm cold extremities. Had I read something somewhere? Was it Cro-Magnon racial memory brought suddenly to the surface? I decided, eventually, that it was so plain simply because, in duress, it *was* so plain—as plain as the method for hoisting half-ton logs to the necessary roof, as plain as the caribou that starving Eskimo hunters "see" on the other side of a mountain pass with only stray tracks as indication.

We *knew* this stuff. It was *life*. It was much more obvious than the vocabulary needed to harmonize conflicting perceptions of human relationships. That was *new*, and hesitant, and necessary too, but the current *Oxford English Dictionary* has *hundreds of thousands* more words (*psychiatry, codependent, relationship*) than did Shakespeare's dictionary. And the 1600s were just *yesterday* in the millennia of *Homo sapiens*. We still learn! *Ancora imparo*.

When I'd put his mittens back on and explained, "I'm *hurrying* already," I grabbed black hanging moss from the surrounding trees and lit a wad of it under the branches. (The tinder was obvious.) The flame took off at once. I continued adding sections of the tree until the flame was too hot to approach.

Janus was impressed. He circled the fire. "Ha!" he said. "Ho! Whoo-hoo!"

I took the harnesses off the dogs, then piled snow in front of the sled to anchor it. I took out the cooking pots.

Our fire, now wanly flaming, had sunk a foot down into the snow.

"Bye-bye," said Janus forlornly.

"Wait," I said. "I have an idea."

I hastily whacked down a little tree that still held green needles. Because I had started whacking so intently, without any initial pause, I grunted a benediction with each blow: "Sorry, sorry, sorry."

When the tree sagged and fell, I hacked it into three-foot lengths. Then I lifted the dying embers atop two lengths of green log by digging the freshly cut pieces into the snow of the fire pit and levering them up. I quickly fed more dead branches atop, dropped to my knees to blow, resurrected the flame, and finally planted the last two green wood lengths at the edges.

And so we learned how to make a fire atop snow: with a slow-burning resinous base. Of course!

While Janus torched a stick by holding it near the fire, then waved it brightly over his head, I melted snow in a steel pot.

The daylight faded. I increased the flame. The pot rested securely on the hissing bottom logs.

Fun!

We fed the dogs the way we always fed them, with strokes and love. When we'd set up our tent and snuggled into our down bag it was the way we always camped out in winter, with ease and wonder.

In the morning we climbed to the crest of the foothills, me pushing the sled, Janus pushing the dogs: "Atta boy, Nortee!"

On the other side was a glacier, miles across. Far below, we could see the curving, concentric ripples of crevasses on its lower lobe.

Farther up, we could see the ice walls from which it descended. We could see no sign of life anywhere, until I said, "Do you know that the glacier is alive?"

Then, suddenly, to both our eyes, the landscape woke.

The glacier made sounds—creaks and booms and grunts. The mountains seemed to move in shadows that lengthened visibly with the rapid circuit of the low winter sun. In silence, a slough of an avalanche spread down a slope near the terminus. The wind became breath.

I knew that snow peaks changed from year to year, the result of glacial action or, as the legend suggests, the result of a silk cloth, carried in the bill of a passing bird, that is draped once a year across the summit of the tallest mountain. But even as we looked, our own perceptions—which we expressed as "See that cave up there?" or "Look!"—also changed.

Here landscape was not backdrop. Mountains—in the Himalayas, in the South Pacific, in Japan, in Andean America, even in Greece where Western civilization acquired its expression—house, or simply are, God. Mount Sinai is sacred. The Athabaskans revered Denali. Kanchenjunga, at 28,169 feet the planet's third-highest mountain, has never been climbed—not from lack of ambition or will or technical ability, but because it's holy. God is not backdrop, except to those more involved in their own pursuits.

We were pursuing nothing in particular. We were just screwing around in our backyard.

We reached Mountain Lookout that afternoon. The map I carried had a different name for the high, windswept summit at the far end of the whale's-back range of foothills. But I knew most of the men who had first ascended to these heights and registered their claims with the U.S. Geological Survey, who made the maps. Those men—the climbers, the adventurers—were my age. They lived in Talkeetna or came into town seasonally. This land had not been explored, except by miners who kept to the creek bottoms, until my generation. Just as the common names of plants at upper latitudes varied (bearberry or crowberry or mossberry—*Cassiope stelleriana*), so could the names of the hills. They were ours to define.

We stood watching the long view until a flock of white ptar-migans exploded from a grove of stunted alders down the slope. They rose like a hundred white balloons. They streamed up and away and then circled back behind us.

Janus followed the flock's flight with his whole body, then, facing me on the sled runners, commanded, "*Go!*"

I wheeled the dogs around and we returned to a weathered band of black spruce on the lee side of the ridge. The ptarmigans—all one hundred of them—had blended back into the snowscape.

The disappointment of losing them was mitigated at once by building a new bonfire. One of the arts of parenting is the art of distraction. I used the twig ends of dead branches to make the fire. My unintentionally theatrical blowing on and cussing at the smol-dering twigs entertained him.

The air was colder at our few-thousand-foot-higher camp. The winds were gustier when they blew down from the crest. I worried that I was pushing the child too hard. But he had no perspective to determine "hard" or "normal." To him, the places we traveled were not out at any edge, known or unknown, named or unnamed. They were just where we were, curled inside our tent with a pot of spaghetti, wrapped up giggling in down.

We pissed together out the tent flap in the middle of the night. We woke in the morning with the same simultaneous stretch of arms. When we saw our breaths rising from our mouths like white plumes, we both grinned and blew streamers like dragons.

"Did you know that Cyrano wanted nothing more at the end of his life than his white plume?" I asked the child.

He ignored any speech from me that had a didactic tone. He snuggled closer beside me, examining his breath.

We got dressed and went outside. While I fussed with kindling— no black moss at this elevation—Janus, with confidence and pride, announced that he was going to poop all by himself. He unzipped his snowsuit, shrugged out of the arms, dropped the top half of his suit, bent over, and shit into the suit beneath him, pissing up one dangling arm. When he saw what he had done he laughed.

I laughed, too. "Almost!" I said, carrying him quickly back into the tent to change him into the extra snowsuit I'd brought. I'd brought a lot of extra stuff—clothes, treat food, picture books.

He had assumed his responsibility, and if it hadn't been accomplished without its own evident lesson, he had tried.

We resumed our duties: mine to build a fire, the boy's to play. I eventually lit the fire using a wad of pages from *Walden* as kindling. I carried the book because I'd never read it. I mean no disrespect in reporting that it illuminated the Alaska Range winter.

As soon as I got the fire going, I knocked down the tent. I laid the elastic-corded poles in the snow, rolled the yellow nylon tent fabric into a cylinder, and hurried back to the fire to keep it from languishing. While I cut down another head-high dead trunk, Janus gathered the four gold aluminum-anodized poles—each ten feet long—and stuck them upright in a row, then pulled the rolled tent to their base.

"Tun!" he cried.

I turned from my fire tending and saw four long gleaming poles wavering against the sky. "Yep, sun'll be up soon," I repeated dutifully. I was busy.

When I had the fire roaring, I went back for the cooking pots. I glanced at his game and stopped dead.

The winter sun at 10:00 A.M. was rising from behind the glaciated Talkeetna Mountains across the valley to the southeast. The sun, from where I stood, from where he had cried, shone directly through the tall poles. The tent fabric was bright at their base.

His boreal Stonehenge would be disassembled without a trace in an hour. But I saw it. I was staggered. I am sure he had no awareness that the sun would rise through the arms of his invention. It was only built as a game because we had no Lego blocks. But it was built to imitate light, which was familiar. I didn't even acknowledge in words what he had casually created.

He didn't care. He was involved with hoisting another flaming poking stick over his head.

What impresses me about any art, no matter how accidental or childish, is not that it exists—codified, preserved—but that it hints at how much more there must be residing in human capacity. In the creation itself is the wonder, not in its longevity.

We ate, loaded the sled, and drove back up the slope. A steady breeze met us at the top. We started down toward where the high hill met the terminus of the three-mile-wide Kahiltna Glacier. The farther we went, the stronger the wind blew. It came from the stretch of the glacier that had been hidden behind a range of successively taller foothills.

Within a few minutes we were headed at a twenty-degree angle to a wind so strong that spume rose around my legs, half burying the sled. The thermometer read ten above. The windchill was at least twenty below.

I stopped the dogs to turn them around. "Norton! Come here!" I yelled.

Janus rose up from his nest and said, "Dod!" with great surprise.

Norton gladly swung the team so that their tails and our backs were to the wind.

"Listen!" I said, bending down close to Janus. "You're not old enough to do this."

He just stared at me, obviously annoyed. The edges of his snowsuit hood flapped around his face.

"Aw, come on," I said. "It's too cold for you. This wind'll make your nose fall off. It'll freeze your eyelids shut. Let's go back somewhere and make a really big bonfire. Maybe we can find some more birds. Or a fox! The foxes are all white now, too."

I knew that I was struggling with my own inclinations as much as with his—higher! farther!—but I also knew that we had no business pushing ourselves too far. At least not yet.

He was mollified at the mention of birds and foxes.

We returned along the trail we had made. We neared our camp of that morning. Already windblown snow had softened the edges of our impressions in the landscape. I could barely make out the dogs' frozen feces, our dwindling tracks. I wanted to point out to the boy how incidental we were here, but he announced, "Look!"

He had recognized the half-dozen remaining stunted trees where we had last stopped for the night. It was an obvious identification. But I had been concentrating on everything that was transient. I'd have made a lousy Eskimo.

Most high-northern-latitude people have a different name for each variation of the snowscape that we were traversing—snow that's wind packed, that's sled crusted, that's deeply drifted on the lee side of a slope. I began to acquire my own vocabulary.

We made it home that night. I made a fire in the cookstove before I unharnessed the dogs. I wrapped Janus in a sleeping bag on the floor before I stoked the stove.

Log homes hold heat much longer than conventional houses do because the dense logs radiate the warmth they've acquired even after the furnace has cooled. But they take longer to heat. A bucket of spring water we'd left on the floor remained frozen solid for an hour.

After I fed the dogs, we carried a dinner of raisins and cold-hardened cheese upstairs. It was almost warm up near the ceiling, but we still burrowed in our bag, from recent habit, and checked for visible breath.

We played Let's Think of All the Good Things That Have Happened Today. I recounted strong dogs and bright mountains and exciting wind and bonfires. When I glanced over, Janus was asleep in the crook of my arm.

In the middle of the night I woke, startled.

He was laughing aloud in his sleep.

We hauled firewood, the boy sitting comfortably atop the six-hundred-pound loads of birch. We built a kitchen counter, and he lacquered it black, using a stick to spread the gunk over a piece of carved plywood. We skidded along the bare floor in our socks.

When I noted how empty of furnishings the house remained, I wasn't dismayed. This was a house built for a boy. There were few impediments to the circuit he liked to make of the poles I'd erected in the center of the floor to support the roof and upper floor logs. We could bounce a ball off the walls, and did.

One evening, when we went for our walk, we discovered an ermine in the woodshed. The ermine rose up from among split birch and boldly denounced us for coming too close.

"That's why we don't have any mice living in the house," I explained.

Janus grabbed some birdseed to feed him.

"No, we can't give him seeds because he eats only meat," I said.

We had no meat to leave him. For the first time I wondered seriously how long we'd live here without even trying to hunt.

The next day it snowed. Clouds from the south enveloped the hills, then the ridge beyond our creek. The temperature rose radically.

The following morning I decided that we should keep our trail to the road open. It was becoming swamped by new snow. I harnessed the dogs, who were eager to leave their chains, and we headed into the sodden storm.

I covered Janus's sleeping bag with my army-surplus rain poncho. He was still unhappy. We were wet, and the wet exacerbated the cold. We were colder at a damp thirty-two above than we had been at ten below. This is why knowledgeable bush Alaskans live in the arctic desert of the Interior.

When we reached the road, after hours, we warmed up in the heater blast of the Chrysler New Yorker. Then, as long as we were in the car, we drove up to the highway to leave a "We love you" message for Melissa.

She answered the phone at her preacher's house, our surest point of contact.

She seemed excited to hear my voice. She was even more pleased to hear Janus shout, "Mama!"

In a slip-sliding hour and a half by car we reached Talkeetna. I trusted the dogs to hunker down where we'd stopped them and I'd overturned the sled.

At the preacher's, with warm nods and smiles all around, Melissa said she was ready to go "home."

Her decision seemed a miracle. A miracle contradicts the normal course of nature. The natural course of pain and resentment plows right into antagonism and easily rationalized revenge.

Melissa was a tuning fork resonant with the heart. Some people in Talkeetna joked about her responses to her life—harmonious one day and loudly dissonant the next. Others admired her honesty about herself. I knew, because I knew her well, that her reactions were always based in reality, though at times I was startled by their intensity and variability. Reality is intense and variable, too.

And here we were, nodding and smiling at each other. Maybe tragedy wasn't inevitable, Western mythology notwithstanding.

But before we even drove together as far as the Petersville Road, Melissa and I were fighting.

She banged on the car's passenger side window with her fist and decried my lack of support, my cruelty, my weakness.

I shouted my "rational" replies.

Janus sat rigid in her lap.

The car didn't become stuck in the snow that continued to fall because I didn't lift my foot from the accelerator.

I was so upset I responded like prey at bay. Melissa, of course, responded just as predictably to bared teeth. And Shiites continue to kill Sunnis, and rightists continue to torture leftists, and dispossessed Eskimos drink themselves to death.

Recorded history is a litany of strife. I don't know why I thought I could avoid it.

At the trailhead, Janus and I went home alone. Melissa, still wearing her hopeful parka and boots, drove back to Talkeetna.

When I tried to call, "Good dogs!" my voice broke.

But by the time we reached the tundra, Janus and I were examining fresh moose prints in our trail. The prints were stomped eight inches deep in the snowpack. The dogs stepped deftly among and across the craters.

"A big bull," I said as we both peered off the side of the sled, dogs pulling steadily.

"Yep," he replied.

I had no experience to judge bull tracks from cow, but I'd seen enough moose prints to tell big from small. It occurred to me that it might be obvious to a tracker whether a print was made by male or female. I didn't want to deceive Janus about anything out of my own ignorance. I decided then to learn to understand all the variations of our world's signs—not just animal signs, but climatic and geologic and astronomical, too.

It also occurred to me, as we continued silently through the vault of the tundra with clouds low overhead, that I was suddenly no longer overwhelmed by my concerns about what had happened between Melissa and me. Those signs were important to understand, too, for all our sakes. But they weren't the whole world, and now not even immediate. I had much to learn about forgiveness *and* moose.

With hope and anticipation I whistled the dogs into a trot. Janus, who had been kneeling to study the trail, rolled back to lean against his sleeping bag pillow. From where he reclined he pointed at the lead dog, though he held his arm high, a gesture more of benediction than indication.

Then I, too, saw what he did. The cloud cover ahead of us, north, had begun to draw back from the horizon. A sliver of green light glowed above the distant line of trees.

"It's the aurora!" I cried.

When we got home we completed our chores and then lay in bed. I told him stories about moose and mountains and boys. The house was still warm. We were comfortable.

That became our winter: forays into Talkeetna, where Melissa gracefully or angrily explained my personal incapacities, but where, too, I got from the little Talkeetna library *Tracks of North American Mammals*, and *Birds of Alaska*, and *Alaska's Wildlife*, and *Glacial Topography*. Then there were dogsled runs back home—either me solo when Janus and his mom resumed their very lovely and very important bond, or boy and dad together when it seemed prudent to allow the healing process to continue unimpaired for her.

When I came home alone, I was often too depressed to do anything. I sat upstairs praying for all the capacities I lacked. I had driven Melissa away because of my adamance and relentlessness. I didn't support her in her needs. I couldn't help her fears.

When I was with Janus, we explored and looked at pictures of animals and made up stories about ermines who stood up to shout, "This is *my* home and not even big dogs or bears can drive me away from the woodshed!"

We went on less extended dogsled trips because the winter was growing more severe, but still we went, on warmer days, to see where our creek melted out of the frozen tundra or how far the dogs could follow the trail of a wandering moose. We fed birds from our hands.

By early March—a season of bright sun and deep but settled snowpack—Melissa and I were no closer to mutual understanding. Janus, two months past his second birthday, was no closer to unimpeded speech. But occasionally we all shared an unexpected intimacy, spending a rare night together in a little cabin Melissa had rented off the Talkeetna Spur Road. Janus was plainly happy when Mom and Dad could talk to each other softly, casually. Mom and Dad tried to maintain it.

The closest Melissa and I came to reconciliation was one of those nights when we lay together in a window alcove of her rented cabin after having exhausted our ability to verbally resolve our differences. Melissa wept quietly. I held her, helplessly. Then, bumping and thumping, Janus came down the stairs from the sleeping loft, on his butt. The kerosene lantern had long since gone out. By starlight he ran up to us, unzipped his Dr. Denton pajama suit, and announced gladly, "'Ere, Mom, you hab tum chi-chi. Den you be *awww* better," as he climbed into her lap, his bare chest exposed. We all fell asleep together, holding tight to each other.

Mostly, however, Melissa was resentful that I had abandoned her for the "woods." To me, of course, it was home, a place where Janus was at ease. I had neither the financial nor the emotional means to sustain two homes. Though I tried. The "woods"—Janus's continuous home—was becoming continuously comprehensible. My understanding of people—and all our adamant demands and desires and needs—was becoming continually less so.

Family, by definition, is people, all of us, together. It can't be ignored. It's elemental. But wilderness, by definition, is the absence of people. And it seemed, for its peace, its necessary perspective on how easy life can be if its signs are heeded, just as elemental. And Janus was very happy to be home.

With the late-March nights freezing the day-melted snowpack to a concrete crust, Janus and I returned to Talkeetna. We had discovered that the brilliantly colored little birds that streaked past the window were white-winged crossbills, according to our books, and "uncommon" in the upper Susitna Valley. We had tracked a big predator ("Wolf!" I cried, but then demurred. "Or coyote. Or maybe just a fox. We'll look at our book when we get home") to a ten-foot-tall glacial boulder atop which was a pile of scat. That became Wolf Rock.

Janus liked to go into Talkeetna, never insisting but always gladly, so that he could be with his mom and his two best friends, Ado and Tarus, the four- and six-year-old sons of the late mountain guide Ray Genet and his widow, Kathy. Janus's buddies were maniacally adventurous, so much so that Melissa was apprehensive about their excursions anywhere beyond her watchful sight. I noted—to myself—that she voiced no concern about Janus's going off with me. I was also aware that, for all the difficulties of her life in Alaska, she never even hinted that she'd rather return to New York.

Then, with Melissa's approval, I went off for "just a look-see" into the mountains by dogsled with Mr. Mike.

As a single parent with a "support network" consisting of five dogs and an ermine, I needed to gain perspective on the way I was raising Janus. Since I knew of no book on the art of wilderness parenting, I felt a strong need to learn more about what the land offered and demanded. With no social circles to expand, I began to go in widening spirals into the source of *my* sustenance.

Mr. Mike, the middle-aged, mild-mannered chief engineer at the upper Susitna Valley microwave relay station in Talkeetna, was in "real" life a nineteenth-century (or eighteenth, or seventeenth) explorer who, for fifteen years, each spring on vacation, took his dog team somewhere remote. His goal in life, ignoring the incidental desire to hang on to his job until retirement, seemed to be to become a colorful old-timer with more stories about bears and mountains, terrible cold and death-defying storms than the first Alaskan pioneers. As far as I could tell, he had already reached that point.

But he had never ascended the Coffee River to its headwall glacier, crossed an unexplored high pass onto the upper Ruth Glacier, one of the Denali massif's largest, then to run down the Ruth for thirty miles back to the forests of the Susitna Valley.

On that trip he taught me, by example, how to yank a fully laden dogsled onto one runner while traversing a slope that dropped into an open creek. He showed me how to read the signs of potential avalanche. He explained that the wolverine tracks we followed into the high pass were indications of a plausible trail because wolverines were the most astute long-distance travelers in the north.

Together, as we waited out days of immobilizing storms, we learned how easy it is to eat nothing for three days, supplies exhausted, plans awry, and still have the strength to snowshoe a trail ahead of the dogs in sodden, peanut-butter-thick, late-spring glacial snow without falling in crevasses.

In answer to my anxious questions about our fate, he was so incapable of expressing even the most hypothetical fear that I, too, began to acquire a confidence that experience cannot create but only validates.

That confidence was more necessary than a leakproof roof.

I brought back a raven feather and a chunk of melting blue glacial ice for Janus. Camped at the entrance to the Great Gorge, a short run into the massive Ruth Glacier Amphitheater, precipitously beneath Denali, I remembered my vow to bring Melissa into the snow mountains so that together we could be at the heart of the world. To her, I brought back that vow renewed.

Mr. Mike and I, led by the World's Best Lead Dog, Norton, who had negotiated the last of the crevasses in a whiteout without a snowshoer to chart the way, returned to Talkeetna amidst the last, rotting snow.

Janus and Melissa accepted my offered gifts eagerly and warily, respectively. Then Janus and I went home, bumping and bouncing in the sled.

I felt energized. I asked him how the time had been for him in Talkeetna.

His description was not the usual kid response of "fine" or "okay." He didn't tell me of his games or his friends. He said at once that he'd seen *two* rabbits, a raven in the tree outside his mom's house, *lots* of other birds, and a moose—a big moose—that didn't seem to know him even though he called to it.

That was the moment I relaxed, for then and forever, about his fundamental emotional health. Many children in Talkeetna were the product of broken homes—most children in America have known some marital difficulty—but this child was sustained by the wider world, by moose and birds and snowshoe hares.

When we came to the big tundra lake there was open water lapping atop the ice at the shore. But there was a bright raised strip of compacted trail across the middle of the lake. I hesitated to attempt the direct route, but Norton tugged, and so we started onto the lake. Norton was right: beneath three inches of water the trail was solid and then rose above the water within a few yards, looking even more solid.

I could see frozen bubbles in the black ice on either side of the trail, but I didn't worry: the ice was thick. When we reached the center of the lake and the black ice had melted to blue water, I worried. But there was no turning back now. There was no way to turn. The trail was a floating bridge. Janus stood between my legs, a foot on each runner, practicing driving the sled up the tundra "by himself."

Then the ice ribbon sagged. Before I could shout any command other than, "Hang on!" we were floating. I was up to my waist, Janus up to his neck.

"Gee!" I screamed, driving the dogs, now dolphins, to the right, across the stretch of open water to mushy ice ten feet away.

The dogs swam, the sled dipped but floated, its wood buoyant. I frog-kicked, one hand like a vise on Janus's parka. When we all trembled atop ice that didn't crack beneath us, Janus said, "Made it, Dod!"

"Good thing you hung on," I said.

The dogs, without request, pulled farther away from the lake's open middle.

"I *dwown* if I let go, and I hung on," he announced proudly, almost casually.

"You're pretty good," I said, trying to be casual now too.

I was startled to realize that I had been chuckling to myself even as we had drifted through the freezing water. I knew—perhaps because I was aware that wood floats—that we weren't going to die, that panic was needless.

But I also knew, intellectually, guiltily, that this was a terrible way to raise a child, like heaving him from a pier into the ocean saying, "Okay. Now *swim.*"

He didn't seem to notice. "Yep, made it," he said.

When we reached the shore I wrapped him in my parka and then ran behind the sled until we got home, where I stripped off his clothes and buried him inside blankets and down, which he liked.

That night, in bed, we replayed our adventure. "And Janus held on to the sled until Norton pulled us out of the water," I recounted, "because Janus knows what to do."

He asked for that part to be repeated three times. Then he said, "But my mom don't know, okay?"

I promised him that we wouldn't worry her unnecessarily.

By the middle of May, the winds had shifted to blow from the south, from the Pacific, carrying warmth and the scent of the first green buds pushing up through the still-frozen ground. With the snows confined to patches on the north side of slopes and the first summer vegetation no taller than our shins, we tramped for miles, just to tramp. For a few weeks at this time of year, before the jungle erupted, and for a few weeks in fall when the foliage collapsed, before the first snows, the landscape was exposed like bones.

We found bones—scattered skeletons of birds, the rack of a moose, a skull! It was small, with sharp incisors. A marten? A fox? The boy, too, treated it with reverence. What made the skull more worthy of deference to the life it had contained than the wishbone of a bird? I couldn't say, but I noted that such totems of life induced an instinctive hush.

One afternoon we ambled down the tundra to check on the beavers in the big tundra lake. We planned to sit on their lodge and watch them swim back and forth with branches in their mouths, slap their tails when we threw sticks into the water (boys throw sticks into the water as instinctively as they kneel silently over skulls in the forest). But the lake was calm, and when we reached the lodge it was ripped open.

"A bear!" I said. "A bear tore the beavers' home apart and ate them!"

There could be no other explanation. We found no sign of the beavers. The dense mound of mud and limbs that had walled their lodge was broken and strewn. I couldn't have dug through it with a shovel.

Janus was impressed. He was also wary. He asked me where the bear was.

I said it was way away in the woods.

He asked *where* way away it was.

I said bears don't attack people unless the bears are surprised.

When we walked home I sang songs—loud songs. I sang songs about boys and moose and birds and summertime—but not bears, at his request.

In the first week of June, with the season more advanced than I had remembered it—seasonal variation? greenhouse effect?—we went down to the creek in our shirtsleeves. The temperature was in the seventies in the sun. The sun was everywhere. The creek, surprisingly, was low. Janus decided to take off all his clothes and wade across a riffle. The water was cold. It came up to his waist— shoulders hunched, arms drawn up to his head, fingers dangling— but he made it across, and then, eagerly, came back.

"Made it!" he announced.

I had nothing to reply except, "Yep."

I thought about reminding him that he *always* made it, but then I decided, "Nah."

He knew.

We certainly had our struggles, because he was raised more in mutual pleasure than in disciplined stricture. Any "No, that's *wrong*" from me was greeted with a cool consideration rather than an immediate compliance. But he ended up more prone to nurture life than to control it. Although, when it pertained to his dad, his disposition was to win. And so I would tell him just one more story before sleep.

By midsummer, Alexander came to visit.

He had sent a mailgram that by coincidence I found in the post office box the day after it arrived. I had not checked the mail for almost a month. Janus and I were on our way into Talkeetna.

"Now's the time," said the mailgram. "I'm ready. I'll be at Anchorage International on United 1746 at 4:00 P.M. Thursday. I expect moose Wellington."

I reached the airport ten minutes after his flight had arrived.

He was pacing the waiting area. He was surprised to realize that our meeting, though late, happened at all only because of coincidence.

"You're *that* far away from reality?" he asked, incredulous.

"*You're* out of touch with reality," I countered.

He laughed at my indignation. "After twelve hours of travel, with two in Chicago reading magazines at the newsstand without paying for them and an hour in Salt Lake fending off Mormons with pamphlets, I'm grateful. *Now*."

"I just want you to know what it's like to live here," I groused.

"Really difficult," he said at once.

"You don't know!" I said, and immediately thought, with love and then sadly, of Melissa.

We got a flat tire driving north. My spare was flat, too. I hitchhiked back to a gas station, thirty miles away. When I returned, two hours later, Alexander was grinning.

"Ah yes," he said. "I now understand. It *must* be difficult to be too dumb to check your spare."

We reached Talkeetna in the radiant twilight of midnight.

Alexander was completely exhausted. But he was tranquil. We got out and stretched in front of the cabin Melissa had rented. "I raced out from La Guardia because I needed a respite from all the little complications of my life," he said. "And though you've done your best to keep me anxious, I can't tell you what peace there is here."

Wildflowers bloomed along the side of the road. Nocturnal birds sang in the trees.

"You're starting to see what I see," I said.

He came around the car to hug me. "I see a liar who wrote me about how *easy* life is in the woods," he said. "But I see that you're right, in your way. And I'm looking."

Melissa's roadside log cabin seemed idyllic beneath silver-point cumulus and spruce. "She said it was all right to sleep here," I said.

"You've told me six times already," Alexander replied.

When we crept through the door Melissa was waiting for us. She lay in the alcove, a kerosene lantern lit. She rose in her nightgown and came to hug Alexander. He lifted her off the floor.

"As soon as the door opened," she said, "I *knew* that blessings had entered here."

"No thanks to Nanook," said Alexander. "Did you know that your pimp-mobile runs on three cylinders and barks?"

"We have to be quiet," she whispered. "Janus is asleep upstairs."

At the mention of Janus she turned to me and easily put her arms around me. I knew suddenly, too, that blessings surrounded.

"Are you hungry?" Melissa asked Alexander softly.

He shrugged. Then he stepped a few feet to the stove, rose up like a shock victim in an oxygen tent, inhaling deeply, and said, quietly but emphatically, "Mrs. Paul's fish sticks with *mayonnaise*!"

Melissa laughed aloud, then quickly put a hand to her mouth. "Salmon *en croûte* with mustard glaze," she hissed.

We ate sitting on the floor with knees touching. The kerosene lantern illuminated our faces. Blue light came through the windows.

"Why did you come?" asked Melissa.

"Because I knew that your lives in this kind of world were so much more sustaining than mine in the city," he replied.

"Ha," said Melissa.

"Ho," I said.

"And I didn't know anyone in Tibet," he added.

"It's *more* complicated out here," Melissa said, "because we can't escape from each other."

"Sort of like telephone answering machines," he said wryly.

"We're going to hike home and then climb Denali," I explained to Melissa.

"Rick does seem to have an awareness of the land," she said to Alexander. "Or else he's just been very lucky. But he'll be a good guide."

I was surprised to hear her supporting me.

"I've already made out my will," said Alexander, "and told my mother that I love her."

"Just make sure you remember what *you* want here," she added, "or he'll try to take you too far."

"From the top of the summit," I announced, raising a finger over my head, "we can lift into stars."

"I'll wait to see if we can get past the bears first," he said.

Alexander woke early. He nudged me, then nudged me again. "I always wake with the dawn," he explained. "I can't help it."

"It's been 'dawn' the whole night," I said.

"Guides don't snore until noon," he said.

I went upstairs to kiss Melissa and Janus in their sleep. Janus lifted his arms to my head and said, without quite waking, "Dod."

I heard the door open and Alexander go outside. I lingered anyway.

When we reached the end of the road to start on the trail, I handed Alexander a mosquito head net before we'd even gotten out of the car.

He put it on at once, grimly. "I feared as much," he said. "But what do we wear against bears?"

"Faith," I said. I had taken an empty tin can from Melissa's trash in which I put pieces of gravel from the road, but I didn't show it to Alexander at first. I figured that our conversation would make enough sound to alert any bear to our passage.

I'd never actually seen a bear on the trail.

But as soon as we broke out onto the tundra, where I had planned to expound on the beauty of open space after the narrow path through the jungle, where I had kept up a monologue on the fecundity of the boreal summer, we saw a black bear cavorting on the other side of the lake. The bear ran, rolled, dug its muzzle toward some mouse or scent in playful game, and disappeared into the trees.

"That's what I've been so worried about?" said Alexander.

"That was probably Bob," I said. "He's our friend."

Alexander watched the spot where the bear had slipped into the woods. He watched the spot for a full minute. "And 'Bob' is now so far away that there's not the slightest chance that he might be . . . there," he said, but it was more a question, and it wasn't spoken with any suggestion of relief.

"Well, bears can be almost as unpredictable as people," I said.

Alexander gave no indication that he was ready to move.

"I've got bear repellent in the pack, too," I said, dropping my pack to take out the can. "See? A metallic noise spooks them." I rattled the can filled with stones.

Alexander lifted his mosquito net and took the can in hand to study. "Much better than a big gun, I'm sure," he said.

"My lead dog is almost the size of a small black bear," I said, trying to be encouraging.

Alexander waved the can as much to fan mosquitoes from his face as to test its efficacy. "No good Buddhist passes a prayer wheel on the trail without spinning it," he said, "just to acquire a little more notice from the gods."

We talked loudly as we continued up the tundra. "You didn't tell me that this stuff is like walking through quicksand!" he shouted as we squished across the wettest part at the perimeter of the lake. "I'm getting very *ti-ered*!"

"That's what keeps us safe from salesmen playing with the *dooor* buzzer!" I sang.

With each step, Alexander shook the can like a marimba.

We took a rest break once we'd reentered the forest a few hundred yards from the house. We were both sweating. The sun on the tundra had been unshaded. Alexander coughed up some phlegm and spit a hawker into the head net he'd forgotten he was wearing. He wasn't amused. He took off the head net and shook it clean. I noticed that he didn't swat at the mosquitoes that immediately swarmed to his face. He had acquired his morality in a monastery in the Himalayas. He made me feel guilty for my own casual killing.

"Let's just get there," he said, putting the net back on, finding no rest.

When we got there, Alexander didn't stop. He dropped his pack, then his head net, and walked around in the breeze of the clearing. The dogs barked wildly. The mountains dominated the horizon.

I waited on the porch. When he returned, he held up a finger. "First, I feel safe, finally, with the dogs around. Second"—he raised another finger—"I can relax without those science-fiction mosquitoes and without worrying that we might have to hike forever. And third"—he held up all ten fingers—"I have more energy, suddenly, than I can remember in . . . a long time. In a long time."

"So does that mean you like it here?" I asked, relieved to see that his answer was so plain.

Alexander was the first visitor to the homestead since the house had been built. His reaction was vital to me. I had feared that he might see nothing but rural poverty and a weirdly wrought log cabin and a tenuous toehold in the overpowering forest.

"That depends on whether we have to eat roots and grubs," he said.

"Beans and rice," I said.

"What happened to moose Wellington?"

"I haven't yet decided to kill animals for food," I said.

He sighed. "And here everyone expects me to return with a sampler of seal blubber and raw whale meat and, of course, a coonskin cap."

Norton suddenly came bounding up to me with his chain streaming behind him. I staggered back as he jumped at me. On his hind legs, his muzzle pushing at my face, he was as tall as I was.

The rest of the dogs broke into renewed frenzied howls.

Instead of stepping away from the huge, unfamiliar husky, Alexander dropped to his knees and said, "Here, boy."

Norton turned and, with a two-year-old's enthusiasm, leaped at him. Alexander wrestled him to his back while Norton kicked.

Alexander stroked his belly. Norton lay inert.

" 'And then when the wild wolves attacked,' " I narrated, " 'Pierre of the North Woods soothed them with his touch.' "

"Mainly because Pierre saw that their world was more embracively joyous than the world where Pierre waited at curbside for a cab to La Guardia while a cokehead tried to get him to sing 'Raindrops Keep Falling on My Head' in falsetto."

"Pierre," I said, "who yearns for a coonskin cap, would never use a phrase like 'embracively joyous.' "

"Pierre figured he should adopt the effusive speech of Nanook, his host," he explained, nuzzling Norton.

We hooked Norton back at his house, then fed the dogs. Alexander showed no sign of being jet-lagged, sleep-deprived, culture-shock blasted.

I took him on a tour down to the spring, of which I was proud.

"That's a hole in the ground," said Alexander.

"Yeah," I said. "I know. That's our spring."

"That," repeated Alexander, "is a hole in the ground."

"Well, actually," I explained, "the spring bubbles up *atop* the ground, but I dug a little pool to be able to dip from it."

"I'm afraid there's gunk in it," he said gravely.

I knelt down and with my fingers sieved up floating pieces of leaves and stems. "Just organic matter," I said.

Alexander lifted a hand, waggled a finger, and called, "Waiter! Here! I'll have a mineral water on ice with a . . . twig."

I ladled five gallons into a plastic bucket. "This is dishwater, too," I said. "And because we don't use soap, it then goes into the dog buckets, still warm and scented."

Alexander bent over the pool and, surrounded by overhanging ferns, lifted a cupped palmful to his lips. He drank.

"Forgive him for all the times hence he might take this for granted," he said simply.

When we went inside the house Alexander said nothing. He looked around. The room smelled faintly of pine, and glistened.

"And that's your stove," I said, nodding toward the bright chrome trim of the wrought-iron cookstove.

"That's what I helped bring here," he said matter-of-factly.

He went upstairs while I lit a fire. I heard the floor creak when he sat on the bed.

"Last week I rode back with Joe Papp from the Hamptons," he said without raising his voice, "and had a few drinks from the limo's bar and was amusing. I got out with an invitation to a dinner party, then showered and went to Studio, where I seduced the top model for Calvin's new Obsession campaign. The next morning I sent you the mailgram."

"Even Pan got sated," I called.

"No," he said, after a pause. "I like the life. I've chosen it. For now. I know I'm living out this society's fantasies. *My* fantasies, too. That's what worries me."

I was silent. I put a pot of beans on the stove.

He continued. "In ten years—what? The power of guiding my own business to a listing on the New York Stock Exchange? Returning to Darjeeling to do another hundred and eleven thousand one hundred and eleven prostrations so that I can become holy? More grapes?"

"I simple homesteader, sahib," I said. "I have no answer."

"So I wanted to see what you'd found out here," he continued, "because I really couldn't imagine it."

I heard the flooring creak again. I could hear him draw a deep breath.

"And it's still hard to believe," he said softly, though his voice carried. "Any of it. The bears or the wolves or the sanctity."

"You haven't even met Janus, either," I said. "He's a lot of my reason for being here."

"He knows," he said.

By the time our dinner was cooked, Alexander was asleep. I didn't wake him. I ate, went outside, and just stood. I hoped that we wouldn't have bad weather on Denali in a day or two. That was as far ahead as I could imagine. It wasn't troubling.

I woke to a snort of laughter.

"Sorry," said Alexander. "I was thinking about Armageddon."

"That's funny?"

"Well, not that. Just you."

I tried to retrieve my dream of riding on the back of a moose.

"I mean," he said, "I walk through the steam rising from manholes on lower Broadway and worry about how long it'll be before Manhattan sinks into the sea. The millennium is, after all, approaching. But it just occurred to me that you'll be sustained here."

"I'm scared of the blast of my own gun," I said.

"Oh, raw meat, beans, wood grubs—whatever. I wasn't thinking of survivalists in camouflage fatigues peering through periscopes from bomb shelters. But we've all grown up terrified of *some* allegorical bomb: cancer, aging, loneliness, despair—some inevitable catastrophe that a world obviously out of whack reminds us of every day. But *this* world isn't teetering on the brink, not out here. I'm . . . well, I'm surprised."

I sat up. "But what about Darjeeling? What about your Rinpoche's monastery? What about *that*?" I asked, pointing to the framed picture of the Himalayas that he had given me when I left New York.

"Oh, I told you years ago how I had to bribe every Indian official almost continuously to remain there on my tourist visa. And even in the monastery there were politics. *You've* walked through Nepal. You know that every arable acre is tilled. There are people everywhere and they all have their petty demands. Tibet's an occupied territory. I really don't want to talk about it."

I hadn't meant to argue. I was sorry that I had disturbed his reverie.

"We can pick fiddlehead ferns to sauté for breakfast," I said. "There's a grove down at the creek."

"Beans and rice are fine," he said. "I'd like to pass through this land altering it as little as possible."

He ate two big bowls of reheated, imported food.

Before we left for the road, we climbed up to the roof of the house to study the mountains. I named each peak that I knew—Mount Silverthrone, the Moose's Tooth, Alder Point, Mount Deception, a dozen others—announcing their elevations. Even as I tried to make the Range familiar to Alexander I was aware that it was a useless task: from a distance the peaks could be charted, but deep among them was another world beyond facile description.

Alexander listened dutifully. When I finished he said, "So now I guess we know where all the crevasses are."

We boarded up the cabins against bears, nailing scrap plywood over the windows. Any bear could rip through the shield at will, but I needed some semblance of security to leave the homestead unattended by guard dogs.

I planned to take them into Talkeetna, in the back seat of the Chrysler New Yorker. Alexander and I would be gone for ten days or so, and the dogs needed to be fed.

Then we harnessed the dogs to the sled. I had never before run them in the summer. I didn't tell Alexander. He was surprised enough to think of all seven of us in one passenger car.

I didn't tell him because I didn't want him to worry about my ability as a guide. Would I take him on an adventure I knew nothing about? Of course! But I wondered, just before I released the line holding the sled to a tree, what it *would* be like to run five manic dogs over roots and stumps.

"I'll wait for you on the tundra," I said. I unclipped the line.

The dogs took off like an Indy 500 pole car. When we crossed over the first exposed tree root the sled lifted off the ground as if from a ramp. In midair, the sled banked to the left. I leaned to the right. Spruce needles scoured my face.

The sled hit the ground on one runner. I removed my feet from the runners to stand on the brake: a semicircle of aircraft aluminum with two six-inch steel wedges angled down like fangs. The brake ripped two grooves in the earth. When we passed over buried roots I shot up, atop the brake, like popcorn. I held the bowed handlebar at chest level in a death grip. It was suddenly obvious that if the sled slammed into anything—trunk, stump, boulder—I'd break ribs before somersaulting.

"Whoa!" I screamed.

Norton slowed. The trailing dogs took his slack as a sign to pass him.

We careened down the trail.

Suddenly Dick, the wheel dog, the dog closest to the sled, planted both hind feet and began to crap. He was dragged by his neck line. The sled slowed from warp speed to supersonic speed.

"Good boy, Dick!" I cried. My molars crunched together as I jerked up and slammed down.

Zoom, in front of Dick, moved by his sudden activity after a morning of torpor, eased himself, too. Dick leaped to the border of the trail to avoid stepping in Zoom's relief.

I kept my jaws clamped tight.

The sled angled sideways to glance off a birch trunk. Then Van Dyke, deciding that it was now or never, began her toilette, decorously waddling with spread hind legs while her urine splashed from side to side.

The initial rush was eased. The dogs couldn't regain their momentum with my feet planted together atop the brake.

When we entered the tundra the brake dug up enough innocent matted plant life to mass a mound of ballast. The sled runners, no longer greased by dew-slick roots, bogged. We stopped.

I was panting. My armpits, my crotch, my palms were soaked with pungent adrenal sweat.

"Stay whoaaaa," I growled.

The male dogs casually lifted one leg and marked their turf. All five looked round with pride. They were well-conditioned athletes in their prime who had just set a record.

Five minutes later Alexander came running up, his pack slapping against his back. He looked anguished.

"Are you all right?" he gasped.

"No problem," I lied.

"Is that *normal*?" he said.

"I'm not sure," I replied.

"That," he said, "I believe."

I asked him to kneel in the sled as we went down the tundra. The extra weight and the drag on the runners kept us all at a fast walk, though the dogs strained.

"So is this traditional Eskimo technique for summer travel?" he called over his shoulder.

"This works," I said. "Thankfully. Doesn't it beat walking?"

Alexander took off his pack and sat on it, legs stretched out. "Onward, vassals!" he said. He picked salmon-colored cloudberries as we passed.

At the bottom of the tundra we stopped to unclip each dog, except the leader, from its tug line. They all remained attached to the main line only by their neck cords. Even then, with the dogs pulling only by the collar, the sled resumed a jolting pace through the forest. Alexander, unwilling to remain in the sled without thick padding, walked, jogged, stumbled, and swore.

We didn't speak again until we reached the creek. I had my hands full trying to keep the sled from launching into trailside trees. Alexander had his lungs full trying to keep up.

It was early July and the creek was low, its flood runoff abated. But it was still an obstacle.

"Now what?" said Alexander when he'd caught up to the sled.

"Now I don't know," I said, and then added impulsively, "Okay! Let's go!"

Norton stepped into the current and without pause began swimming to the far bank. I hopped off the sled and ran, precariously, across the cottonwood bridge. Norton clambered up the bank, shook himself cursorily while the dogs behind treaded water, and then pulled the rest of the team out of the current. The sled stuck against the shore, listing, but floating.

I pulled the prow free and, voilà!—we were across.

"Saber," called Alexander from the other side of the creek, refer-ring to his parents' golden retriever, "would have taken the sled over the bridge."

"But wasn't that just the way it should be?" I insisted, flush with my newfound ability. "Wasn't that easy?"

Alexander mumbled his reply into his head net as he carefully crossed the bridge.

While the dogs finished spattering us with their fur-wringing shakes, Alexander said, "Honestly, now. How much of your life here is so ad hoc?"

I grinned. "All of it."

At the road, we put our packs in the trunk, Norton between us on the front seat, and the other four dogs in the back with enough room left over for the president of Chrysler Motors.

We unloaded the dogs at the sitter who cared for Denny's team. As we chained them up, corralling my pups by the collar to keep them from Jake's jaws, I tried to explain Denny to Alexander. I was aware that I exaggerated almost everything: "One of the best bush pilots in Alaska." "An American hero who spurned material comfort for a wilderness Xanadu."

Six months prior, on a weekend stint in Anchorage to make some fast dollars, I had, while driving my cab, sipping at a bottle of Harvey's Bristol Cream sherry that I kept between my legs (work in Anchorage had become *old*), written a longhand entry to the "Best Bear Story" contest being run by the lesser of Anchorage's two daily newspapers. The prize was two hundred bucks. When the paper's outdoors editor tracked me down a month later—by coincidence I was in Talkeetna ("Yo! Rick! Someone's on the phone in the Fairview for you!")—he'd asked, "Is this all true?" I laughed. I asked him how long he'd been in Alaska. "Two months! From Chico, California." I explained that *every* Alaskan bear story is true. "Out here," I'd said, "we have no need to exaggerate."

I got my two hundred dollars.

After securing the dogs we went to the airstrip, where we had chartered a flight with one of the air taxis. Melissa and Janus were there to meet us.

"This is your uncle Alexander," I said to Janus, who immediately hugged Alexander's thighs.

Alexander picked him up and said, in a stage whisper, "Will you let your mom come with us for a few hours?"

Janus was perplexed. Melissa and I were more so.

"We want to fly her to the mountains," Alexander explained to Janus. "She'll come right back very happy."

Janus gave Alexander a scrunched-faced, one-and-a-half-lidded wink. Alexander laughed and wrapped him closer.

All of the tumblers of the combination lock fell into place for me. "Just to Base Camp," I said, ad hoc, to Melissa. "Just to fulfill my vow that we'll go into the mountains together."

Melissa looked stunned. "I'm not . . . I'm not prepared at *all*," she said.

"Would you like to come?" asked Alexander.

"Well, of course," she said. "But . . ."

She took a step back and said to me, "Look, I baked you coconut bread and made pita sandwiches to take with you. Just cooking for you again before a climb is weird enough."

We called "Aunt" Tanya from her helicopter maintenance across the airstrip to care for Janus.

The plane took off with Alexander in the copilot's seat and Melissa and me wedged together atop our gear in the back. As soon as we'd crossed the Susitna flood plain to cruise above the seemingly endless forest, I began, once again on the mountain flight, to laugh a lunatic laugh, for no reason, for every reason. "Look!" I said to her.

She looked at me. Her eyes were clear. She reached for my hand.

When we landed on the Southeast Fork of the Kahiltna Glacier, all eyes were on the mountains. We jumped out as soon as the plane had taxied to a stop. We carted our gear away from the makeshift runway. Our pilot went up to the tent of the radio operator to chat.

The peaks overhead reflected cloudless sun. The air was warm. A three-man expedition waiting to return to Talkeetna from their climb lounged in their polypropylene underwear, indicating no hurry to leave the glacier.

Melissa, Alexander, and I stomped in different directions in the snow, trying to reach some private perspective with which to see each other and ourselves. Alexander said nothing. I said nothing. Melissa, after a while, called to me, "I guess this is some kind of completion." In the brilliant light I could see, even from a distance, that her eyes were filled with tears.

At the moment that I reached her to take her into my arms, the pilot shouted, "Gotta go!"

Our parting was unexpected, and much too soon, but definite. She ran for the plane. "Janus needs you," she said from the door of the plane.

Alexander and I watched the Cessna 185 quickly become a gnat against the snow peaks. Then we set up our tent.

I am privileged to quote now from Alexander's diary that he kept for his latest and, ultimately, last lover.

Monday, 7/4. I wish you could see where I am: a snow-crusted glacier 7,200 ft. up a narrow valley surrounded by incredibly cut peaks, where the sun is so bright on the snow that a day without goggles would mean blindness, and Sun Block 15 does little. Every once in a while there's a roar as rock and snow crack free and avalanche down one of the surrounding peaks. It stays light here all night, making it hard to decide when to sleep—we had dinner at midnight after being flown up in a small plane that passed within 20 feet of one crest.

There are at present only three other people here besides us, and some thirty-odd people out over the next 10,000 feet in various stages of assaulting the mountain, Denali. On June 24th—ten days ago—a woman fell into a crevasse and died, in the area we'll be going thru tomorrow. I've had more of a sense of danger in this state than in New York—down in the forests from grizzlies, up here from crevasses, falls, and cold. No one's fooling around here!, and everyone's so competent. All the senses are sharpened as needs become simplified, and with it grows a detached calm that's so rare where there are people.

Tuesday. Last night two climbers snowshoed in from the 14,000-foot camp and advised us to go up at once because the crevasses were opening, and would soon be impassable. So at 9:30 in the night we hastily packed up and left Base Camp. The glacier remained in light for several more hours afterwards. It was fantastic to be traveling over a snowy terrain in the softened light, slowly plodding as Rick dragged our sled. There *were* many crevasses, and in two places holes where people had broken thru, as we'd heard. As one of us would cross, the other would be on guard to plunge his ice axe into the ground so as to anchor himself from being likewise pulled in by the safety rope connecting us.

Thursday. Yesterday we woke to sleet and a virtual white-out, which occurs when a cloud shares the same space as you. Cold, damp, and very strange. The sky and ground are all the same color, glowing, eerie, refrigerator-white. Rick was all for packing up camp and hiking higher but I wouldn't hear of it.

Saturday. 12,000 feet. Yesterday the morning had been "the usual" but the sky had cleared enough to energize our departure. The trek began with a straight-up ascent of a very steep hill, no mean task at this elevation dragging a sled, up to your knees in snow. Each step was slow and painful. At this altitude it's colder than below, cold enough for snow. I woke at 2:00 A.M. to a tremendous wind ripping our tent, and I was sure it would be torn away at any moment, leaving the purple cocoon of my sleeping bag exposed to the elements. After an hour, however, the gusts did die down. We had planned to hike another 1,000 feet to "Windy Corner," beyond which you can't go without crampons, but I have lost my desire to do so, and am feeling cranky, tired, and a bit headachy. Besides, not many views are any good in a storm, and tho Rick claims it's clear up there, I don't believe it.

5 hours later. Practically kicking and screaming, I agreed to go up to the pass with Rick, mainly because lying in the tent all day had made me very cold and restless. The closer we climbed, the clearer the sky grew, until incredible vistas began to appear behind us. At the top a whole new panorama unfolded of Denali, still misted, the West Buttress gleaming in the sun, Mt. Hunter spectral above the clouds. Words cannot describe the joy of the moment, more than the sum of the exhilarating climb, the pure air, the utter quiet, the majesty of peaks. The light highlights any object with a preternatural glow—rocks thrust up, cracked and split by sun and snow. Everything seems so perfect, pure, and beautiful; earth and man so far away. The exhilaration, freedom, and peace that I felt while up there are beyond anything I've ever experienced. I had, for once, a sense that all was well, and that living held so much potential, and was worth all the confusion. How great Man would be if he lived on mountains and not in cities! How clear everything is, if only for moments, in a world of such purity and beauty! We hiked thru the snow around the Corner, heedless of the dictum that crampons were needed to prevent slipping off the icy slope into crevasses, knowing we were blessed and immortal this one day.

On the eventual way down, Alexander confided that he'd been sick for months before coming to Alaska, though he was vague about describing what his ailment entailed. "But I'm whole now," he said, grinning.

I assumed that his illness had been malaise. I didn't question his joy.

When we staggered into Base Camp the radio operator greeted us with, "Phone call for you," looking at me.

The jest, though inexplicable, seemed droll. "Tell 'em I'm still in the stratosphere," I said.

Then I heard the radio crackle with, "Rick? Are you all right?"

It was Melissa, from the office of our air taxi. It was a preposterous coincidence. But I dropped my pack and went for the mike.

"How did you know we were back?" I said.

"I knew," Melissa said.

"We didn't make the summit," I said.

"Thank the Lord," she replied.

A few hours later Alexander and I were airborne. The plane droned above chasms of blue crevasses, then banked into the slot that would bring us out into the upper Susitna Valley. We slipped between black rock and white snow. And then we saw green.

It was like descending in *Apollo 11* to discover a coconut palm oasis on the moon. It was Arcadia. It was *alive*. It was home.

But then, for the first time in my three—now four—crossings of the valley by airplane, I noticed dark grooves in the tundra. I saw a straight, thick line, then two, like ballpoint pen scratches across a map.

"That's from ATVs!" I shouted at Alexander where he sat next to the pilot. "All-terrain vehicles! Balloon-tired go-carts. Hunters use them to rip up the land on their way to blast game!" The machines, new to Alaska, becoming exponentially more popular with each season, allowed motorized access to summer lands that previously had been the province of hoof, foot, and paw.

I climbed closer to his ear. "People are starting to find ways into this valley," I cried. I had been secure in the isolation of our homestead, but now, suddenly, I could see the proximity of others like me—just like me: *Homo sapiens* spreading into every ecological niche—but who had come for different reasons.

"Can you see those tracks?" I demanded loudly, though I was leaning right beside him. "This valley could be overrun like everywhere else! What are we going to do?"

Alexander didn't turn from his window view. He seemed unmoved. He said simply, "Just what you're doing now."

I was suddenly as reality-overturned, as mood-swung, as full of not-quite-contained fear as when I'd first come out of the forest to try to talk with Melissa in the Teepee about her religious conversion.

Before I could reply Alexander calmly added, "Haven't you just seen what can never be lost?"

250

The plane hit an air pocket. I jerked up, bumping against his head.

"What's necessary," he added, reaching out to touch my forehead, "will remain."

I drew back to pursue my case, to make him see that even here—here!—in one of the last untrammeled landscapes on earth, holiness was beginning to be reduced to just another Winnebago overlook. But he wasn't paying attention to me. I felt like a shareholder trying to interest a Buddhist monk in a hundred-point drop in the Dow Jones Industrial Average.

I looked out the window. I now saw no tracks. I saw only amber tundra, sea green forest, blue lakes that had been dug into the earth by the advance and retreat of glaciers.

The plane veered and swooped in a sharp descent. My stomach veered and rose into my throat. We roared over a log cabin. Forest—then a tiny clearing—became forest, forest upon forest. The pilot glanced back to give me a nod while I struggled to choke down the bile in my mouth.

The cabin, I knew dizzily, had been my home, visible for an instant, and then hidden again in trees. Finally we crossed the Anchorage-Fairbanks highway and then, a minute later, the Susitna River, to land smoothly on the small airstrip of Talkeetna.

Alexander got out to hug Melissa and Janus. I dropped onto the runway with my head reeling from air sickness, but also from what I'd just seen. When Janus ran to me, I lifted him up, fell to my knees, and drew deep breaths to establish my equilibrium. His touch made it easy.

"Well, you certainly look like a climber," said Melissa, standing over us. "Blasted and burned and glad to be back."

"It's still all there," I said. "Still."

She squatted beside us and hugged us both. "You too," she said.

I could see Alexander going into the air taxi office to pay the bill, but I was too weak to argue with him over the tab.

"How are you?" I asked Melissa.

"Just waiting," she said easily. "As always. But learning how to make the time for me good."

The summer in full bloom was too overwhelming for me to pursue the conversation. The breeze was warm and river-bottom humid. The scents were giddy—pine and flower and earth and the warm glow of my boy. Some kinds of isolation do heighten fear and joy.

Alexander came back to ask if it was all right for him to head back to New York. I was dumbfounded.

"So soon?" I said.

"I'd like to take what I've found home. I want to just sit with it for a while," he replied, "before it fades. I don't doubt that it will fade."

Janus asked for some ice cream, "Now."

Alexander, just for an instant, was uncertain. Then he said, "I *love* ice cream."

"I told him we'd all have a party when you got back," confided Melissa.

Alexander hoisted Janus to his hip and said, "*I* want *two* scoops."

I said an unusually quiet goodbye to Alexander at the Anchorage airport. Then I returned to Talkeetna, where Melissa explained that her ease, while Alexander and I were climbing, was due to an "internationally known" climber whom she had "just begun to know," who "accepts me for just what I am."

I slept in the back of the car that night. I slept twelve hours, grateful for her calm, hurt by her distance, but serene.

The next day, without the slightest ripple in parting from Melissa, Janus and I went home. "I love you!" Melissa called, indiscriminately, as we drove away.

Janus was overjoyed to have all the dogs piled in the car around him. He crawled from front seat to back, petting each dog. "Nortee! Dick! Zoooom!"

Midday sun heated the car. The electronically controlled windows, lacking electronics, unable to be rolled down, encapsulated us in doggy-breath-damp, greenhouse-hot warmth. I savored it.

When I tried to tell Janus about the mountain realm where I'd just been he paid little attention. He'd seen the mountains, stood on their flanks, stared into their winds. What could I say that he didn't already know?

Besides, this was deep summer, in a tropical car. He helped me to admit that just where we were was exciting enough. Especially since I knew, but he didn't, what a dogsled ride over roots and stumps would be like.

We clipped the dogs only by their neck lines. I rested Janus atop a pack filled with cans of tuna, sliced pineapples, peeled tomatoes, and our just-in-case rain gear. He leaned back against a plastic garbage bag in which were the down parkas and bags Alexander and I had used.

The extra weight in the sled slowed our passage enough to keep it fun, as opposed to terrifying.

Then we slid over a huge conical mound of bear scat.

The dogs began tugging faster.

My knees went weak, which, in fact, aided the ride for me. But if we ran into a bear on the trail, I'd have no ability to stop the dogs from eagerly accepting the challenge.

"Well . . . I don't care if it's rainy or cold / Long as I got my Janus Lee-oh / Riding in the basket of the sled," I began to sing at the top of my voice.

I had read that for every one bear encounter there are three hundred times when the bear, in its superior wisdom, shies away from the meeting.

"And . . . I don't care if it's hard or a joy / Long as I got my Wonder Boy / Riding in the basket of the sled."

"Dod," he called. "Shut up."

He wanted to listen to the forest, not to me.

I lost firm control of the sled only once, descending a small hill where the trail bent around a tree at the bottom. I dragged behind the sled on my knees (big bruises the next day), my bloodless hands glued to the handlebar. Janus's head slapped against one of the wood railings of the sled. He whined. I pulled myself back upright on the runners and stopped the team. I held my boy until he didn't hurt. Then we continued.

When we got home, while the dogs rolled on their backs scratching and the boy rolled around with them, I ran to the little cabin—our storage shed now—and returned with a discarded throw pillow and some twine. I cut the foam of the pillow in half with the machete and lashed it to the upper railings of the sled where a small head might get whanged on a rough trail. One more unexpected difficulty had been surmounted.

After chaining the dogs we took the plywood from the windows. Janus was surprised that the threat of bears ripping into the house required such safeguards, but he didn't seem even remotely concerned that such an event would happen.

I yanked a nail from the base of the split-log door and we went inside together. I felt as though we were entering the great hall of Valhalla, the final resting place, the reward-that-doesn't-vary. Janus paraded around the floor, touching the table, the kitchen counter, the stove. He turned to me where I still stood beside the door and said, simply, " 'Om, Dod."

" 'Om," I replied, bass voiced, raising one hand palm out.

He narrowed his eyes trying to decide what I was really trying to say, then announced decisively, "Time to eat!"

I fired the stove and made pasta.

That evening, on our ritual walk, we found the outhouse's two-inch-thick construction-grade Styrofoam seat (a decided creature-comfort advantage of woods life compared with the cold porcelain of cities) clawed to pieces. But we found no other evidence of the visiting bear.

Then we walked along the creek. We followed the game trail on the bank through towering grasses. The boy made forays into vegetation twice as tall as he was.

He found a duck's nest. There were six eggs in it.

"Let's take one!" said the eager hunter.

I told him they should remain where they were so their mama could hatch them.

He asked, carelessly, if he could throw one in the creek, hoping to lay his hands on anything that could extend his power.

We left the eggs where they were but read, that night in bed, from a paperback that Alexander had mailed us a year ago, *Care of the Wild Feathered and Furred.* It described how to heal broken wings and shotgun survivors and abandoned infants. Chapter 1 counseled leaving nests alone.

The next morning we crept quietly through the grass, to see the female burst from her nest ten yards away. Janus was the one who decided not to get any closer to the nest.

On our walks we explored the forest fearlessly. Even on the occasions that called for prudence (dogs barking down the ridge in the morning, fresh scat by the creek the night before), when I carried along the shotgun, Janus gave no indication that he worried. He didn't try to stay close to me. Nor, however, did he try to march away to "prove" to himself or to me that he was brave. Either action would have revealed apprehension.

I knew that the upper Susitna Valley had no history of epidemic rabies among its fox or coyote population, as cyclically infected the higher arctic. Predators such as wolves or wolverines simply didn't attack people. And we were too far removed from axe murderers and serial assassins for *those* fears to intrude on our sleep or to figure in even the most far-fetched scenario.

We were surrounded by a world that we accepted as an ally, not an adversary. It was plain what a profound security that might grant to a child.

Then the first run of salmon came up our creek. We were walking along the bank on the way to check on the ducks when the water swelled in a long line down the center of the creek, like a serpent arching its back. We both stared, open-mouthed, as a three-foot-long submarine streaked silently past an inch below the surface and a yard from where we stood.

For an instant I was shocked that something so large could have passed so close so quickly. Then I just marveled.

Janus skipped the anxiety and went right to the elation. He

looked as if he were going to jump in. I quickly put a hand on his shoulder.

The creek was narrow at the point where it ran below the house. It was also, in spots, in the periods between rains, so shallow it seemed unlikely that so massive a fish could travel up it. The salmon had journeyed thousands of miles from the open ocean up the Susitna River to this unnamed tributary to spawn. The sight of it, now, as it hovered in a pool upstream, was miraculous.

Janus raced along the bank. The fish turned and darted back downstream. We followed it up and down, down and up, until it simply vanished. For the next two hours we sat on the bank waiting. I had never seen Janus so still for so long. I finally had to drag him away, promising we'd return the next day.

The next day there were two fish, then three, then four. Janus was entranced. He was also annoyed that I refused to take one. I knew that in time I would, as easily as dipping into a holding tank. If not one of these seal-sized king salmon then the smaller silver salmon or "little" five-pound pink salmon. But not yet. Now it was enough just to watch. I wanted Janus to appreciate only their presence. He did.

When the summer began to fade to autumn—mid-August— when the winds first shifted to begin blowing again from the north, we picked berries from around the house. Fifty yards down the trail to the road was a blueberry patch that extended so far and so fruitfully that we could have launched a business had we been willing to pick nonstop. In a contiguous clearing of moist tundra, cloudberries were the dominant vegetation. We made pots of "Eskimo ice cream"—traditionally cloud- or salmonberries whipped into seal fat but currently, as of this generation, Crisco in place of seal blubber. We added gobs of honey.

By the first week of September the sound of our world had shifted from a green and silver ringing in the forest canopy to a flaxen rustle. The wind was louder, but, without the thrushes and wrens and larks and sparrows and warblers and flycatchers and swallows, we heard the sound as soft, as the last tremulous stroke of a bow across strings before silence.

We lowered our voices unconsciously on our walks as we pushed through grasses that no longer bent but now snapped. I admitted— and it was startling to do so—that vegetation at latitude 62 north lived for barely three months: the first buds in early June, full leaf in July, death beginning with the last days of August. Only three months! The tip of the Antarctic Peninsula is the same latitude south.

But during the two-week interstice between last leaves and first snows a new awareness of the land became possible. No longer was the focus on detail: web and flower and narrow game trail in tundra moss. It wasn't the enormous open vistas of winter, either. Attention was drawn to the intermediate places: the revealed hollows of flat- tened brown ferns where moose had slept, the exposed holes high in old birch where squirrels hibernated, the chevron of swans beneath the lifting stratus of morning fog.

Even the garden we had carefully created brought the unex- pected. In a matted-grass clearing of a small saddle where our ridge dipped behind the little cabin and the sun shone full, I had turned up chunks of sod and Janus had whacked the pieces into dirt with a machete. The clearing wasn't overhung by trees, like the spot that Melissa had chosen for a garden two years before. But after the ground thawed he and I had had time to dig up only a small plot in which to plant. The surprise was that it produced vegetables: four huge heads of broccoli, two perfect heads of cauliflower, even some brussels sprouts. Though we had *looked* at our budding garden often, we had tended it rather cavalierly. It was as yet so small that there were few weeds to pull; the grasses towering at the perimeter of the clearing were so dense that they acted as a natural fence.

My major construction chore over the summer had been to build a root cellar. The foundation for the greenhouse had been laid with a crib of logs and now awaited the real work of first hauling by winter dogsled and then securing large sheets of double-pane glass. But more important than getting a jump on the growing season in a greenhouse was preserving our food. Even a salmon would keep fresh in the cool of a root cellar.

Over the course of a month, I had dug a four-foot-deep, four-foot-wide, seven-foot-long hole, hacking into dense glacial pebbles, rocks, and boulders. It was "no fun" for Janus, and so construction was slow. I partially lined and fully roofed the pit with logs, then covered the whole thing with dirt and sod. But I hadn't yet built a door. Now I hurried to build one, because we had grown something to put into the cellar. Janus was not pleased that I worked most of a day framing the door, but I explained how important it was to bring a task to completion. He ate stalks of broccoli raw, like candy, waiting for the door to be over and done with.

When I finally finished it I quit to play with him. It was rare that I put him second behind any project.

In the morning, before hanging the door, we went down to the garden. The vegetables were gone. Moose prints were inches deep in the soil. Janus was happy that the moose liked our food, too.

We still gave our thanks at the dinner table for the bounty of our world, which we shared, intentionally or otherwise.

Inevitably, inexorably, the animals and fish and birds, who fed upon each other, came to be food for us, too.

We began to hunt.

For my years in New York I was a macrobiotic vegetarian, eating only grains and vegetables. My metabolism at high northern latitudes, however, was not well served by only grains and vegetables. I knew that I needed more calories, and so took to eating—especially in winter—a half pound of safflower oil margarine a day. I gained no weight; nor did I gain vitality.

I still lacked something that I worried might be meat.

I knew that all upper-latitude people ate meat as the elemental part of their diet. Eskimos ate seal and caribou. Athabaskans ate moose. Laps ate reindeer. European arctic explorers ate pemmican—a dried paste of meat and meat fat.

My horror of meat was mostly because commercial meat is a biological time bomb of artificial growth hormones and antibiotics, seasoned with pesticides and herbicides and ammonium-based fertilizers in those cattle who feed on chemically greened hay.

But I was also conditioned by my upbringing to view all hunting as licensed murder.

Janus, however, assumed that killing was what happens, like bears feeding on beavers, like ermines feeding on mice.

In the third week of September, with ice beginning to limn the edges of the tundra lakes, I hiked home alone after bringing Janus to his mom in Talkeetna. The foothills were covered with what Alaskans call "termination dust"—the first, higher-elevation snow of the winter.

As I walked up the frost-tinged tundra I brooded about another winter of garbanzo beans and rice. I didn't particularly mind it, but it seemed somehow wrong: those foods came from thousands of miles away.

I stopped at the border of trees to watch a flock of Canada geese sing their way south. After I started into the woods on the final stretch home, I saw the moose. He was ten yards from the trail.

He had a rack so large I didn't know how he could move between trees. But at the edge of the tundra, amidst stunted black spruce, his head was as high as the trees.

He eyed me calmly.

I stood for perhaps five minutes watching him watch me. He made no movement.

Eskimo culture assumes that all large game give themselves to the respectful hunter. With appropriate, heartfelt gratitude from the hunter, even whales will wait to be taken.

I went on home, greeted the dogs, took the shotgun from its place above the door, and returned slowly along the trail.

The moose was waiting.

My heart wasn't pounding, my hands weren't trembling.

I aimed, fired a magnum slug, and, while my ears rang, saw that the moose hadn't fallen.

I'd missed. From ten yards.

I closed my eyes and considered, again, whether what I was doing was right. It seemed evident to me that living where we did without living naturally, as the environment defined it, was a preposterous refusal to accept the interdependence of all forest life.

I said a prayer of thanks, raised the gun, and hit the moose in the neck. He crumpled.

I was surprised that I felt neither remorse nor excitement. I felt only as though I should skin and gut him well, wasting nothing.

A long-ago Buddha laid down his life in front of a hungry tigress with a starving cub. I had my own cub to sustain, but I knew that now, when I died, I wouldn't be entombed in a box. My old bones would nourish other forest life.

It took me six hours to separate the hide from the flesh, pull out the steaming viscera (arms plunged up to the elbow), and cut the carcass into two-hundred-pound sections that I could haul home on the dogsled. A seasoned woodsman would have done it in thirty minutes.

I hung the sections—four haunches, ribs, neck—on a line strung across the little cabin. When I finished, by gasoline pressure lantern, I cut a piece of meat to eat raw. It was sweet. It was rich. I understood why Janus was so eager to practice his instinctive hunting.

I left the rack in the forest—a source of calcium for shrews and squirrels. The thought of hanging it on the house was grotesque.

Two weeks later, when I brought Janus home, he was startled by the hanging meat. When, after a long silence, he touched it, he became very gradually excited, first staring at his hand, then touching other parts of the moose, then asking, eagerly, what was leg and what was back and how the whole thing fit together.

I carved off a chunk to fry. When he tasted it, hesitantly, he pronounced it "good," then let me eat the rest. But I could see in his eyes that he, too, had come to a new understanding of the land, and was grateful.

When the snows came, it was like old times. Living on an established summer homestead had been new to both of us. But when we had trails to break and mountain canyons to explore and kerosene lanterns to light by 4:00 P.M., we had come full circle.

Janus raced outside in the first wet inches of snow to build a truncated snowman. In ten minutes he held up his hands to be warmed. I lifted my shirt, accepted his hands on my belly, and one year was fused to another, in grins.

. . .

When the snows deepened and the creek froze, we decided to visit Rex and Penelope. They were just three or four miles away, but because there was no trail between us, the effort to reach them was as complicated in summer as it was easy in the snow with the dogs.

They were glad to see us. They were also relieved. A new guard dog had begun barking as soon as we entered their clearing. Rex burst onto the porch with a rifle.

"Thank God!" he shouted when he recognized us, stomping out to shake my hand.

I saw, when we'd stopped, what had concerned him. To the side of their house was a large generator, with electrical lines extending to two different sheet-plastic buildings.

"Just one more year," he explained, seeing my glance, "and we're done."

"What?" Janus demanded, unwilling to be left in the dark.

Rex bent beside him and said, "Broccoli. Me and Penelope are farmers, and we decided to grow broccoli."

Janus was satisfied. I was surprised that I hadn't before understood why they had moved so far into the forest.

"Rotating crops, huh?" I said.

"Gotta start 'em early. That's the key."

Rex led us on a tour of their operation. I lost count at two hundred potted plants, each six feet tall, in rows beneath lights, with stoves and fans and buckets of fertilizer. "Do you know how much snow we have to melt for water?" asked Rex.

I told him that I admired the discipline it took to sustain such a scale.

When we went inside the house Penelope said, "We've wanted to be neighborly and visit, but you can see how much work's involved here every day."

I told them that I planned to grow soybeans in my greenhouse as soon as it was finished. They seemed to have forgotten their initial impression of me, but suddenly I could see them return to gentle smiles.

"Soybeans," said Rex, as Penelope heated water for Janus's hot chocolate.

"Soybeans," he repeated, his smile widening.

"You'll certainly be able to make a lot of tofu," called Penelope.

"You know," said Rex, leaning back in an armchair, "we couldn't figure out what you were doing out here. And now, to tell the truth, I understand it even less." He sat up, then reached over to where I sat with Janus to pat my knee. "But we *need* people like you to . . . uh . . . provide perspective."

"Just like we need the mountains," I said.

He nodded. "Beans and mountains. I guess that'll keep anyone going."

I laughed, then asked for information about our local area of the Susitna Valley. I was looking for gossip. They were direct.

"No, there's been no one else we're aware of," said Rex, "except for a couple of retards who tried to find their land last spring near here. They slogged around in the snow without snowshoes, got lost, didn't have the brains to follow their own posthole tracks back out, and spray-painted HELP on the tundra in twelve-foot letters with the can they carried to mark their corners. Then they waited until a plane spotted them and a rescue chopper picked them up. But otherwise, no, it's still just you and us and that's it."

"It'll be different, though, in ten years or twenty years," said Penelope from the kitchen. "It's harder than I thought to live here, but my God"—she poked her head around the partition and smiled—"it certainly is beautiful."

"I saw ATV tracks gouged in the tundra last summer," I said. "It upset me."

"The yahoos'll stop coming out here when the oil revenue dries up," said Rex, "or when one of them gets eaten by a bear."

"I've never had a bear problem," I said, "even with a half ton of dog food stockpiled."

"Well, I had to shoot a griz this summer," Rex said, "when he got too close to the house for comfort."

He saw my shock at once and tried to explain himself. "He was getting aggressive," he said, but his voice was lame. "He could've wiped out our whole operation."

"Bears lived here before us," I said, and was immediately annoyed with myself for sounding so docile.

I could see that Rex wasn't persuaded by my argument.

"And there are only two hundred brown bears in all of Denali Park, you jerk," I continued, rallying. "These are creatures who know how to live here *well*, easily, joyously! Without all the crap we need to haul into the forest to survive. This is the last place on earth where they don't have to run scared. And you're blowing them away? Because they're *here*?"

Penelope stepped out with a mug of hot chocolate to stand above me. "Well," she said.

Rex reached for his pipe. "I got *that* message," he said.

Penelope looked at Rex. Rex looked at me. Janus was looking at the hot chocolate.

"So we learn," said Rex, simply.

I glanced down, embarrassed for my outburst. I wanted to apologize, but when I looked up Rex was still staring at me calmly. I saw no anger, no judgment, and not the slightest need for excuse.

"Want some starts?" he said. "You've got a greenhouse. Make a thousand dollars a plant."

I was speechless in the face of such a casual response to confrontation. I realized that human relations don't have to be complicated, even when there are complications.

Penelope handed Janus the mug. He was glad.

"Thanks," I said to Rex. "But no, I've got my hands full already," I explained, lifting one hand from Janus in my lap and resting it again on his leg.

Janus and I returned home by the last light. The air was cold, the forest deep in blue, but I had to give no instructions to the dogs and no protective comfort to Janus, who reclined casually in his bag. Everything was easy.

The next evening, after our walk, I decided to write a magazine article. I had been thinking that day that we had, in fact, no cash crop, and sporadic sleepless work stints in Anchorage were debilitating. I gave Janus his Lego blocks, sat at the typewriter that I'd placed on the dinner table, and, a half hour later, turned from my pages to create an even greater guilt than that which I felt toward Melissa.

Janus, for the last fifteen minutes, had been tugging at my sleeve, demanding that I play with him, even hugging me ingratiatingly.

I turned, midsentence, and, leaning down to him, yelled, "Leave me alone! I told you I'm trying to work!"

I saw my face reflected in his wide eyes, but my expression in his pupils was distorted, as if I were looking into mirrored sunglasses.

He backed away. I sat upright.

"Oh boy. I'm sorry," I said.

He sniffled, hands lax at his sides.

"I'm really sorry," I repeated, reaching to lift him up.

That was the last time for a year that I typed anything other than letters. Until we went upstairs to read and tell stories and sleep, we built a big, *big* Lego block tower.

The next time Janus went into Talkeetna we returned home with Ado and Tarus. Kathy, their mom, was very glad for the respite from single parenting. Ado and Tarus were twice as glad: they'd never ridden on a dogsled before.

I piled secondhand foam pillows the length of the sled, burrowed the kids into down bags, admonished all three boys to be aware of keeping their hands *and* their feet *inside* the sled *always*, and took off.

Within five minutes, as soon as the initial burst of speed had slowed, all three boys were out of the bags. Ado, a slaphappy sort, and Tarus, two years older and normally brooding and intense, were both animated with delight. They didn't want to miss anything.

"Cool!"

"Oh wow, this is *fun*!"

"Make them go *fast* again!"

"Let's chase a moose!"

They crawled up and down the ten-foot-long sled basket, keeping their hands and feet mostly inside.

Janus knelt in the back of the sled. He was very proud that his two best friends appreciated his world, but he revealed it only through his eyes, which shone. His composure surprised me. I had expected him to show off, like a kid.

When Ado called, "Janus! Do you get to do this *all* the time?" Janus just nodded. He knew it was wonderful. Since his friends did now, too, why be demonstrative?

On the tundra, Janus showed them how to land surf—standing up in the sled as we traveled—then remained mainly in the rear while Ado and Tarus took turns trying to hang ten off the prow.

For the next few days we all fed birds from our hands and built snow forts and looked for overflow on the creek and followed the new tracks of a moose. We took the dogsled onto the tundra to "go fast" and romped with the dogs in the yard. At night, we played freeze tag in the house.

I watched Janus carefully. I worried that with the years he'd grow to need other people more and more, that he'd chafe at going "back into the woods," that one day I'd get a postcard from West Hollywood saying, "Dad, it's just overwhelming. The lights on the hills are so bright. Everyone's so well dressed! I think I've found an apartment . . ."

But I saw that, while he was having a good time with his boy buddies, he wasn't having a *better* time than otherwise. Like a field biologist or prospector or solo climber or John Muir, he was comfortable with himself and his world. The animals and the land were his friends, too. What he seemed to need, conclusively, was love.

On the long journey returning his friends to Talkeetna, I said, "Well, I guess you're going to miss Ado and Tarus."

He replied, honestly but without regret, "Mm-hmm."

I brought them all out again once more that winter, when clouds warmed the land. It had been my suggestion, not Janus's.

. . .

On a late-February day when the sun rose far enough above the horizon to provide the first radiant heat since October, I explained to Janus that the traveling season was coming. I told him that I was going to the Brooks Range for a month but that he could play with his friends in Talkeetna.

He wanted to go with me.

We had gone on dogsled trips together twice that winter.

He didn't understand why I would now go into the mountains for so long without him. I tried to make him understand how remote the Brooks Range was. "Look on this map. Four *hundred* miles from where we live is the Brooks. It's the only mountain range on earth that's completely above the Arctic Circle. Remember that giant map covering the whole wall of the library in Anchorage? It has empty white spots on it. That's *unmapped* land, never seen by—"

"Yeah, yeah," said Janus, pouting.

The Loussac Public Library in Anchorage, a new glass-and-chrome edifice stocked with an impressive number of oil-revenue-funded volumes, listed in its state-of-the-art, computerized inventory one hundred thirty books on "Antarctica," forty-one on the "Amazon," but just six on the "Brooks Range." Three of those six were fifty years old.

Where else on earth was there such unexplored, unimaginable wilderness?

I'd seen the Ice Age landscape of the upper Susitna Valley. It was the same environment—cave bears and glaciers!—that had shaped human evolution across fifty thousand years of blinding winters and brief riotous summers. Our now-instinctive dispositions toward herding and aggressive dominance and awe had been sorted and codified amidst such wilderness as still existed only marginally. Even now people were intruding on the Susitna Valley—here I was!—signaling the end of the last great perspective we'd ever have on our origins. We wouldn't find it in satellite transmissions from the moon.

Nor from the three-thousand-year-old *Tao Tê Ching*. Nor from any-thing *we* had recorded.

I wanted, I needed, to see the seven-hundred-mile-long Brooks Range.

My partner, Murphy, with whom I agreed to travel because it seemed less irresponsible than going alone, was a photographer recently arrived in Alaska. He had settled north not for big bucks or for job offers better than other offers (he was good) but for the Alaska that few eyes had seen. He, too, even after a sea kayak trip down the southern coast of Chile, held no preconceptions but only fantasies about what we might discover on the slopes of the high arctic within an ocean-mirage sighting of the North Pole.

Over beers on Fourth Avenue in Anchorage (Y'upik Eskimos dancing traditional dances to the beat of the sallow-faced country-western house band; eighteen-year-old U.S. Navy sailors on leave in one of their recruiting-advertised "exotic" ports chatting with gig-gling aboriginal village girls), we had decided to go in winter. The Gates of the Arctic National Park, through which we'd travel, was visited by Sierra Club types and journalists only in summer, and then but rarely.

In early March, at thirty-five below zero Fahrenheit, we started from the place where we parked our cars. We'd had only a vague idea of where we might jump off from the North Slope Haul Road, a narrow gravel conduit from the Fairbanks end of Alaska's truncated road system that then cut through the central Brooks Range to Prudhoe Bay, where huge trucks in convoys continued to bring shipments to the oil development on the Arctic Ocean. The road was owned by the oil companies and restricted to their private vehicles.

We drove to the foothills of the range without seeing any warning—no armed sentries or checkpoints—except for a sign half buried in drifted snow reading PRIVATE ROAD.

Plainly, the 412-mile-long winding rock road with only two gas stations and the most severe shifting weather on the Triple A's maps held its own intractable restraints.

We parked outside a trapper's cabin in Wiseman. The current 250-page, nationally distributed, Alaskan-produced authoritative guide to Alaska's road system listed Wiseman as a "ghost town." In all the reading (six volumes) and talking (every professional guide I knew in Talkeetna) that I'd done, I learned that only two communities had ever existed in the length of the Brooks. One was a tiny Eskimo village across the Arctic Divide on the Anaktuvuk River. The other—Wiseman—had been abandoned at the end of the Alaskan gold rush.

Behind the trapper's house was a bigger cabin with a satellite TV dish near its front door.

Forty or fifty people, it turned out, lived in Wiseman: two trappers, a dogsled racer, hunting guides, and aging miners who still worked their claims.

Such was the knowledge about remote Alaska even in the 1980s, even within Alaska.

The trapper, who had immediately come out of his house to introduce himself ("They call me Mad Joseph"), was shy and cordial. He invited us inside to meet his wife and six-month-old baby girl. He pointed out the start of his trail that would take us through one pass into the heart of the mountains, where we'd then be on our own.

When Murphy and I went outside we untied the sled from the roof of the car. As we harnessed my dogs, Mad Joseph reminded us that at 1:00 P.M., the heat of the day, it was still thirty-five below. Then he wished us luck.

Murphy, on skis, took off ahead of me. Five minutes after my dogs and I streaked past him he was lost to my sight within the thin spruce cover of the lower hill slopes. While I waited for him to catch up, I took a spare sled line from the top of my pack, fixed it to the back of the sled, and stretched it out ten or fifteen feet along the tracks of the runners. When he reached me, Murphy, an excellent skier but no match for a dog team, fastened the line to the middle of his poles. Holding the poles horizontal to the ground, he gripped them with one hand on either side of the line.

"Who knows?" he called, to say that he was ready.

I towed him like a water-skier. He lunged and wobbled and then found his balance. He grinned. That was how we discovered how best to travel.

During the next few days, I put into the top compartment of my pack a white ptarmigan wing with bloodstains on it, the silken tuft of arctic fox fur from the trampled ground beside the wing, a fragment of a caribou antler, a chunk of lichen-red shale, and a swath of wool sliced from the hide of a Dall sheep that was, as we could see from the fresh wolf prints twice the size of those made by my large dogs, still in the process of being eaten.

They were for Janus. For Melissa, I didn't know what to bring, though it seemed important that I carry something back for her, too. On this wilderness trip I had, as always, regrets. I waited for the revelations.

We passed beneath the Frigid Crags, past Boreal Mountain, into the Valley of the Precipices. We careened up miles of glare-ice overflow. Caribou tracks covered the ground in places like birch leaves in the autumn forest. The temperature remained a constant twenty-five to thirty-five below.

With each succeeding river canyon that we crossed, the peaks angled in wildly different directions like storm-whipped waves frozen at the End of the World, the signature of the geologically complex Brooks. While Murphy took pictures and I took mental snapshots, we repeated, independently of each other, "Yes."

It looked to be about as far into true wilderness as we'd get in our lives, as it was *possible* to get.

When we crossed the Arctic Divide in high-pass winds so violent the dogs' noses bled, the spruce that had lined the southern slopes vanished. There was nothing on the northern slopes but rock and wind-sculpted snow extending as far as we could see. But we were running downhill now, following a drainage toward the Arctic Ocean. Setting up camp that night was grim work. Murphy frostbit a finger or two. I was hypothermic. But when we collapsed into our bags we both exploded with the laughter of children.

Then we reached Anaktuvuk Pass, pop. 200.

When we came over the final ridge, where dozens of caribou antlers stuck up through the snow, the village was so tiny below the surrounding unvegetated peaks that I thought at once of the remote Himalayas. As we got closer in a wind that blew the sled from side to side, I saw that the village was not built of moss-chinked rock and stretched hides, but of plywood and sheet metal, with typical American telephone poles carrying wavering power lines in a grid above the town.

We cascaded down the slope to the edge of the settlement and came to a stop beside a huge diesel truck. There were two Native guys inside. The driver rolled down his window and said casually, "Hey. Pretty wild," meaning me and Murphy.

The truck carried the chemical waste of flushless toilets— "honey buckets"—to a dump site outside of town, as the driver explained in answer to my first blurted question: "What *is* this?" A decal on the side of the door said SANITATION DEPARTMENT, NORTH SLOPE BOROUGH, ALASKA.

I was disoriented by the imposing truck a hundred miles from any other road, but the sanitation workers didn't seem at all startled by a dogsled coming out of the mountains. We chatted for a few minutes—"Pretty cold, huh?"—and then a snowmachine streaked between houses up the wind-scoured gravel main street at the far end of which we stood.

It was one of the village elders, the man who welded broken snowmachines and kept the only working dog team in the village, who prepared income taxes and presided over the crucial school board in a community where more than a third of the residents were school-age, and who never, never, unlike the younger mayor, unlike the much younger bucks, flew to Fairbanks or Barrow to "party."

He stopped at our side, cut the engine, and grinned. Even beneath his wolf-ruffed parka hood his eyes sparkled. He was a mensch, a magus, the sachem figure of the village.

He escorted us to his home. Inside, the walls were covered with the world's largest collection of ritual Eskimo masks—the faces fashioned from caribou skin and wolf fur.

His name was Orv and he was a pure-blood Norwegian from Minnesota.

For ten years, with his lovely, twenty-year-younger wife (just as white as he was), he had lived in Anaktuvuk, teaching school, fixing broken plumbing, arbitrating disputes, giving dogs to residents determined to return to the "old ways" who then gave the dogs back to him in favor of 500-cc Ski-doos.

Orv took us on a tour of Potala Disneyland. We saw the electric sauna and Olympic-size swimming pool in the new kindergarten-through-twelfth-grade school (computers, full-court gym, complete wood- and metalworking shops). We saw the twenty-machine laundromat. We saw the $250,000 garbage collection truck with 000006 miles on its odometer—its cab filled with drifted snow—that was supposed to but didn't work in the high arctic. We saw caribou hides and wolf skins draped over the porches of oil-heated houses inside which, by satellite, twenty-two channels came in loud and clear while the aboriginal residents, fans all, tuned in Super Station WGN to pick up the Cubs games.

Murphy took no pictures. "This is all too bizarre," he explained.

Orv, better able to explain, told us that the oil tax revenue accumulated to the North Slope Borough—six villages, five thousand people in an area not much smaller than Wyoming—in less than a generation had converted a hunter-gatherer people to the American dream, where money was easy and All-Star second baseman Ryne Sandberg was a hero. Cargo planes brought in goods—VCRs, sirloin beef, full-sized yellow school buses, Tupperware. Inupiaq was spoken in every Native home.

At an early-April Easter Sunday gathering of all the white schoolteachers in the village—which was all the teachers, which revealed as much as anything—Orv and his wife, Anne, introduced Murphy and me to the dozen assembled people and then disappeared. We met an almost three-hundred-pound man who raised Pekinese dogs for show, which he kept in paper-lined cages inside the house. "Come to Papa," cooed the fat man, holding out a piece of ham, calling one precious dog that had a satin bow in its neck fur. We met an English teacher who broke into a beaded sweat visible on his forehead when I asked him what he planned to do after retiring from teaching in Anaktuvuk. "Oh," he said, eyes becoming glassy. "Oh. Well. I make forty-five thousand a year teaching in the bush, you see, and retirement from twenty years' service gives me twenty thousand a year, you know. And I, well, I . . . I really don't know for sure just *what* I'll do. But I'm going to hang on! I *am*! I've only got two years to go! Just two more years! I'm going to make it!" We met the school principal, who in answer to my innocently social query replied, "What do *I* do? Hmm. Ahh. I run things. Yessss. I'm in charge. Heh-heh. I am in charge. Ha-ha!" He seemed so precariously sane that I turned my attention to the baked turkey.

When Murphy and I had finished stuffing ourselves, we retired from our generally ignored status as visiting guests. We raced through the unabated wind and cold back to Orv and Anne's.

"That was the most incredible, Felliniesque, culture-shock nightmare I've ever seen in any travel I've ever taken," I announced.

Orv blanched. He looked down. "They *are* a little different from the rest of the village," he said.

"This is how the Eskimo kids learn about the wider world?" I cried. "From those loonies?"

"Twenty-five years ago Anaktuvuk didn't exist because the people were nomads," Orv said. "But now every Native village in the state has telephone and television links, and enough oil money to bring us all into the twenty-*first* century."

"And yet they still make masks and wear wolf," said Murphy.

"Oh, they haven't forgotten everything," said Orv. "Yet."

That evening, Pat and Ben came over to visit. They were both in their early twenties. Pat's face was as puckered by new frostbite as if he'd just slathered himself in Clinique Gelatin Masque. They both had long black hair held from their faces by animal sinew headbands. They looked like fierce warriors. Orv introduced them as the best trappers in the village.

"Heard some mushers were passin' through," said Ben with the gentle singsong inflection of Inupiaq.

"Thought we might show you where we laid our lines," said Pat.

They asked where we were headed when we left Anaktuvuk. Murphy and I said we weren't exactly sure but we'd be glad to know where they'd set their traps.

"Well, pretty much everywhere," said Ben. "I guess you might not miss 'em no matter where you go."

Murphy said that before we'd reached Anaktuvuk we had seen, to our horror, a bull caribou caught in a trap with the flesh peeled from one hoof to the bone.

"Yeah, well, we brought him in yesterday," said Pat. "That happens sometimes."

They showed us on a map where their traplines were. Pat took a pen and drew loops through every possible pass leading from the village across the mountains, including one pass that seemed impossible, the contour lines rising almost solid to a notch and then plummeting five hundred feet to a canyon.

"We're going there," I said impulsively. I wanted to explore the least plausible routes.

"No problem," said Ben. "I guess we'll pull the traps in the morning."

"We set for wolf a lot," said Pat, "and don't want your dogs to step in one."

When they'd bowed away with handshakes and polite goodbyes, Orv said, "These people have only two speeds on their snow-machines, on and off. Pat frosted his face last week when he went out in a storm to check their lines and ran out of gas. They run out of gas more often than you'd believe because they're so completely confident in themselves that they *know* they'll survive, even in a blizzard fifty miles from the village."

The next morning I stood at the picture window watching massive winds thrum the power lines. My dogs were in the front "yard," each cowered in a ball against the cold. Anne, handing me a coffee mug, stood silently for a minute and then said, "I just wish there were more dog teams here and more people who remembered their traditions. So much has changed so quickly, even since we first arrived."

Every house had a flattened streak of oil-furnace smoke whipping from its chimney. Every house had a snowmachine outside. I could see a Chevy Blazer, its exhaust streaming to keep the engine from freezing solid. The village had two and one-half miles of road of any kind, all leading to the general store, where the cars went, heaters blowing.

"The oil won't last much longer," she said simply.

Then a Pekinese darted toward my tethered dogs. They leaped up. Norton and Dick together yelled, "Snack time!"

"He *never* lets them run free!" cried Anne. "Hurry! If your team—" But I was already out the door hollering.

For the rest of the day Murphy and I sorted gear. He was amused that I wanted to investigate the most remote valleys that our maps suggested. "It's *all* remote," he said, though he wasn't arguing.

In the morning we started out on Pat and Ben's trapline trail, then lost it as we started up the first slope. We reached that notch beyond which was the steep drop. We unpacked the entire sled to ferry the load down the cliff while the dogs slid unharnessed around us. Halfway down, grooved into the snow, we saw snowmachine tracks undercut by the winds to stand two inches high, as plain as an interstate highway marker.

Two days later we did, in fact, descend a creek valley where there was no evidence of human intrusion. But that meant nothing.

The Brooks Range, for all its mystery, was not removed from the rest of the world. Transarctic jets drew white lines in the unspeakably blue sky. Prehistoric people had wandered the hills with skin tents setting stone deadfalls for clothing fur.

I suddenly came to terms with wilderness. It had never been removed from *anything*—migrating animals or the hunters who pursued them or the rest of the world. The truth of wilderness was that it was interconnected—mountains to creeks to the sea, trappers in the Brooks Range to Wrigley Field in Chicago, I on my ridgeline to Melissa in Talkeetna. I'd found places where no man had walked before, but it didn't separate me from men. In those places I valued my isolation from distraction, but disconnection is the province only of hubris and lunacy. And Janus acted as if he lived at the heart of the world, not at its edges.

For two years I had had a recurrent dream. I had never before in my life had recurrent dreams, though I courted the ones about flying. I dreamed of heavy equipment blowing black smoke from their diesel exhausts as The Road Up The Ruth Glacier got pushed across the Alaska Range to the other side. Each time I awoke sweating, only to begin laughing out loud. A road up flowing, splintering ice where snow fell year-round? Ho!

Alexander had been right. That which sustains will remain, and though it can be glimpsed in a landscape, it resides in grace. Grace assures mercy. Mercy forgives.

I no longer blamed Melissa for not wanting to live deep in the forest. I didn't even blame myself for my failure to support her.

As the dogs pulled steadily down the unnamed creek valley, I admitted that I'd probably forget my high resolve. But it was a place to return to, as irreducible as the snow mountains.

When I got back to Talkeetna, Janus was impressed by the booty I had brought him. I promised to bring him a polar bear claw the next time I went to the high arctic, along the coast, onto the sea ice. I had seen the lambency of the Arctic Ocean from the hills.

The world was vast beyond imagining. Still. Of course. Even now. It had never been otherwise. If we looked.

Melissa kept her distance, but now I could see how connected we all were, unavoidably—anxious animals drawn back to familiarity after forays into the enormity *out there*: the arctic littoral or our own guilts and fears.

I offered her what I had found. I told her that I wasn't resentful, that I loved her and wanted her to be happy.

Janus I didn't have to forgive for anything, and in my love he was happy.

That seemed to be how all human relations transpired: starting in love and ending, eventually—with grace—in forgiveness.

Time returns in a vast closed curve to the place of its starting, where, by a dim foreknowledge of this, men find heart to live. What else is living good for unless it brings us back to love?

I pushed the limits of my experience to explore the unknown. What did I hope to see? More light!

But family was a beacon that could be touched and held, and, in the eyes of my son, never wavered.

"Now we go 'om, Dod?" he asked.

Melissa opened her hands and turned her palms up, gracefully.

"Now we go home," I said.

9.

ONE DAY IN SUMMER, 1987

I woke early. I lay in bed with one hand behind my head. In the other arm Janus slept.

I stared out the window that was just above the foot of the bed. I'd built it low so that a child could rest his arms on the sill. Against the blue summer sky the upper part of a spruce, through the window, stood motionless, the icon of the boreal forest. Though it was only 6:00 A.M., the sun had risen hours ago. The light was equatorial, as intense as sheen off the ocean.

Alexander would be dead soon. He lay in bed in his parents' house staring at the wall. The form his AIDS had taken was neurological. Thought was difficult, grand emotion impossible.

I watched the spruce for a long time, thinking little, feeling less.

I had flown to the East Coast a month previously when Alexander told me, almost grudgingly, that he couldn't care for himself anymore. He had returned to live with his parents. Until then, he had successfully hidden the extent of his illness.

When I arrived at the Philadelphia airport I had been fasting for a week, even through the creekside wedding celebration of Rex and Penelope when they culminated their adventures together by hosting a festival. I had found, three years ago in my depression at Melissa's departure, that fasting induced clarity. I needed clarity now. I needed to see the extent of my sorrows without being overwhelmed by them.

As I came off the passenger ramp I saw Alexander's mother, a woman of vivacious energy, waving enthusiastically at the back of the crowd. I shot up a hand and waved as I pushed toward her.

Then Alexander stepped from behind her. He was skeletal, as if he had become the patrician artist of ninety he might have been, as if, after an annual retreat to a monastery, he had emerged with flesh taut across his skull and with fingers thin in ascetic abnegation. I saw him as he was, in time greatly foreshortened, but inevitably. His smile was wry—full of irony at his condition and full of amusement at seeing me with my carry-on backpack slung over a shoulder.

He leaned on my arm as we walked out of the terminal. I had counted on him to show me, across the years, the requirements of art and the paths to God. I held his hand.

We spent a week together, speaking little, sitting side by side for hours, once walking, slowly, into a nearby field where a massive oak windbreak, branches rippling in the summer breeze, roused him to say, "Here's where I come to return to the boreal forest." He tried to add something, pointing above the trees to bright cumulus, but his energy failed. "Mountains," I said for him. He grinned.

When, at the moment of our parting, his mother backed her Oldsmobile station wagon out of the garage, I, from my passenger's seat, gave Alexander, who stood immobile in the doorway to the house, the thumbs-up. He was much too vital a presence, even in his devastation, for a wave goodbye. It wasn't until I'd hugged his mother at the airport bus terminal, repeating my amazement at her strength and love, that I finally, after ducking away, wept.

The twelve-hour flight back to Alaska was a blur, as were the weeks following.

Janus stirred in the crook of my arm. He opened his eyes. "Good morning I love you," he said. That was our standard morning greeting.

I drew him closer to me. He was five and a half years old—*very* big—but still my little boy.

He raised himself up. "Let's go fishin'!" he said.

I didn't reply.

He rolled over onto my chest. "Time to get up!" he said. "It's mornin' time!"

I didn't move. The spruce was incandescent—a burning bush!—but it remained in its frame, beyond a pane of glass, and I couldn't remember why it had once seemed to fill the room.

"I can hear 'em jumpin'," said the boy. He sat up on me. "*Big* ones!"

I noted, vaguely, that the weight pressing me down was no more than fifty pounds, and warm, and vibrant with love. I began to suspect that I could in fact rise from bed.

The child put his hands to my face. "I'm gonna give the first trout to *you*! Because I loooooove you," he sang.

"Thank you," I said quietly.

He didn't know what I was really thanking him for, but he grasped at once that my gratitude was deep. "So how 'bout if we have some carob chippies for breakfast?" he suggested.

I smiled. "Forget it," I said.

"But it'll be a super special treat!" he insisted. "I need *energy* to catch the big ones."

I had accepted Melissa's cyclical expressions of love and helpless anger now that we were irredeemably separated; familial devastation is always hard, and there is no blame. I had come to terms with the continued intrusions into the upper Susitna Valley by writing a column for the *Anchorage Daily News*'s Sunday magazine; my hope was that my descriptions of the enormous beauty residing here would mitigate state development plans that would reduce this land to another paved Yosemite Valley. Even though my father had suffered a mortal stroke while I was exploring the Cathedral Spires of the distant Alaska Range two years ago, that inevitability, too, was part of life: he had lived long and well and left an abiding legacy of benevolence. But the extinction of Alexander's light seemed random; it had neither meaning nor hope.

Human events had become too tragic for me to find absolution even in our wilderness home, where sustenance was visible. Pestilence and war reared and snorted on the horizon alongside famine and flood. I shied from the sun on bright spring days because the ultraviolet radiation streaking through the depleted ozone layer at this latitude burned my skin after an hour.

Janus bounced up and down atop my chest. "Hey!" he said. "This is *mornin'* time!" He refused to accept my lassitude. "Let's wrestle!"

I blinked. I tried to hug him close but he spun away. From the time we first came home together we had nurtured each other. We had adopted rituals: after "I love you" came wrestling.

I propped myself up on my elbows. "I'm gonna get you in a headlock," I said dully, trying to find the energy to move farther.

Janus carried the requisite energy to me in a bound. "*You* need to get out of a headlock!" he shouted, burying me in pleasure.

We spent fifteen minutes trying to pin each other. He won, as was normal.

Then he moved on to the next morning game. "Time to play Magic Butterfly," he said.

Magic Butterfly required me to pretend that I was asleep so that the creature burrowing under the blankets could reach a hand from his cocoon to stroke my face gently. I scratched my cheek and muttered about flies in the house. Again the touch from beneath the covers roused me. "Oh, look," I then said, according to script. "It's a wing! It's the color of . . . the aurora!"

And the Magic Butterfly revealed himself by rising up, arms slowly winging. "I . . . am . . . magic," said the Butterfly.

"You, you can *talk*," I said.

"And I can give you anything for you and all the animals," said the Butterfly, soaring around the bed.

The Magic Butterfly then accepted flowers (presto!, wild roses in my grasp) from which to sip nectar. The nectar got converted, back under the covers, to a "special" honey that all the animals could eat for a treat. The animals from all over the forest came to the honeypot that—just look!—never ran dry.

Bears and ravens and foxes and wolves and little mice and big moose arrived in a thundering herd that made us dive into the cocoon so we wouldn't be squashed. Above us was an earthquake that made the whole bed shake like a dad bouncing up and down making guttural noises (pause for gleeful laughter). When there was calm I peeked out to report on how the animals had liked their honey. I saw—Oh no! Duck!—a river of pee coming right toward us.

Anything scatological is funny to a five-year-old. He laughed so easily and so gladly that the last of my lingering inertia was lifted into familiar activity. We went downstairs to make rice cream.

I stoked the cookstove. "Put some socks on, the floor is still cool," I said, as much of a ritual as anything.

"Okay," he replied, not bothering to put socks on, as usual.

He gathered his books. He studied pictures of birds and fur-bearers and fish in our various *Field Guide to North American . . .* primers. His favorite was the *National Geographic* bird volume with paintings of every species in stages ranging from "immature" to "in flight."

I went outside to examine the day on my way to the little cabin where I'd grind rice for breakfast. The hand grinder remained where I'd clamped it five years ago.

I rarely had a full day's supply of ground grain or split wood in the house. My chores commonly took me outside, if only to walk ten paces to the woodshed. This was a conscious choice in reaction to my old urban life where daily routine was confined to interior spaces. I was aware that, even in the upper Susitna Valley, most other residents moved quickly from box to box: house to car to bar to store to house, as if security resided not in the world itself but rather in its containment.

While we ate we practiced words. I penned, in capital letters, "MOON," and "DAD," and "MOUNTAIN," and "THE BOY IS GOOD." That was the most formal of our schooling. I'm a big fan of words, but in their place, in their time.

The rest of home school was spontaneous. Two elements didn't vary: love and happiness. Today, because we were going fishing, we would study *thinking*. I had long since abandoned "Be careful" as a reminder of the risks inherent in our world. *Care* comes from the Old Saxon *kara*, meaning "sorrow." I had adopted Contemporary Aretha Franklin: "You better *think*." Standing on a midstream rock above a neck-high pool required attention.

But first we greeted the dogs. They had become personalities as definite as members of any family, with the same quirky demands. Bruno, a young prince who would eventually be the next leader, wanted to be petted first. Maya, long-legged and high-carriaged, named for Maya Plisetskaya, the last of the great Russian prima ballerinas, needed constant reminders that she was beautiful. Huge red Dick only wanted an extra bite to eat, which Janus carried from the previous day's fishing: a tail fin. Poor Van Dyke, who had been dingey ever since she'd been kicked in the head by a crazed moose, raced in circles nipping her tail; we were never sure just what she required, but we went over to humor her so she wouldn't feel left out. Norton, the king, the Alpha dog, suffered us our slowness in reaching him because he knew the love we gave him would be unequivocal.

Other dogs had come and gone. These were family.

We let one dog run free—Bruno today—to accompany us down to the creek. Bears at the peripheries of our influence were common in summer. A dog helped us know when they wandered too close.

For a few hours of silent concentration the boy stood on his midstream rock holding a spool of monofilament line with a size 10 hook attached, waiting for trout. He normally had the sporadic concentration of all kids, yet he barely moved for the entire time that the fish darted toward and away from his line. I can remember no precedent in my own childhood for such sustained intensity. Eskimo hunters poised above seal breathing holes on the sea ice were the only association I had.

When he saw that his bait had dissipated he tossed the line up onto the bank where I sat so that I could impale another orange salmon egg. No words were spoken. The fish might hear.

We were focused, the boy on the fish, I on the boy. He was illuminated in sunlight coruscating off the water. He was surrounded by flora that grew taller by the hour, as if caught by time-lapse photography.

"Got one," he announced with the dispassionate tone of a professional. He yanked on the line. A fifteen-inch rainbow trout trailed beads of shimmering water as he swung it up onto the bank. I whapped it on the head with a pair of needle-nose pliers and pulled out the hook.

We grinned at each other. I pierced another egg onto the hook. He stutter-stepped atop his rock, stretching his legs, and bent again over the current.

I leaned back in the grasses. I squinted up at the sky.

"You can die, Alexander," I said to myself. "It's all right. Don't struggle. We're here. Just look where we are. The world is rich beyond imagining, still. Remember how we used to joke that there might not be anywhere left to go, everything known, everything already described? Remember how bleak life seemed when all hope was blown away by the intimation of inevitable tragedy—lost love or winnowed possibility or obtuse human righteousness? *I* remember! But look. Here is only light and land, as anywhere. But such light! And the land presupposes nothing except its continuity. I haven't escaped sorrow, not even here, of course, not even on an unnamed creek in the boreal forest. But there's so much life. Still. Alexander."

My eyes began to fill with tears. Bruno stirred from his place in the sun. He crawled over to nuzzle my arm. I reached out to hold him to my chest. He burrowed his nose into my shirt—Alexander's shirt.

The boy looked over with an expression of, "Hey! Keep the dog from scaring the fish!" But then he laughed. He had no reason to laugh, no reason in particular. We gazed at each other. He winked. Five years old! And he gave me the thumbs-up.

A lone mallard at the warp speed of ducks on the wing streaked down the creek corridor. The boy glanced up. "Female," he said, noting its muted plumage. Then he bent back to attention.

. . .

We cooked the trout over a fire outside the front door of the house. Or, rather, *he* cooked the fish. He gathered slivers of split firewood from around the chopping block. He plucked darkened moss hanging from the low branches of the spruce encircling our clearing. Atop the moss he placed the wood shards and then built a teepee of branches left over from felled cabin logs, branches that, to my amazement, had not decomposed at all but rather revealed the longevity of the forest's skeleton. He took his knife—a single-bladed pocket Gerber, a knife that he would have coveted if he had known how unusual it was for a child to be entrusted with his own blade— and cut an alder branch. He whittled the stick to a point and handed it to me.

My only role in the cooking was to ram the stick through the fish's mouth, along its gutted middle (he had made the cut and removed the inner organs), and securely into the tail. With the fish skewered, I handed it back to him.

He roasted it over the flame until it was ready to drop off. Then he plopped it onto a plate.

"For you!" he warbled. He took a bite or two, but the idea of eating something that he'd just been studying as it moved cautiously around him must have made him feel like a New Guinean child sampling human flesh. "Good! But you eat the rest."

After lunch ("*Now* I get some carob chips, okay?") we went for a hike. I lifted him to my shoulders and held on to his feet while he gripped me under the chin.

"No bugs up here, neither," he called.

We had noticed that the dense mosquito swarms—which made head nets and gloves mandatory—lasted only for three weeks, from mid-June to early July. We kept the bed net suspended from May to September, but we didn't need protection outside once the peak had passed.

"So where should we go today?" I asked.

"Janus Rock," he said. That was the glacial erratic nearest the house, a low boulder covered in moss, atop which he could clamber unaided. We also had Norton Rock, fifteen feet high, named for the climber who had made the first ascent; and Wolf Rock, where we once had found moose-hair-filled scat; and Climbing Rock, with live birch growing from its apex, though the route up to them required some skill; and Secret Rock, which was reachable only by dogsled in winter after a circuitous journey to a distant tundra meadow, where the Denali-shaped rock jutted from the center of the clearing.

These chunks of mountains were visible reminders of the glaciers that had recently scoured the land.

The trail to Janus Rock was only fifty yards in length but it passed through a microcosm of our world. Right behind Bruno's house, at the start of the trail, was a tree fort I had built with the same vague carpentry with which I had built everything else on our ridgeline. It was a platform of odd scraps of wood that allowed us to reach the height of the birch leaves (a million per tree!), which we studied for infestation so that we could pluck the insect-chewed ones to send them spinning to the ground like pinwheels.

This day we passed up the fort. Beneath it, around the base of its tree, was a carpet of dogwood and trailing raspberries. It was part of our normal idyll to lie there for a while and suck on berries, but we passed that, too.

The trail then went through tall grasses into which Janus dove to hide after dismounting from my shoulders. "Pretend you can't see me!" he cried, crawling a few yards away. So I pretended, though as soon as he stopped moving he was as invisible as a fawn. I kept walking up the trail slowly, waiting for the "Here I am! Did you see me?" I could see only that this child was, in fact, a small forest animal.

We had gone to Anchorage together that spring on a supply run. Janus's greatest fascination was riding on a public bus. I saw him in his seat not as a stiff-backed rube gawking at the big city, but as wide-eyed wild child impressed by the marvels of the Modern World.

Within ten paces we came to a clearing of wildflowers. I had taken a few trees from here for the house. The revealed sky had nurtured wild geranium and arctic larkspur. Beneath their leaves, closer to the ground, were white ladies' tresses and yellow saxifrage.

We tried not to pick them. Picking wildflowers was reserved for special occasions like renewing the vase on the dinner table or going to see Mom or suddenly announcing, "For you, Dod, because I love you!"

On this walk we discovered an unusual pink flower that might have been a spring beauty or a wedge-leaved primrose or maybe even a dwarf fireweed. "We'll look it up," said Janus, putting one in his pocket. Until cross-referencing it with our library at home, he suggested calling it a "pink beauty," and so it remains, to us.

A spruce chicken burst from the side of the trail to flap heavily into a nearby tree. Spruce grouse live their entire lives within a few acres of their birth and seem to have the limited consciousness of most intensely provincial residents. It's always perplexed me how these birds, which are so slow to fly from danger and so loud in their dodo meanderings, could have survived as a species amidst fox and wolf and marten and hawk.

A few years ago I had shot one as it sat placidly in the bough of a spruce directly above our spring. From the first summer on the homestead I had worried over how to keep them from shitting in our water supply as they pecked at gravel for their crops and then expressed their gratitude annoyingly. I had concocted all manner of preventative covers and scarecrows and Better Gravel Pits and finally, in the flush of my acceptance of meat as a basic element of our life, had said, "Should we try to eat one?"

Janus had been enthusiastic.

We discovered that its gullet was filled with spruce needles. That impressed us both. Why are spruce grouse so slow and careless? Look: they have an endless garden of food right where they roost. The boreal forest, for them, is a paradise beyond any need for struggle.

Janus had eaten most of the hen. I was surprised. Then I realized that the taste was scented by the familiar forest.

When he would dawdle over his dinner, we still played a variation of "Here comes the train into the tunnel." But for us it became "Here comes the bad hunter into the Magic Cheetah's mouth." The Magic Cheetah disdained, above all, hunters who blasted our friends so that they could put the dead animals' heads on their walls. The Magic Cheetah roamed the forest protecting the animals and their children. The Petersville Road provided a rocky entry into our valley for trophy hunters who could not claim subsistence privileges, who did not *live* off their kills. They hired guides for bear. They coveted the racks of moose. We had seen them in September: camouflage-uniformed, beer-toting, eco-oblivious "sport" hunters who never came near our homestead but whose guns we heard in the distance.

The Magic Cheetah, like the Magic Butterfly, was not my invention. We had read about cheetahs in a glossy *Ranger Rick*, Janus's favorite magazine. Cheetahs were elegant and endangered and *fast*. They did seem magic. I couldn't take pride that I had influenced his conceptions. Magic Anythings came from the natural world, a more immediate presence than even a dad.

"Let's get her!" shouted the boy, watching the hen's flight.

I reminded him that in this breeding season, she might be a mom with babies. He stalked through the clearing searching for chicks.

When he abandoned the hunt ("I just wanted to *see* 'em!"), we hiked on to a spruce sapling that grew to the side of Janus Rock. In the winter I drove the dogs farther down this trail to get at stands of firewood: trees far enough away from the house so that we didn't notice their removal. When I returned with a sled full of birch—a six-hundred-pound load as manageable as a freight train—I sometimes ran right over that sapling, unable to turn the sled.

In summer we tried to root the battered tree more securely into its soil. Each time we passed it on our walks we fussed with the way it was leaning, with the state of its health. If it grew to become a shade tree for Janus Rock, a source of pleasure to squirrels and spruce chickens and grandchildren, it wouldn't become a monument to our attentiveness. It would be just another tree. The energy we put into its life was as casual as the time we took to replace the moss kicked loose from Climbing Rock, as common as the berry bushes we planted by spitting out seeds or shitting in the woods.

We never felt compelled to hurry back to the outhouse when we were out and about. We wiped ourselves on leaves or green hanging moss. That created moments of stress for me in more populous realms: "I have to poop!" "Okay. I think there's a restroom in the store across the street." "But I have to go *now*!" "All right, come on, let's hurry!" "What about behind those flowers?" "Uh, no, *no*, I mean, it isn't appropriate here. Come *on*!"

I admit, however, that there is a great grinning bond rural folk have with each other—especially if one of us is a kid—when we look up and down the alley and then unzip our flies.

When we had crawled up onto Janus Rock and flopped in its crowning moss-filled depression, we lay staring up at the trees. We were in one of the many spots that seemed unique to us—like the seat on a stump amidst a thicket of magenta fireweed down the slope from the house, where bumblebees browsed; or the cave created by the crater and overhanging root system of a wind-toppled birch, where the tree still sprouted leaves though it lay on its side; or the fern grove under the alders behind Dick's house, where a machete in the hands of a boy sculpted secret hideouts that could only be appreciated by an adult who kneeled low, "So no bugs can find us under the leaves."

We just lay on Janus Rock, hanging out, looking around at Things. Swainson's thrushes—the mysterious echo birds whose identity we had tracked by their trill—darted in and out of their nests, carrying insects. Pink-belled blueberry flowers dropped from their stems, leaving new green berries.

Through a slot between trees (an opening created by House Log # 101), the five-mile-wide terminus of the Ruth Glacier defined the end of the rolling forest. It was ten miles away.

On the other side of the Range, the Peters Glacier had surged five miles that very year—towers of blue ice hundreds of feet tall toppling in advance of the glacial sheet. It was undeniable evidence of the greenhouse effect, a reminder of our tenuous grasp on the planet. I was very much aware that our valley had been subsumed by Pleistocene ice for almost all of human history. It was the newest arable land on the planet.

The boy considered nothing so encyclopedic. But he, too, appreciated the miracle of the valley.

Suddenly we both sat up.

"Shh!" he said.

We stared at the alders east.

My heart, as always in these situations, pounded. He was cool.

"Moose," he suggested.

"Oh Jesus, I hope it's not a bear," I thought.

He stood up to see better. I glanced to the house where the shotgun hung, loaded with magnum shells.

The brush rustled again. He was excited. I was protective.

A moose lifted its head from its browse and eyed us.

The boy knelt down. "There!" he whispered. "See it?"

I saw it. I relaxed. I drew a very long breath. We had never even come close to being attacked by a bear. Many times we had been confronted on the winter trail by moose who lowered their head like water buffalo and snorted. But moose don't *eat* people. They only induce apprehension when the snows are deep and our trail provides the only firm footing.

"It's a cow," I said softly.

"How can you tell?" asked the field zoologist.

"Well, I guess it could be a young bull who hasn't grown a rack yet," I whispered.

"It's a cow," said the boy, "because she's got a calf."

I surveyed the brush. I started to tell him that there was no calf. Then I saw it, motionless at the side of its mother. "You're right," I said.

"I know," he replied.

This was not an unusual pattern for us. His perceptions of forest life were consistently more astute than mine.

Once a bird too swift for a raven and too small for a raptor streaked low overhead as we wandered through a clearing. "What's that?" I cried.

"Downy woodpecker," said the boy so quickly I didn't believe he'd even seen what I was talking about.

"Look!" I insisted. "It landed in that tree! Can you see where it's perched? It's a woodpecker. I bet it's a downy."

"Didn't you see the red cap?" he said.

When, in summer, we hiked the trail to the road, leaving the sled at home in clairvoyant deference to prowling bears, he rode in my single-compartment Lowe pack—a vastly more efficient means of travel than having him walk with me ("Look! A sulphur butterfly! I need one for my collection!" "I'm gonna pick a *ton* of tundra cotton for my mom!" "Let's just take another little break here, okay?"). He regularly noted, even from his high perch, scat on and off the trail, tracks in the earth, and low spiderwebs blocking our path, which we then stepped around, respectfully.

I no longer argued with his perceptions.

When the cow and calf turned away, he jumped off the rock. "Hurry!" he hissed.

I hoisted him to my shoulders and set off into the brush.

A year ago, in midsummer, we had gone out onto the tundra with Ado and Tarus and three male dogs whom we had allowed their freedom for a romp. The sight of the dogs' sun-lustered joy was one of my great pleasures. This was their heaven.

They had, immediately upon reaching the amphitheater, lowered their ears, dropped their tails, and slunk single file into the band of trees bordering the western edge of the tundra. I was perplexed.

Then we heard a bleating like the sound of a goat with a harvest knife at its neck.

I shouted, "Don't move!" to the boys and ran after the dogs. I crashed through the brush where they'd disappeared and stumbled into a hollow. Norton had a moose calf by the throat. Dick gripped its haunch. Bruno growled at the cow five yards away, keeping it back from the fight.

"No!" I screamed, battering Norton and then Dick with my fists. "No! Whoa! No!"

I wrestled loose the two dogs beneath me. I yanked them off the calf by their collars. I commanded all three back out onto the tundra with curses. They complied.

It was only after I had returned to the boys to explain what had happened that I began to shudder. I had just pulled a wolf pack from its prey.

Janus, when he understood the situation, had booted Norton in his bloody muzzle. "*Bad* dog! No! You *don't* kill the baby moose!"

Norton had cowered.

The calf had lived.

Now we hurried after the cow and calf for no reason other than that we wanted to *see* them. We had once followed a porcupine to where it climbed a stunted swamp spruce to stare at us. We had tracked a snowshoe hare until its trail in the snow became a series of bounds too far across the tundra to pursue.

The moose we lost, too.

We were still practicing how to track.

We paused in a bog of cloudberries, limned by one of the arms of our extensive blueberry patch.

"Let me down," the boy decided.

He marched over to examine the progress of our blueberry crop. In another few weeks we could begin our picking. Some years the berries, especially while still green, were infested with a worm that aborted their growth.

"No worms!" he announced, splitting a budding berry between his thumb and forefinger. "It's a sign!"

I laughed. "A sign of what?" I asked. I thought he was mocking me.

"A sign of blueberries," he replied simply. "Let's go swimmin'!"

Usually we carried an inflatable raft from the house to the smaller of our two tundra lakes. We then pumped up the raft with a bellows. The lake was maybe a hundred yards across and no more than four feet deep. The upper foot or two was solar heated. The bottom was spring fed and cold. Five small islands seemed to float in the lake: stepping on one made it sink a bit, bubbles at the edges rising through the vegetated mat. There was Norton Island, the three Poop Islands ("Dod! Come quick!"), and Manhattan Island, the largest, in the center of the lake, which we reached by rowing. I had named only one.

Janus now, for the first time, didn't insist that we bring the raft in order to swim. He wasn't much of a swimmer. But with each leap into the lake he acquired a little more confidence.

We had pursued the moose to within sight of the open sky of the tundra. We pushed through an alder thicket into light.

A mare's tail of clouds was dissipating west. The white mountains were north. Without the shade of trees the late-afternoon sun was so hot that Janus stripped to run naked.

Any lingering mosquitoes were exiled by a steady warm breeze. Dragonflies buzzed our heads. If we stood still they would land in our hair.

Janus didn't stand still. He raced into a shallow pool of horsetail grasses, stumbling, splashing, rising with earth dripping from him. "It's *warm!*" he yelled. "Come on!"

I didn't come. I was the gallery in the Colosseum. I gave the thumbs-up when he dove for a butterfly and rose sodden. I shouted my applause when he ran in spirals imitating nectar-bound bees.

When we circled the lake he found a tadpole nest, a gelatinous sac of frog eggs moored to the shore. While we studied it, a lesser yellowlegs sandpiper flew shrieking overhead. We agreed on its identity.

I took off my rubber boots and rolled up my pants so that we could play Run Around All Over. We shouted to hear our own voices returned from the trees in echo. When we tired, we examined long-leaved sundew—an insectivorous, glue-tipped plant—to see if any bugs had become trapped.

Finally we decided to swim. "You first," he said.

I took off my clothes, dove, sidestroked, and kicked back onto the shore. I had never, after my traumatic high school plunges into cold chlorination, been an eager swimmer. But I didn't want my boy to fear anything.

He jumped in, gasped, thrashed, and grabbed my hands to lift him out. "Did it!" he said. "Hotcha-roony! Yeah! All right!"

"Next time we'll swim to Manhattan Island," I said.

"Next time we'll bring the *raft*," he said.

We dried in the sun and then ran home to take a sauna.

The last of my construction on the ridgeline had been a seven-by-seven-foot sauna with a sod roof. I had built it from leftover logs, which determined its size. I had wanted a sauna, but the immediate impetus had been Epoch Dogsled Excursions ("Adventures into the farthest reaches of the Alaska Range"). For a season, to make money, I had guided clients from the "lodge" toward the mountains. A sauna had mitigated the absence of plumbing. I hadn't lacked for business, but I had been seriously deficient in desire. I didn't *want* our home to be public. I earned more that season than the couple of thousand dollars a year that it took to live well in the forest, but I valued our solitude more. I didn't care if I had to write schlock articles about "wild Alaska" for airline magazines or, like most others in the bush, work sporadically for the state in jobs like clearing a path for the Anchorage-Fairbanks power line, or even accept welfare. I wanted our home to be inviolate. It didn't require much. If we embraced the proximity of wild game, living off it to the extent that the Native population once had, we would require little else.

Our garden was flourishing. Beneath wood ashes and dog shit compost it was rich. But I wasn't yet ready to clothe myself in fur sewn with sinew. I still had much to learn.

In the sauna we had no choice—wilted by two-hundred-degree heat—but to relax from any demand.

Janus took the high seat beside me. He leaned against me. "I'm glad we saw that cow and her calf," he said.

I agreed.

We began to drip with sweat.

"I'm glad we found that frog nest," he said. "Wasn't it *fun* to go swimming?"

I said that I liked catching the trout, too.

He nodded. "Yep," he said.

We splashed water onto the stove to create steam and then hurried outside to dunk our heads in the rain barrels beneath the roof.

"Hoo!" we cried. "Ha!"

When I was a teenager, I read somewhere about an order of nuns in the south of France who prayed on their knees ceaselessly, in turns, for the continuation of the world. I believed in them without question. I pictured these luminous women with clasped hands in isolation, begging for mercy for us all. I imagined their hearts to be so pure and their plea so plain that no god could refuse them.

A year after moving to Alaska I saw a small item in the *Anchorage Daily News* mentioning that the Order of the Perpetual Adoration of the Blessed Sacrament, which had convents in very few locations, one of which was in the south of France, had been given a retreat on South Lake Otis Parkway in Anchorage, where the nuns lived in seclusion. A mysterious photo of the mother superior accompanied the article. She glowed. I smiled for days. A sign!

At times, at home, when the boy crawled into my lap for no particular reason and said, carelessly, "I love you," I thought that we were, in our retreat, offering something to some small part of the wider world similar to the nuns' service to the whole planet, though certainly ours was not by design.

Maybe we were so grateful for just where we knelt when examining plants that our happiness blessed a world worth continuing. Maybe the ease of acquiring our sustenance (spruce chickens! salmon! fiddlehead ferns!) helped balance the wealthy's need for *more* and the poor's struggle against starvation. Maybe we just validated a landscape that was a world away from a *New Yorker* cartoon that shows a child recoiling in horror, clutching his mother's hand, pointing up the sidewalk. "It's a *tree,* dear," reads the caption.

I was often aware of the grace in our life, but it wasn't our doing. It just was, like angels.

When I was at Harvard, where most people were on the fast track to diversified portfolios and rental property, I first saw that privilege doesn't necessarily bring contentment, though, of course, the most successful 20 percent of America lives as well as or better than the aristocracy of the ages. Charlemagne or Atahualpa or Louis XIV didn't have VCRs or Mileage-Plus coupons.

We had fifteen-inch trout below the house and a tundra meadow. I wanted Janus to understand how fortunate we were just for what we had. But he responded to all my parental admonitions with an implicit, "Uh-huh."

Still, I was consistent, if not incisive. And my enthusiasm at what was common was pervasive, if not poetic.

The boy dodged my zeal and found his own. He needed neither dads nor nuns to sustain his world.

He had seen mountains and valleys and the aurora. They would remain.

I knew of nothing more to teach, or desire, or hope.

10.

JUST HERE

It's impossible to live in isolation and not reach out toward the rest of life.

Lonely people long. Saints pray.

The rest of life can be other people or God or the land where animals look for or provide food.

I can't judge which is more worthy to reach out toward.

It's all requisite and, with a moment's reflection, surrounding.

True isolation is, ultimately, a feeling of being disconnected.

A wilderness homestead can certainly seem, to conventional perspectives, isolated.

But for me it is connected to so much of the rest of life that I can't feel lonely.

When I stomp out across the tundra in pursuit of game or firewood, I am very much aware that the reasons for my excursions are identical to those that motivated our ancestors from the time the

Ice Age required an immediate link to the animals and to the gods who sustain us all.

I'm also aware that the boundaries of my world are defined by roads and airstrips and microwave relay stations. When the wind blows hard from the east I can sometimes hear the heavy bass pulsing of the Alaska Railroad train halfway across the valley on its run between Anchorage and Fairbanks. When, eerily, I do hear it, I wonder who is in the baggage car huddled around the wood stove.

I've come to accept the need for other people, which is often as simple as family. And my love for Janus remains, as all love should, unequivocal.

I've also come to feel a part of the land without the anxiety that made the first days so hard. I admit, however, that there are moments when the brush rustles and I worry about my readiness to provide *me* as food.

On rare winter nights when there is no moon and no aurora and the arctic cold clarifies any lingering cloud, there are so many stars that they irradiate the sky. They *are* the sky, a single enveloping glow, a presence more immediate than bright pinholes in a black void. There is no way to feel removed from such light.

In the Eskimo tradition, the culminating moment of a successful hunt comes when the intermingling of all life (animal flesh into human flesh, flesh into earth, earth into flower) is so apparent that celebration is less a matter of ritual than spontaneous joy.

Christianity calls the same thing an epiphany, when God reveals His inescapable presence, His love *everywhere*.

Ho-san, a proponent of Zen, said the same thing: "Starvation and sorrow! / Hide in this cave. / What's this? A bone!"

Every spiritual tradition on earth allows for the sudden mystical appreciation that living is, ultimately, sacred, and worth the effort, that what is returned, after struggle, is divine.

The point of all these revelations, it seems to me, is less that they occur than that they are sustained. Even the Buddha rose from his bodhi tree to bring a semblance of what he'd discovered into daily life.

Like all revelation, what we've seen here, at latitude 62, illuminates our world (a piece of moss, a moose skull, the peaks at dawn) only for its moment. How it then resonates through our lives is not universal, and not mine to insist upon even for my son. I can't extrapolate and call our world "good," or "better than West Hollywood," or *anything* except right outside the door.

I now must, of course, go out of that door, both to verify what I'm trying to say and to get another log for the stove.

. . . Okay. The stove is stoked. But before I even stepped out the door I had to stop. The moon is nearing full. A stiff wind from the north bends the tops of the trees. The trees are right *there*. The difference between our warmed little box and the rest of the world is inescapable.

I can call it invigorating or humbling or wondrous, but it needs my description as much as it needs my presence.

I came here because I thought there was something powerful and proximate that I lacked. I still lack it. I stand in my doorway and breathe a presence that will be powerful and proximate long (long, long) after my wood stove and log walls are gone.

I take my sustenance not from this homestead—the garden and salmon stream and moose—and not from my son's happiness and ease, but from what remains beyond me, which is, just is, and will be when my posturing in doorways is done.

From beside me on the floor, a polar bear paw from the arctic coast in one hand and a tall Lego block tower steadied in the other, Janus cries, "Dad! Watch this! It's *amazing!*"

Marvin and Anna moved into town from Dead Dog Ridge so that their now three children could have access to public schooling. They sold their remaining dogs. Marvin takes his pride in remaining the best pitcher for Talkeetna's summer softball team, the Mandingos. Marvin and Anna don't often get back up to their cabin, but when they do, it's an adventure.

Rosser, with his family, lives in Fairbanks, from where he sets out to work, through the Laborers' Local, on the Slope, earning good bucks. He gave all his dogs to his cousin, who competed in Alaskan long-distance races and managed to avoid finishing last.

Denny married the second-grade teacher of his son when he was still flying in western Alaska, in Bethel. They all now live in suburban Fairbanks in a fancy home, with a V-8, chrome-trimmed, four-by-four, one-ton Chevy crew cab in the driveway and a Bible on the night table. He still has a working dog team, staked in the backyard. Denny is the most experienced pilot for a Fairbanks air taxi company. He adopted a fundamental Christianity in recent years, in part to expiate his "hedonistic" past but mainly to remain true to his desires. "I love my family! And I want us all to serve God."

Pecos drew the first position for the first Yukon Quest thousand-mile sled dog race. Unlike other contestants, he was not sponsored by ARCO Petroleum or R. J. Reynolds Hi-Pro dog food, but "self."

Russ quit his lucrative Anchorage job as a programmer and, with Gloria's support, spent a year, with their two boys, traveling the country investigating spiritual communities. They found greater affinity with nonprofit hospices than with long-hair communes. Russ returned to Anchorage to work as a masseur in old-age homes. They are now in the process of selling their downtown home in order to move to an isolated tract, subdivided from original homestead land, overlooking Alaska's rich Kachemak Bay.

Murphy turned down an impressive job outside Alaska to remain the *Anchorage Daily News*'s photo editor. His superiors, with bemusement, allow him his desire to take his vacation time "out in the cold" instead of in Waikiki.

Orv and Anne, now retired, maintain their involvement with Anaktuvuk, though most of their time is spent building a remote homestead in the Susitna Valley.

Norton, the sentient lead dog, can now count backward from ten, in addition to always finding the best possible trail between two unknown points. I admit that I have no videotape of these accomplishments.

I think of Alexander almost every day, still.

Talkeetna was named one of the fifteen best sporting towns in the country by a slick and facile national outdoors magazine. Boulder,

Colorado, and Bozeman, Montana, also made the list. Brightly colored plastic pile clothing has replaced wool as the local fashion of choice. The population has swelled to five hundred, and voted, in a fiercely contested election, to install a public sewer system. Tourism is now the mainstay of the economy, but trappers and miners still wander into town to buy a round for the house in the Fairview.

Our homestead now has solar-panel-generated electricity, from which we run the radio/tape player, three light bulbs, and a hand-held ham radio for emergencies. That's it for our power demands. At first it was exciting to install a source of electricity but, gradually, it became clear that we didn't *want* a Cuisinart or dishwasher or television or telephone or computer or sump pump. We still go outside in the morning to the outhouse. The view there is of glaciers, not linoleum. We still haul water, singing. But we no longer run the dogs to the road in summer. We take them halfway—to the bottom of the tundra, where we clip them to an aircraft cable stretched between two trees. From there we hike the remaining miles. When passing cantilevered roots and jutting rocks I am amazed that we never splattered the sled or our skulls in the years before it became easy for a young boy to walk the verdant miles through berries and bears. We still have no other neighbors within more than a hundred square miles.

Rex and Penelope moved to Saint Croix, where they bought a scuba-and-glass-bottomed-boat tourist operation. Rex is the captain of their forty-two-foot cruiser. He wears a Hawaiian shirt and sandals. Penelope volunteers time to a local hospital. When I'm able to reach them by phone on their veranda they still speak of coming "home," which I check for them, once in the summer against bears, and once in the winter against excessive snow on the roof.

The upper Susitna Valley, like the Arctic National Wildlife Refuge, has become a political battleground between forces demanding and decrying development. Loggers lobby for roads. Wilderness guides point to studies tabulating the megadollars spent by visitors seeking wilderness. The state implacably grinds toward ski lodges and "access" trails and the paved parking lots of Yosemite Valley, "for income." Until Gabriel blows his trumpet ("West End

Blues," I hope), that tidal encroachment across the remaining land seems difficult to contain. At the moment, however, there are only legislative plans and much grass-roots opposition. The landscape continues.

The cottonwood bridge across our creek, impossibly, has not been moved by recent floods that destroyed both a highway and railroad bridge linking Anchorage to Fairbanks. The cottonwood's bark had been stripped by spring ice jams, its banks undercut by meandering oxbows, and its strength tempered by time. But when we cross it, it doesn't budge.

The shotgun that was acquired against aggressive bears we now use only for hunting, not for protection. A bug-spray-sized canister of Counter Assault—aerosol-propelled cayenne pepper—allows us to explore the forest without fear of having to blow away, with a grain-and-a-quarter magnum slug, a she bear protecting her cubs. I know two men who have turned aside charging grizzlies with a burst from their little cans. We carry it in our tackle box down to the salmon creek. We have, as yet, never even come close to being attacked by a bear.

Melissa married a wilderness guide, a soft-spoken man with great integrity who works as a carpenter when he isn't taking clients up Denali or down white rivers. They live in downtown Talkeetna, which Melissa calls, gladly, "home." She rarely ventures out into the land, but she remains within it. We talk easily about the needs of our son. She still hopes to open her own restaurant, but in the meantime she is the most loving, supportive, amusing, and accepting mom a boy could ever want.

Janus climbs, skis, mushes his own dog team, rafts rivers, hunts spruce chickens with his own .22, and fishes intently from June through September. This season he caught twelve silver salmon, two forty-pound kings, and his personal best—an eighteen-inch rainbow trout—among many others. He gave away most of his catch, as is his wont, to our postmistress, to his buddies in Talkeetna, to needy locals in the area who looked, to him, "like they might want a fish." He has now entered the Talkeetna Public School, right into its third grade, after years of sporadic but rich elementary education investigating glaciers and tracking game. "He fits right in!" says Mrs. Clark, his teacher, who mines gold in summer on the family claim. For large parts of the school year he has maintained, with his mother's blessing, his connection to the rest of his world. We still play Magic Butterfly upon awakening, though mostly now to get to the part where the bed shakes in giggles, before wrestling.

I have never again run into "Mel Anderson."